Business Studies AS

The Complete Companion

AQA

Jenny Wales

•

Neil Reaich

Published in 2004 by:
Nelson Thornes Ltd
Delta Place
27 Bath Road
CHELTENHAM
GL53 7TH
United Kingdom

04 05 06 07 08/ 10 9 8 7 6 5 4 3 2 1

A catalogue record for this book is available from the British Library

ISBN 0 7487 7667 2

Illustrations by Harry Venning and IFA Design Ltd, Plymouth, Devon
Page make-up by IFA Design Ltd, Plymouth, Devon

Printed and bound in Spain by Graficas Estella

Contents

Acknowledgements

The authors would like to thank the following businesses/individuals for their support in writing this book:
DJ Wildrich, Yeo Valley, Wadworth's Brewery, Harriet Kessie Hairdressing, Disneyland Resort Paris, CMRC, Carphone Warehouse, Virgin Mobile, The Co-op in Aldbourne, Discarray, Indulge, Chester Zoo, Claire Wilson and Terry Warlock.

Art Directors & Trip Photo Library: p110 (top)
BMW: p7
Cadburys plc: p22
Canon (UK) Ltd: p86, p118
Corbis Images/ Patrik Giardino: p104 (left)
Future Network plc: p64, p76, p82
Martin Sookias/Office World: p6
Microsoft: p88
PA Photos/John Stillwell: p140
Press Association/ Barry Batchelor: p168
Rex Features Ltd/ Richard Young: p11, Rex Features Ltd/ Jeremy Sutton-Hibbert: p32, p34, Rex Features Ltd/ John Wright: p36 Rex Features Ltd/ Frank Casimiro: p42
Science Photo Library: p100
Sue Sharp: p20, p21, p29
Tesco Stores Ltd: p134, p154
Thomson Holidays: p8
Toyota: p124
Virgin Mobile Telecoms Ltd/Copyright © Virgin Mobile Telecoms Ltd 1999–2003: p72, p92, p96, p170

Picture research by Sue Sharp.

How to use this book

In your Complete Companion you will find all the support you need for your AS Business Studies. Each topic has been broken down into sections which are each covered on two pages so they can be easily understood and build a comprehensive understanding of the specification.

starSTUDY

The 'Star study' is a short case study which aims to help you work out what the theory really means. The questions are not just comprehension but ask you to make connections so you understand the theory and can put it to work.

Text

The links in the icon tell you what these sections are about. They tie the theory together with the real world and provide analysis and evaluation of the ideas.

IN THE KNOW

'In the know' provides all the knowledge you need. It is the basis for all your answers in the exam. The rest of the material on each page helps you to put this knowledge to work so that you can apply it in different situations.

Critical thinking

In exams you get good grades when you show you can analyse and evaluate business ideas in different situations. The 'Critical thinking' questions give you the opportunity to practise these skills in the context of the ideas on the page.

KEY TERMS

You will find definitions under the heading 'Key terms'. They are explained further and used in context in other places on the page.

Next steps

'Next steps' asks you to use the concepts and ideas in situations you know about. It might be your school or college, a business you know well or your local area.

Assessment

There are assessment opportunities throughout the book. These combine case study exercises to practise using the knowledge and skills you have acquired with real exam questions. They all provide you with assistance. The practice questions all have help! which gives you hints and tips about answering the questions. The exam questions show you the concepts and ideas which are being used in the case studies. Identifying these is very important because it gives you clues to how to answer the questions.

Marketing

Module 1

Marketing and accounting & finance

What is marketing?

starSTUDY

Jo and Adam designed and made their product and set about selling it. They liked it so much that they were sure that everyone would want to buy it.

1   What had they done wrong?

What can marketing do?

Marketing is an essential part of almost every business. Even a business that claims that it never advertises will need to know about the market for its products, the prices charged by its competitors and how their products are evolving. This is all marketing.

Most businesses are selling in competitive markets so it is important to make sure that:

- the product is right for the customers
- the price compares well with competitors
- the promotion of the product attracts the greatest number of customers
- the place where the products are sold reaches the maximum number of customers.

Know the market

Effective marketing is based on knowing everything there is to know about the market for the products you are selling. The size of the market is essential information. If people's total spend on a product is low, there is no point in investing heavily in it. The key is then to find out everything you can about your competitors and customers. There are lots of questions to ask.

KNOW YOUR COMPETITORS

- What share of the market do your competitors have?
- What is the image of their brands?
- What are their strengths and weaknesses?
- How do they distribute their products to their customers?
- Why do their customers not buy your products?
- Is there anything new going on?

KNOW YOUR CUSTOMERS

- Who are you trying to sell to?
- What do your customers like and dislike?
- What image do they have of your product?
- Are they loyal to your product?

GET THE PRODUCT RIGHT

- Product: its design and functionality
- Price: right for your target market
- Promote the product: with the right image, in the right place, at the right time
  - Place the product with the right distribution methods for your customers.

Product or market oriented?

Jo and Adam had got it wrong. They decided what they wanted to make without finding out if anyone wanted to buy it. They were **product oriented**. This isn't always wrong because some well-known products such as the Sony Walkman have come about in this way. Drug companies also carry out research and development which leads to new products but they often have an eye on the market. More research goes into cures for high profile diseases with lots of sufferers than more obscure ailments.

A **market-oriented** business will work out what the customer wants and set about providing it. Whether it is a new product or the development of an existing one, matching the customers' wants is more likely to meet with success. Market orientation is not just about the product itself but also the other aspects of the **marketing mix**. The business needs to know about the price people are prepared to pay, where they see promotional material and activities and how they will set about buying the product. Customer service is an increasingly important aspect of selling a product. Poor after-care can mean that customers don't return. Carphone Warehouse works hard at this. 'Why win an argument if it means losing a customer?' is one of the principles it expects its staff to work by. It expresses the point of view of a market-oriented business selling a service to its customers.

A successful business combines the strengths of both strategies. Few businesses are starting from scratch, so they have assets. Combining knowledge of what the market wants with the strength of these assets is often the best way forward. It is known as **asset-led marketing**.

Next steps

1 Choose three products that you use frequently and work out:

   a the target market

   b how the price compares with competitors

   c how its promotion differs from its competitors.

Critical thinking

Work out what marketing might be carried out by the following businesses:

1 A beauty therapist who works from home and finds clients by word of mouth.

2 A fizzy drinks company.

3 A person setting up a website development service.

4 A sports car manufacturer.

KEY TERMS

Marketing involves finding out about your competitors and customers so that you get your product right and sell it effectively.

Marketing mix combines the product, its price, promotion and the ways it is distributed – often referred to as 'place'. Together these make up the marketing strategy.

A **market-oriented** business will focus on the needs of the customer before developing and marketing a product.

A **product-oriented** business will focus on the creation of a product rather than considering the needs of the market.

Asset-led marketing involves building on the strengths of the business and customer needs.

The **target market** is the section of the market in which a business aims to sell its product.

Making marketing work

Specification Content

Strategy, analysis and planning

starSTUDY

Getting it together

What the marketing department wants to sell

What the finance department budgeted for

What production wants to make

What the customer really wants

1 Explain why each department wants something different.

2 What does the customer want?

3 Why is it important that all the departments of a business work together to decide what to sell and how to sell it?

Does it meet the objectives?

The purpose of a marketing plan is to help the company achieve its objectives.

 go to → *Find out more about marketing objectives on page 18*

Some businesses want to grow, some want to be more distinctive, some want to build on their strengths and others want to develop new products. Sometimes they have to dig themselves out of a hole. Whatever it is, the plan should be devised in conjunction with senior staff in the business so that the whole process is **integrated**. Before a plan turns into reality – there are more questions to be asked.

What are the **constraints**?

KEY TERMS

Integrated marketing means that all aspects of the business are involved in developing the marketing strategy.

Constraints are factors that limit the activities of a business.

Product differentiation means ensuring that your product stands out from the rest. People will buy it because it is special, not just because it is cheap.

The marketing model is a process that helps a business to make marketing decisions scientifically.

Market analysis uses a range of techniques to discover what is going on in the market.

Vision tells us where the business wants to be in the future. It is often an ambitious view of the future that guides planning.

Inside the business:

• The finance department will want to know what it will cost and what the price will be.

• The production department will have to decide if it can be produced.

• The human resource department will want to know whether the business has the right people – and whether training will be needed.

Beyond the business:

• What's happening to the economy? If unemployment is rising, people won't have any money to spend.

• What are competitors up to? If they are cutting prices, you may have to follow.

• Are tastes changing? Can you keep up with the customers?

Differentiating the product

If products are to sell, they have to be noticed – so they need to be a little different from everything else on the market. Being the cheapest is not the objective. If your product stands out from the crowd, people may be prepared to pay more for it.

Product differentiation needs careful marketing. Creating an image requires research about what the market wants and what others are doing. The design needs to be developed in light of the results. Outlets can be identified and types of advertising selected. All this needs to fit together so that the target market knows that your product is something special.

The marketing model

Corporate objectives
↓
Marketing objectives ←
↓
Gather data
↓
Devise a plan   Feedback
↓
Test the ideas
↓
Review outcomes ──

The marketing model aims to ensure that all the information required is fed into the system. Plans are then drawn up and tested before final decisions are made. If it is not working, the information will be fed back into the cycle and it will be redeveloped. Marketing budgets can run into millions, so getting it right is a serious matter.

Businesses generally have a **vision** of where they want to be in the future. The plan must therefore take this into account and not include anything that contradicts it.

Throughout the planning process, the business must always remember the key attributes of the products. Most businesses aim to maintain and develop the value of their brands. BMW wouldn't want to sell more cars by making a cheap, unreliable car because this would threaten the company's good name. The long-term view is therefore important.

Why do people pay a high price for a BMW?

It is equally important not to hang on to ideas that have guided a business when they have become outdated. New entrants tend to come in with bright new ideas and can take a share of the market very quickly if existing businesses do not move with the times.

There are many uncertainties in the process and businesses often have to make compromises. Risk-taking is at the heart of running a business. The degree of risk can be minimised by knowing as much as possible about what is going on.

Clever marketing is a mix of sound information and gut reaction. Sometimes a business makes a leap forward because someone has had a bright idea which people think will make a difference.

Finding out about the market

If a business is to produce and market its products successfully, it must know exactly what is happening in the market. By **analysing the market**, it can decide how to sell effectively.

This involves knowing how much of the market a business has, what sort of people buy the products and where the product fits in relation to others. Techniques for finding out about the market and how it works are to be found in the rest of this section.

Critical thinking

Make a list of well-known products and work out their key characteristics. What factors do you think are important to be incorporated into a marketing plan?

Next steps

Choose a product you know well and work out what the business would want to know before it devised its marketing plan. How would this information affect the plan?

Segmenting the market

starSTUDY

Thomson — Young at Heart

Thomson Winter Sun

Thomson Florida

Thomson — Faraway Shores
Safaris, tours and beach holidays

NEW

Portland
HOLIDAYS DIRECT

GREAT CHOICE
SAVE £££s

Thomson — Cruises

1 Which group of people is each brochure aimed at?

2 What are the differences between the holidays on offer?

3 What are the similarities between the holidays?

4 Why is there a different brochure for each group?

5 Why do you think holiday companies break up the market into different segments?

6 Can you think of any other products that are sold to different segments? Why do you think businesses do this?

Who are the customers?

To target its products effectively, a business must know who buys them. Few businesses meet the needs of the whole market so it is important to know the characteristics of the customers. Different target segments will need a different approach to the marketing mix. An 18–30 holiday will obviously need a different marketing approach from a holiday for families or older people because the products are different and the features that sell the holidays are also different. The information gathered helps to develop a **customer profile**.

They also have things in common. They need flights, hotels, employees and administration. Selling products which have similarities can lead to lower costs because flights and hotel rooms can be bought in bulk. A hotel that is full of families during the school holidays might become an 18–30 venue at other times.

Critical thinking

Newspapers in the UK meet different needs and serve different customers.

Identify the characteristics of each paper and its readers and use this information to decide on segments to put them in.

Next steps

1 Investigate market segments in a business that you know.

2 What are the products? Who are the customers? How are the customers different from the same as those who buy from other businesses?

KEY TERMS

Customer profile is a breakdown of people who buy a particular product. It will include age, gender, region, income and social class.

Niche markets are very small segments with specialist products. They may grow or remain small.

www

http://www.marketsegment.com shows how a commercial organisation offers expertise in working out market segments.

Defining the segments

A customer-oriented business must have a clear picture of the segments that it is targeting. They can be defined in a variety of ways.

• GEOGRAPHIC

People in different parts of a country – or the world – have different needs and wants. A business must take this into account when it develops products and marketing strategies. Ford cars in Europe are very different from those in the USA. Cheap petrol and low speed limits create different priorities.

On a more local basis, supermarkets around the UK stock different ranges of products to fit the demands of the surrounding community.

• DEMOGRAPHIC

The composition of the population influences the nature of products and the marketing activities used to attract different groups. Businesses will look at age, sex and ethnic background, for example. Data also tells them how spending power relates to different groups within the population so they know how to target these segments.

Social class is often used as a measure because it can reflect the demographic mix. It is, however, important to remember that people are no longer stuck in one category all their lives. Education and employment can move people quickly from one category to another.

Social class

A   Directors and chief executives of large companies

B   Solicitors, accountants and head teachers

C1   Skilled workers, bank staff, teachers

C2   Skilled manual workers, electricians, plumbers

D   Semi skilled and unskilled workers, refuse collectors, warehouse staff

E   Casual workers, state pensioners and students

• PSYCHOGRAPHIC

Lifestyle has become a way of defining market segments. People's attitudes affect what they buy. These attitudes may have come about because of an individual's background, education, income or personality. People who are well educated but not high earners may have attitudes that are different from others who earn the same amount.

The categories are not always easy to define and are constantly changing. Different marketing organisations are always finding new ways to describe these market segments. One consistently used categorisation that reflects attitude divides people into innovators, early adopters, early majority, late majority and sceptics. The strategies that a business uses will vary according to the sector it plans to target and the speed at which it wants to diffuse its product.

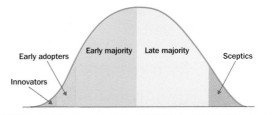

WHY SEGMENT?

Segmentation helps businesses analyse the market they are in and make decisions about where they want to go. It also helps to focus minds on the product itself and how it can best be placed in the market.

Some very big companies have products that span all segments but most will want to be successful in a smaller number. A small business can focus successfully on one segment and get the product right for its customers. It may develop great expertise from specialising.

The different characteristics of customers make business life more difficult. Unlike Henry Ford's early cars – which were all the same and came in black – today's products have to be varied to meet the customers' desires in relation to the price they are prepared to pay.

While focusing on the customers in a segment, a business must not forget that new segments may be developing as customers move on. The niche market, which is a very small segment often containing a new product, is important and can grow into a fully-fledged segment.

SUCCESSFUL SEGMENTATION

Study your competitors

• Work out their objectives and where and why decisions are made.

Study the customers

• Know who buys what.
• Know why they buy what they buy.

Will a segment work?

• Is it big enough to give the return you want?
• Are you asking the right questions about the people in the segment? The questions must relate to the product.
• Are the people in the segment very similar?
• Are they sufficiently distinct from the rest of the market?
• Can you reach the people in the segment?

Target growth

Specification Content

Market size, growth and share

starSTUDY

Market share of newspaper sales

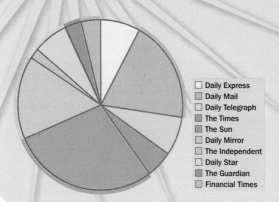

- Daily Express
- Daily Mail
- Daily Telegraph
- The Times
- The Sun
- Daily Mirror
- The Independent
- Daily Star
- The Guardian
- Financial Times

1. List the papers in order of the size of market share.
2. Group the papers into market segments.
3. Choose one of the papers and work out how it might increase its market share.
4. The market for newspapers has generally been falling. Where do you think the competition comes from?
5. Which markets for news do you think have been growing? Why?
6. How might newspapers fight back in order to increase the size of the market?

www

These two sites have plenty of information about national and regional newspapers.

www.abc.org.uk

www.newspapersoc.org.uk

Growing shares and growing markets

Newspapers are very conscious of their market share and total sales. Much of their revenue comes from advertising and advertisers want to know that they are getting their message to as many people as possible. It is an uphill struggle because the market for newspapers is shrinking. The tabloids compete for scandalous scoops, which raise sales and market share for a period of time.

IN THE KNOW

Market share

Market share is the proportion of a market held by one supplier. It can be measured by volume or sales value. The newspaper figures are by volume because they relate to the number of copies sold rather than the value. Value is calculated by multiplying sales by price.

Marketing objectives often include an increase in market share so it can be regarded as a measure of success. As it measures how well a business or product is doing compared with the competitors, it is a clear indicator of whether the strategy is working.

Having the biggest market share makes a product the **brand leader** and can give a business power over the prices being set and help keep costs low because of economies of scale. Success breeds success because being in prime position means that retailers will take the product, without having to be persuaded with big discounts. A famous name also means that customers are more likely to pick up the product.

Next steps

1. Supermarkets are always fighting for market share. Why is market share more important than market growth in the food business?
2. Find out what changes have taken place in market share recently.

KEY TERMS

Brand leader is the product with the biggest market share.

Market mapping involves analysing the market to compare the position of a business or product and its competitors.

Market growth

Market growth measures what is happening in the whole market. It can also be measured in terms of volume or sales. Life is much easier for businesses in growing markets but if their individual growth doesn't match or exceed the growth of the market – the strategy isn't working effectively.

The relationship between value and volume is also critical. Rising volume but falling value means that the unit price is falling. This has happened in many computer and electrical markets. Businesses have to run faster to stay in the same place.

Market growth is usually generated from a feeling of economic well being. Higher incomes mean more spending and growing markets. It is hard for individual firms to influence such growth. Other factors that affect it include:

• changing fashions, such as scooters, skateboards, trainers and so on

• social trends, such as more women going to work and therefore buying more convenience food

• innovation, which attracts customers to new products.

Fighting for a share

Businesses watch their market share rigorously and respond quickly if things are moving in the wrong direction. They have more influence over share than growth because the latter is affected by factors beyond their control.

In order to fight for share, a business may change the activities within its marketing mix. Cutting prices, updating the product, different promotion and having products in the right place through improved distribution are all solutions that might be used.

go to → Find out more about the changes that might be made on pages 30–37

Mapping the market

Once all the data has been gathered, a business will create a map of the market which shows the relationship of a product with its competitors. If you want to buy a new personal stereo, you will be faced with lots of choice. A basic model will have a low price. A top of the range model with the latest styling and features will cost much more. The positions of products can be plotted on a market map.

The labels on the axes will vary according to the product.

Businesses use **market mapping** to decide where they want to go. Burberry, almost by chance, moved from fuddy-duddy/expensive to trendy/expensive but then worked hard to maintain this position by making sure its products were seen on celebrities as well as having a big marketing budget.

A map also shows up any gaps in the market. Finding a niche that can be developed may be a lucrative activity.

Critical thinking

1 What factors affect
   a market share   **b** market growth?
   Why is it important to distinguish between data on the value and volume of market share and market growth?

2 Map the market for fast food restaurants. Use price on the vertical axis and decide on the feature to use on the horizontal axis.
   a Have any of the restaurants changed their position recently?
   b How can the map help a business to plan its marketing strategy?

Researching the market

Specification Content

Market research: primary and secondary, including government statistics

starSTUDY

Gathering data

David Hanson runs CMRC, a market research business in the middle of Croydon. CMRC helps businesses to find out what people think of their products. It uses all sorts of strategies – from focus groups to phone calls. The company specialises in fragrances so it brings people into its offices to smell new products.

Some of the research involves recruiting people from the streets of Croydon to come into the offices to answer some questions about the products.

CMRC carries out **primary research** for other businesses. It talks to people and therefore brings in first-hand information.

Market research can be expensive so many businesses survey their customers and retailers on a regular basis because they have cheap, easy access to them.

1 Why do you think businesses employ CMRC to carry out research for them?

2 Why is the centre of Croydon a good place to carry out research?

3 If you are testing fragrances, what special conditions would you need?

4 What factors would you want to consider when looking at the results of the research?

Critical thinking

A market research company recruits women to test products for them. It sends a product and a short questionnaire about twice a month. What are the advantages and disadvantages of this sort of market research? What factors would you have to consider when looking at the results?

Next steps

1 Have you been involved in any form of market research? What was the product? What was the business trying to find out?

2 Look at some adverts and work out what market research has found out about people's views on the product.

KEY TERMS

Primary research gives a business specific information about how the public views their product.

Secondary research comes from existing information that provides details about the market and other products.

Finding out about the market

PRIMARY RESEARCH

Primary research means asking customers and potential customers questions about your product or a product you plan to bring to the market. It is carried out by market research companies or the business itself. There are a variety of strategies that can be used to find different sorts of information.

QUESTIONNAIRES are

frequently used to find out what people think. The design of a questionnaire is critical to its success. It needs to find out about the respondents as well as their views on the product in order to work out what different people think. The design will differ if the person completes it on their own or with a market researcher. An in-depth interview will use open questions and encourage people to think about how they feel about a product. If the questionnaire is sent through the post, the questions must be short and snappy and easy to answer.Questionnaires are carried out in all sorts of ways.

- Postal/e-mail surveys involve sending out a questionnaire and hoping that people will respond. The rate is often quite low. An inducement might be offered to encourage people to respond. A health club might offer a free visitor's pass. Postal questionnaires seem relatively cheap but the real cost depends on the number of responses.

- Personal interviews give more detailed information but they are expensive because the interviewer has to spend quite a long time with a group or just one individual. The information is often more interesting because the format is less structured and the interviewer can explore areas of interest.

- Telephone surveys fall in the middle. Most are straightforward questions but in some cases interviewers will book a time and be more expansive. The drawback is that people are not always happy about being disturbed by unexpected phone calls which they suspect are trying to sell them something.

- Panel surveys use a team of people whose views are monitored regularly. This has the advantage of showing trends, but it is important to know whether the panel reflects the views of the population. A panel might be asked to test products, report on their purchases or record their activities, like the TV programmes they watch – and the adverts they see.

OBSERVATION is used in supermarkets, for

example, to find out how people shop, what they see and what makes them stop. These are all critical pieces of information when trying to design stores, packaging and promotional features.

EXPERIMENTS are used to compare how

changes affect the market. Two similar towns are often chosen so there is a control group, where nothing changes, and one that tests the new product. Market researchers have to be careful in interpreting the data because it is hard to ensure that everything is kept constant.

SECONDARY RESEARCH

Secondary research is also called desk research because that is where it is carried out. An enormous amount of information is collected by all sorts of organisations and is available either free or at a price. The Internet has speeded up this process considerably. The government provides free data about society, the population, industry and the economy. Trade associations gather data for their members and specialist newspapers and magazines also track changes in the market. These cover every aspect of industry from cars to catering.

Specialist reports are also available but the price charged for them is high and prohibitive for many.

Secondary research can provide a useful background for marketing activities but its main drawback is that it is not tailored to the direct interests of a business.s

Rules for writing questionnaires

Carrying out primary research is an expensive process so why waste money on a poor questionnaire? You want to know who people are and just what they think. It is important to be able to count up the results.

1 Find out who has answered the questionnaire – age, sex, occupation – but don't become intrusive.

2 Know exactly what you want to find out.

3 Don't ask leading questions.

4 Make sure that the people will understand the questions.

5 Ask closed questions in which people put a cross in a box or rank things in order of preference.

6 A few open questions will allow you to find out a little more about what people think.

The questionnaire will vary according to the group that is being tested. *The Economist* uses its subscription members to carry out surveys and asks quite detailed questions about income. If people are to be questioned on a street corner they may be less willing to answer such questions.

Getting the data right

starSTUDY

Selecting the sample

CMRC specialises in finding out what people think about new fragrances. Some businesses want to know how many people like or dislike different versions of their products. Others want to give people the opportunity to discuss their views in greater depth in order to discover their attitudes to products or potential products. CMRC has to work out the number and sort of people they need to ask in order to find an answer which reflects the views of potential customers.

Specification Content

Size and type of sample (random and quota), problems of sampling and research methods, analysing survey results, qualitative research

1 What advantages and disadvantages do you think there are, from a business's perspective, in finding out
   a how many people like or dislike a new product
   b the attitudes of people to a product?
2 What sort of people would you need to question if you wanted to find out about a sports deodorant, a room freshener, a new perfume and a car freshener?
3 What should a market research business consider when deciding how many people to question about a product?

The right choices

Businesses that carry out market research are looking for evidence to underpin decisions. If things go wrong, the decision-makers can blame someone else – the market researchers! Making sure that the data collected is right for the cause is therefore critical. Counting potential purchasers of a new product or having an in-depth discussion with a few potential customers provides different sorts of information that can contribute to decision making. The first is **quantitative data**. The second is **qualitative data**.

It is also important that the people who are being asked are representative of the market as a whole. Even if some elderly people can be found at the gym, asking a sample of the over 80s about the design of new trainers would not provide useful information. Choosing the sample – or **sampling** – must also be done with care.

Quantitative or qualitative?

QUANTITATIVE RESEARCH provides numerical information. It is the answers to closed questions, which often have one-word answers. To obtain such information it is important to ask the right people, write good questions and interpret the information.

QUALITATIVE RESEARCH comes from in-depth interviews and group discussions. Because the interviewer, who is often a psychologist, will be free to follow up interesting lines of thought, the responses will give more personal views. Such research may discover how people think, how they are influenced by others or problems that had not been thought of before. It often takes place in people's homes or a comfortable environment where people can be observed.

Sampling

Sampling techniques help market researchers to ask the right people. The first decision is whether to use a random or a non-random sample.

A random sample gives a genuine cross-section of the population. Once someone has been picked at random, from the electoral register for example, it is important to talk to that individual. It gives good data but is expensive because someone has to visit and hope to catch them at home. It can also be done by phone. The researcher works through a list until they have spoken to everyone.

A random sample can be:

- A stratified sample. A company which makes food aimed at children will want to interview mums and children so the people are selected from this group – or strata – of the population.

- A cluster sample. This is used infrequently but aims to find the views of people who live in particular areas. If a business wants to decide on the location for a new club it might decide to carry out a cluster sample in places where there are many young people.

A non-random sample can be:

- A quota sample. This reflects the target market for the product so it chooses people in the appropriate age group and gender. The business that is opening a new club would want to ask young males and females.

- A convenience sample. A market researcher might stand on a busy corner and catch people as they come by. It is a cheap way to carry out a survey but will be biased by the location, time of day and other factors.

HOW BIG?

Size matters, but bigger is more expensive. A sample of 1000 will give great information, which will tell a business more about the target market and therefore give clues about promotional strategies. It might show that a new brand of makeup appeals to the 25–35 age group. This would enable the company to tailor the style of the adverts and where to place them.

Many businesses use much smaller samples because of the cost. A sample of 100 often gives quite enough information to decide on package design or a new taste.

Interpreting the data

The reliability of the data will be determined by the size of the sample and the percentage of people opting for each alternative. A 4% difference between two fragrances in a small sample gives less confidence than 4% on a

large sample. Businesses generally work to a 95% confidence level so they are happy with a result that is right 19 times out of 20. If the results are closer, it will be necessary to take other factors into account – perhaps the packaging that goes with the product.

Critical thinking

Pizza, pasta or ...?

A catering company with an existing pizza restaurant chain is considering developing a new brand. The first thought of the development team was to move into pasta, but is there too much competition in the field? A Spanish tapas restaurant is another possibility. Choosing lots of little dishes that are good for sharing could be popular.

The company wants to know which would be most popular and the demographic pattern of potential users.

A market research company is asked to find the answers.

1 Draw up a questionnaire for them and decide on the best sampling method to use. You will need to be able to explain the rationale behind what you have done.

2 Select and interview ten people according to the sampling method you have chosen. Write a report on how well the questionnaire worked. What would you have changed?

3 Make a presentation about your findings.

KEY TERMS

Quantitative data comes in the form of numbers and can be used to work out statistically valid conclusions.

Qualitative data comes from in-depth interviews and shows attitudes, opinions and judgements.

Sampling involves questioning a proportion of the population. The nature of the sample will depend on the information required.

Developing marketing strategies

Specification Content
Developing marketing objectives

starSTUDY

Pizza revival

Pizza Express was the UK's first chain of pizza restaurants. For many years it had a great reputation for producing high quality pizzas, just like the Italians make. Suddenly it found itself in difficulties and needed to work out what to do next.

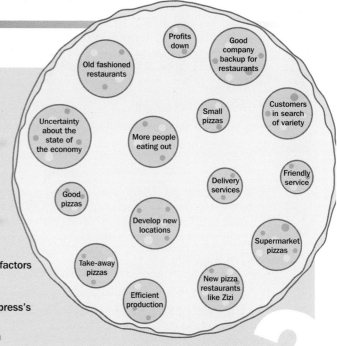

Profits down

Good company backup for restaurants

Old fashioned restaurants

Uncertainty about the state of the economy

Small pizzas

Customers in search of variety

More people eating out

Delivery services

Friendly service

Good pizzas

Develop new locations

Supermarket pizzas

Take-away pizzas

New pizza restaurants like Zizi

Efficient production

1 Divide the factors into those which come from inside the business and those which come from outside.

2 Which of the 'inside' factors are strengths and which are weaknesses?

3 Which of the 'outside' factors are opportunities and which are threats?

4 Can you think of any more factors to add to each of these categories?

5 What do you think Pizza Express's objectives might be?

6 How does this analysis of a business help it to meet its objectives?

What's going on?

To develop a marketing strategy, a business must know what is going on both inside and outside the business. The analysis of Pizza Express shows how a business might go about the process. **SWOT analysis** looks at the strengths, weaknesses, opportunities and threats that a business has to deal with, or make the most of, if it is to thrive. The marketing strategy will be built on statistical analysis of how the business is doing and on market research, to show how customers and competitors are behaving. This information all contributes to the SWOT analysis.

The big picture

A formal SWOT analysis is a major task. The analysis of the world beyond the business can be challenging because businesses only give out the information that the law requires in order to keep their competitive advantage. For many businesses, it involves keeping a constant eye on events.

The SWOT analysis should take account of the views of all the stakeholders both inside and outside the business. They may appear in any box because they can be strengths, weaknesses, opportunities or threats. Whatever their contribution to the picture, a business must decide the significance of their role in order to give weight to views. This is the case for any statement in any of the four boxes. Some are more powerful than others and will therefore have a greater effect on the future of the business.

KEY TERMS

SWOT analysis is used to sum up the internal and external factors that affect a business. Strengths and weaknesses are internal. Threats and opportunities are external. It can be used for departments within the business or for the business as a whole. It is the basis for developing or reviewing strategy.

SWOT

SWOT analysis is a way of analysing a business's situation from both inside and outside the business. 'Strengths' and 'weaknesses' are about the internal environment of the business. 'Opportunities' and 'threats' concern the external environment.

It is a formula that is often used in the marketing department to decide on a marketing strategy, but it is also used throughout the business to help make decisions about future plans. The chart shows the internal and external factors that should be considered.

Internal factors	External factors
The company's reputation: do people come back for more?	The economy: are people likely to spend more or less?
The product: does it match customers' needs?	Competition: are competitors proving to be a threat?
The business: is it producing the products efficiently?	The market: are there any gaps?
The future: are there new products in the pipeline?	New developments: can technology help?
	People: is the changing population opening new opportunities or proving to be a threat?

USING SWOT

When a business is developing or reviewing its strategy, SWOT is a key part of the decision making. It can be carried out in each department of the business as well as for the business as a whole.

The process of working out what is going on internally and externally to the business focuses the attention on the future. It is very easy for businesses to concentrate on the task in hand rather than working out what happens next.

The results are often set out in diagrammatic form. By bringing the information together in this form, it is easier to see the contrasts and similarities within the different boxes.

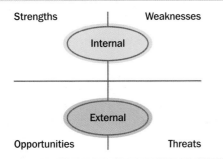

In a large business, SWOT is generally carried out formally as part of strategic development. In a small business it can be carried out without people being aware of the formal process. Just watching what is going on inside and beyond the business means that the person in charge is keeping a finger on the pulse. A competitor may be using a different marketing strategy or a new production technique which has become available that reduces costs and increases quality.

However the exercise is carried out, the objective should be to develop the business's strategy in order to:

• add value more effectively

• develop competitive advantage.

Competitive advantage is a feature that puts a business ahead of its competitors. It may be based on reputation, innovation or the relationship with customers and suppliers.

Critical thinking

1 Why is it important for a business to understand its internal and external position when developing a market strategy?

2 Carry out a SWOT analysis on your school or college. How do you think it should market itself?

3 Carry out a SWOT analysis on Carphone Warehouse or another business that you know. Does its marketing strategies reflect the SWOT analysis?

Next steps

1 Ask someone you know who runs a business, or works in one, to identify its strengths, weaknesses, opportunities and threats.

2 Ask what changes they might make in the light of this information.

Objectives and strategy

MODULE 1: MARKETING AND ACCOUNTING & FINANCE

starSTUDY

Jo and Adam have created a product that no-one wants and it is not selling.

1 How has planning gone wrong?
2 What do you think the overall objectives of the business are?
3 What should the marketing department have done to help the business achieve its objectives?
4 What would you suggest it does now?

> Specification Content
>
> The link between marketing strategy or mix and the objective being pursued: strategies versus tactics

Business objectives → Marketing objectives

Businesses set objectives for the short and long term. The marketing strategy must aim to help the business achieve these objectives. The marketing department will make the plans for marketing activity but the overall plan will be determined at a very senior level because it has to be woven into the business's mission and objectives. These are likely to include the market segment, the area of the world market to be targeted, and the market share the business wants to achieve.

> The impossible is easy.
> Miracles take a little longer

 go to → *Find out more about market segments and market share on pages 8–11*

The plans must be integrated into the business as a whole. There is no point in setting an elaborate **marketing strategy** if the finance department says there isn't enough money to pay for it.

The target should be realistic. Trying to change the image of Marks and Spencer so it becomes the only place to shop for every student is not realistic. People are unlikely to strive to develop a strategy that they know is impossible.

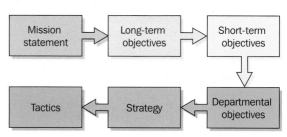

Critical thinking

1 What objectives do you think the following businesses have?

Starbucks, BP, Tesco, New Look, Carphone Warehouse, Levi, Apple computers, Dell computers.

2 How is the marketing department aiming to meet the objectives?

KEY TERMS

Marketing strategy is set in the light of business objectives and an analysis of the business and its environment.

Marketing tactics are the short-term activities often designed to deal with the competition.

Marketing targets are short-term goals that are achievable and can be monitored.

Matching the objectives

Once the business has set its objectives, the marketing department develops its strategy to make it all happen. The routes it chooses will depend on the market for the products although any plan will be a combination of different activities.

> Business objective:
> **We want growth!**

> Business objective:
> **Continuity matters!**

> Business objective:
> **Be innovative!**

> Business objective:
> **Make our products different!**

DEVELOP NEW PRODUCTS, BROADEN THE RANGE

New products can be developed from the existing range or can be a completely new idea. The confectionery market has a constant flow of new products. Some become a permanent feature on the supermarket shelves and others disappear. Cadbury's Heroes opened up a different segment for packaged chocolates. Boxed chocolates had been thought of as a present for females. Heroes are acceptable to a much wider market.

The latest computer games console always arrives with great hype. It is the 'must have product' for many young people. Sony and Nintendo work very hard to bring out the most exciting version.

New products come from innovation. Development of products can be innovative but may also provide continuity for both the business and the customer. They should also be distinctive.

IMPROVE DISTRIBUTION

Products won't sell if people can't see them on the shelves. Shops will only stock lines that sell so the marketing department has to work out how to ensure that the company's products are in all the right places. If growth is the aim, placing the products is critical. Some products benefit from a different approach to distribution. Vichy's skin care range is only sold in pharmacies in order to stress its scientific qualities. It limits the potential range of outlets but makes it distinct from others.

PRICE OR QUALITY?

The objectives of a business may mean staying in the same segment, moving into another one or functioning in several.

Some businesses position themselves at the 'low price–high volume' end of the market. Hi-Tec, for example, makes no attempt to sell expensive products. It knows that there are plenty of people who are unwilling to spend £100 on a pair of trainers. Others aim for high price–low volume or if plans work well, high price–high volume.

Increasingly, businesses have lines in different segments. Famous designers, who sell their clothes for thousands of pounds, also run a range through Debenhams. This was an innovative approach for a department store and left Marks and Spencer standing. Ford bought Jaguar to give it access to a top of the range car market. People who are looking for status won't buy a Ford but will buy a Jaguar.

Sometimes businesses cut prices to compete when under threat from competitors. Sainsbury's always meant quality but when challenged by Tesco, resorted to cutting price and lost its standing with the customers because lower prices meant cutting corners.

INCREASE SALES

A business that is going for growth will often have marketing objectives which include increased profits or sales in terms of volume or revenue. The marketing department will have to devise methods of achieving such objectives.

go to → *Find out more about marketing activities on pages 30–37*

Setting targets

Encouraging staff to achieve the objectives that have been set can be challenging. Tough objectives can be hard to meet and staff can be disillusioned if they can't see success. Breaking the objective down into **marketing targets** makes it easier. Everyone can see what has been achieved – or not. If targets aren't met, the department must review what has happened and revise the plans. It might decide that more resources should be put into the marketing budget.

Reviewing strategy

A business must monitor its marketing strategy constantly. This will be done in the process of reviewing the business's objectives.

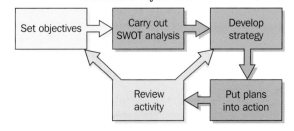

Niche or mass?

MODULE 1: MARKETING AND ACCOUNTING & FINANCE

starSTUDY

Thornton's is a great place to go for presents. To make them even more special, you can have the recipient's name iced on the chocolate rabbit, football or monster. Thornton's Special Toffee is out of this world and all its lines are high quality and delicious. They are all available from Thornton's shops on the high street.

Cadbury's products can be bought anywhere from the corner shop, supermarket or petrol station.

It sells chocolate ranges for everyday consumption and to give as gifts.

1 Where can you buy Thornton's and Cadbury's chocolate?

2 Why do you think Thorton's limit the outlets where its products are available?

3 What advantages and disadvantages are there to Thornton's strategy?

4 What advantages and disadvantages are there to Cadbury's strategy?

5 Make a short list of niche products and mass market products.

Why mass marketing?

Products for **mass markets** are made on a large scale and are therefore cheaper. This means that more people can afford them – so sales are higher. Most of the things we buy are made in this way. Clothes that we buy, whether from high street stores or designer names like Calvin Klein or Tommy Hilfiger, are made in the same way – in large factories on production lines.

The bigger the market, the lower the cost. Wherever you go around the world you see the same brands. Ford cars are to be found from Moscow to Monterey. People wear Levi jeans from Calcutta to California. By selling to a **global market**, total sales can grow to massive scales. The cycle continues as the product becomes available more widely. Production on this scale leads to **economies of scale**.

Businesses have to be careful when they decide to go global. A product name that is acceptable in one language can mean something very different in another!

Why go global?

• Lower unit costs for large-scale production

• Lower marketing costs for selling worldwide

• A national market may not be big enough for a differentiated product that sells to a small sector of the market

• A global market is big enough to bear the costs of innovation. New products are expensive to develop and the market expects them more and more quickly.

What's in a niche?

A **niche** is a slice of a segment. Most markets are divided into segments. In the car industry, sports cars, family saloons, small hatchbacks and people carriers are all aimed at different segments of the market.

A business may start a niche by spotting a gap in the market. Claire's, for example, is a shop that sells all sorts of bits and pieces for teenage girls. There isn't another one like it. The shop is now on almost every high street. It has turned into a successful niche.

- Niche products are often made by people with an enthusiasm for their product. Innocent, which makes smoothies, came about because its owners wanted really fruity drinks made from the freshest produce.

- Thorough market research can also lead to the identification of a niche. By mapping the market, gaps can become clear. Research will tell whether there is a market in that gap. There is no point in creating a product to fill a niche if people don't want to buy it.

go to → *Find out about market mapping on page 11*

- Existing businesses can create new products to fill a niche in light of feedback from their customers. Such niches may grow into mainstream products. As a result, some businesses sell their mass market products to the whole market and have niche products for separate parts of the market. An ice cream company might have its bulk sales but may also sell a special Italian style range at a higher price to a much smaller market. Unilever sells Walls' ice cream to the mass market and Ben and Jerry's to a substantial niche.

Who are the customers?

Customers in a niche market are usually wanting something that is a bit different so they are probably prepared to pay a bit more. This means that demand is inelastic.

go to → *Find out more about elasticity of demand on page 30*

A business in a niche has to cover its costs just like any other so the higher price that people are prepared to pay helps. Some niche businesses sell at low prices but aim to shift more items. Claire's does this. Nothing in the shop is expensive but its customers buy lots of items.

Critical thinking

Make a list of some mass marketed products and some in niche markets.

1 How do the marketing strategies differ?
2 Why do you think this is so?
3 What sort of factors does a business have to take into account when it starts global marketing?

Next steps

Choose a product range that interests you. Try to identify a niche that relates to the product.

KEY TERMS

Mass marketing creates products for the whole market and sells to all customers.

Niche marketing involves products in small sections of the market with specialist customers.

Global marketing involves using the same marketing methods throughout the world.

Economies of scale cause a fall in costs per unit as an output grows larger.

Planning marketing

Specification Content

Marketing planning

starSTUDY

Creating a purple patch

Dairy Milk is a brand that is deeply embedded in the minds of people in the UK and beyond, so Cadbury decided to make the most of it. Wispa and Caramel became part of the Dairy Milk family and new products including Mint Chips, Turkish Delight and Crispies were developed to create a purple patch on the confectionery fixture in the shop.

The packaging of the whole range was redesigned to give a more contemporary feel. The swirly Cadbury logo aimed to give the brand name more prominence and was used across the whole portfolio including Cadbury Dream and Bourneville.

The strategy also aimed at broadening the product range so people would choose one of the products to have with their morning coffee. Crispies was specially designed to meet this criteria.

To catch the public's attention, Cadbury's sponsored Coronation Street.

The whole relaunch cost the company £8.2 million, its biggest spend to date.

1 What were Cadbury's objectives in relaunching the Dairy Milk range?

2 What are the advantages of having a wide range of products under one well-recognised brand?

3 How did the development of Crispies contribute to Cadbury's objectives?

4 Why do you think Cadbury's decided to sponsor Coronation Street rather than another programme?

5 How do you imagine that the relaunch of Dairy Milk fits into Cadbury's objectives?

6 What other businesses use the strategy of turning a family of products into one brand?

Why plan?

A business develops its objectives and sets targets. It then has to work out how to achieve these targets. The **marketing plan** is an integral part of the process. Without it, activities would be haphazard and unconsidered. Imagine spending £8.2 million on the relaunch of Dairy Milk without a plan!

Putting the plan together

IN THE KNOW

ANALYSE THE CURRENT SITUATION

The marketing department must look at the market in general, as well as the market for its products, in order to build a picture of the current situation. Secondary research will show what is happening in the market. Primary research will give a more specific picture of the products involved, the market segments and likely target markets. SWOT analysis will help it to work out the strengths, weaknesses, opportunities and threats.

 go to→ *page 17 for a reminder on SWOT analysis*

DEVELOP OBJECTIVES AND STRATEGIES

Marketing objectives stem from the business's objectives. If the business aims to develop into new areas of the country, the marketing strategy needs to fit. There are many possibilities including developing new markets, increasing profitability, revamping the image, devising new products or increasing market share.

CREATE A MARKETING PLAN

The plan will be determined by the strategies. It has to use a balance of the marketing mix to best effect. This means weighing up the effectiveness of the product, price, promotion and place or distribution to decide the best combination. The amount that is available to spend will also have a strong influence on the plan.

The plan will include a schedule of actions and events which needs to be clear and readily available for everyone involved. People need to know exactly what their responsibilities are. It helps, for example, to make sure that the public relations staff are putting out messages about exciting changes.

MONITOR OUTCOMES AND REVIEW PLAN

Once the plan is in place, a business can't afford to sit back and assume it will all just work. Sales must be monitored carefully to see if targets are being met. If things are not going smoothly, the plan must be reviewed and changes made to achieve better results.

Getting it right

The evaluation of the marketing plan will be determined by the objectives and strategy that has been put in place. The integration of the strategy into the business as a whole is also very important. There is no point in persuading people to buy a wonderful new product if production simply can't make enough to meet demand. This may give a product short-term notoriety but often leaves customers fed up. It is important not to damage the reputation of the business by being over-ambitious.

The elements of the marketing mix that are used will also contribute to the success or failure of the plan. The product is obviously key to success but the other three must be selected to support the product according to market conditions.

The role of after sales support and customer care is becoming increasingly crucial. They are almost part of the product already because people often need help in using today's gadgetry. A business that puts an exciting new product in the marketplace but does not look after the customer is likely to fail.

Critical thinking

You are going to run a disco at school or college. Devise a marketing plan for the event. Remember to keep costs in mind. Photocopying an A4 advert, for example, will cost about 4p a sheet. Your marketing costs take a slice of the profits.

Share your plan with others and evaluate your choices and likely outcomes.

Next steps

1 Keep an eye open for new product launches or relaunches.

2 Work out how the marketing mix is being used.

3 Does it seem to be successful?

KEY TERMS

Marketing plan shows the schedule of marketing activity for a product over a period of time. It will show how different elements of the marketing mix contribute to the strategy.

The life of a product

Specification Content
Product life cycles, problems of prediction and determinism, extension strategies, relationship with cash flow and capacity utilisation, Boston Matrix

starSTUDY
Making music

Vinyl
1950–1985

Cassettes
1970–1995

CDs
1990–

Products come and go but music goes on forever. Since people learnt to replicate music, it has been played on all sorts of different machines and stored in as many different ways. As new ways of playing recorded music have entered the marketplace, their predecessors' lives have been cut short. You can still buy vinyl and cassettes but most buyers opt for CDs.

1 When a new music product is introduced, who does it appeal to?

2 What happens to sales as customers become familiar with the product?

3 What happens to sales when another new music product is introduced to the marketplace?

4 Draw a graph showing the life of a product in terms of sales.

5 A new product is likely to take much promotion in order to sell and generate revenue. Add a line to your graph, which shows the cash flow it generates.

6 In the light of this pattern, how does a business try to manage the range of products on its books?

The product portfolio

Products at different stages of their life bring in different amounts of revenue, so a business needs a healthy mix to maintain a balance and ensure a secure future. The **product portfolio** includes the range of a business's products.

Businesses generally analyse this mix to check on potential future revenue flows. A tool that is often used is the **Boston Matrix** – so called because it came from the Boston Consulting Group, which sells its advice services to business.

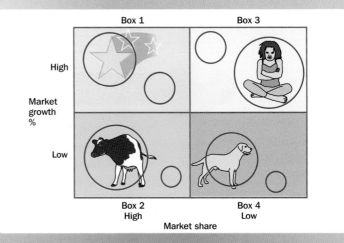

The four boxes of the Boston Matrix help businesses to decide how their products are doing when compared to others. Each circle in the box shows the amount of revenue that a product brings in. A big circle means lots of revenue.

Box 1 High market share/high growth

Stars shine brightly in a product portfolio because they bring lots of revenue, but competitors will want to create a copycat.

Box 2 High market share/low growth

Cash cows are milked to provide money for investment for newer products.

Box 3 Low market share/high growth

Problem children need investment to gain market share.

Box 4 Low market share/low growth

Dogs disappear because they don't bring in much revenue and the market isn't growing.

Every product has a life ...

1 While a product is under development, it is adding costs to the business rather than contributing to profit.

2 In its early stages of introduction costs will still exceed revenue because of promotion costs. This will change as the launch takes root.

3 The growth stage brings an increased market share – or place in a growing market. Profits grow throughout the stage.

4 During maturity sales of the product become more stable.

5 Decline means a fall in profits as customers turn away from the product. The business must do something if it wants the product to continue.

Some products have features which mean that all the businesses in the field move in similar ways. The television, for example, started life in black and white, became colour ... and grew into the television we know today. Others are very personal to a particular business so the **product life cycle** is less dependent on major technological changes.

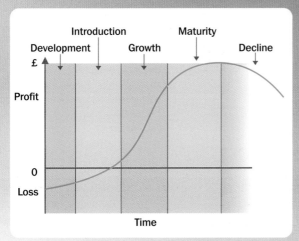

Product life cycle

... BUT A DIFFERENT ONE

Not all products follow exactly this pattern. Some famous flops have hit the market. The C5 was a strange little electric vehicle that was supposed to save city congestion but it did not catch the public imagination and its product life cycle looked very different from the diagram. Some products have very long periods of maturity. Kit Kat has remained almost unchanged for decades. It became chunky but the traditional bar still exists. Nestlé is of course very happy to have products like this in its range.

... OR A LONGER ONE

When a business sees that a product is reaching maturity, it needs to think about what to do next. Making the most of the investment in the product is important, so a plan should be put in place to extend its life.

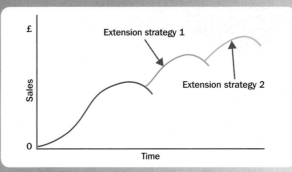

Extending the product life cycle

Businesses try all sorts of ways of extending the life of their products. Sometimes it works and sometimes it doesn't. Coca-Cola decided to give Coke a new flavour but its customers revolted. Classic Coke was quickly reintroduced and the new flavour was forgotten. Cars are updated with little tweaks to their design to give a longer life before an expensive major revamp is necessary.

Success comes down to clever use of the marketing mix. Many products have gone through periods of maturity only to have new life pumped into them by a fresh marketing approach. Lucozade is one of the most famous, having been repositioned as a drink for healthy people instead of being aimed at the sick.

Critical thinking

1 Draw a product life cycle for Kit Kat, skateboards, televisions and Sony Walkman.

2 Select a range of products that you buy and decide whether they are likely to be stars, cash cows, problem children or dogs. What advice would you give the company about future developments?

KEY TERMS

Product life cycle shows the path that many products go through from development to the end of their lives. Many businesses use extension strategies to give products a longer life.

Product portfolio shows the mix of products that a business produces.

Boston Matrix is a way of analysing the products in the portfolio.

What is a product?

Specification Content

Product design

starSTUDY

Stephen's laptop

Stephen needed a laptop to take to clients when they called him in to develop their websites. He went to one of the big name retailers and chose a smart-looking machine with a name he knew to be reliable. He wanted to look professional when he went off to visit his growing client list.

After a couple of months his frustration with the laptop exploded. The battery lasted for about 20 minutes and he was always looking for a socket to plug it in. His clients always seemed to have equipment that worked properly. He just looked inefficient. He rang the manufacturer and was told that the machine had nothing to do with them. The machine had been bought direct from their head office in Hong Kong and was supported by the big name retailer. He tried contacting them and was told that the laptop would have to go back. But it was only the battery... He needed his laptop to go on working so how could he part with it? After spending hours on the phone, queuing for the helpline, trying to talk to someone who could make decisions, he persuaded them to send a replacement battery. When it arrived it didn't fit!

1. What did Stephen expect when he bought his laptop?
2. Why is aftercare so important with products like this?
3. How did Stephen's costs increase because of the inadequate aftercare on offer?
4. Why should a business think about its products as a 'total experience'?
5. Do you think Stephen will go back to this retailer again?
6. Make a list of the criteria that a business should include in this 'total experience'.

What is a product?

Products are all the things that are sold to customers. Both products and customers vary greatly.

Customers may be:

- individuals in the customer market
- businesses in an industrial market.

Products that are sold to businesses include all the resources that they need such as:

- electrics for the motor industry
- concrete for the building industry
- paper, photocopiers and other office supplies for any business

- services such as cleaning, repairs, insurance or banking.

Products that are sold to customers can be:

- shopping products, such as televisions and fridges, which last a long time and are bought occasionally and need consideration before purchase
- convenience goods which are bought frequently for everyday consumption.

The product doesn't stop at the item or service itself. When Stephen bought his laptop, he expected the warranty that came with it to meet his needs, but it didn't. Many businesses find that customers do not return when customer service and aftercare fall down.

Right product – right market

You are unlikely to see frivolous adverts for insurance. Buyers are looking for security, so want to feel safe in their purchase. Fun might not be ruled out but a customer wants to know that the product is sound – especially when they feel that they do not understand all the small print that goes with it. Such security is an **intangible benefit**. Almost all products offer intangible benefits: cars, trainers, phones and drinks – to give but a few examples. Different cars give different intangible messages. It's easy to guess the nature of the message from looking at a product's styling and advertising.

Draught beer has moved into selling with a different sort of intangible appeal!

The tangible benefits are more concrete because they can be measured – the washing machine that spins 1200 times a minute rather than 800; the computer that has a bigger hard disk and a faster processor.

To get it right, a business must have a clear picture of the market. It is important to keep a close eye on both customers and competitors.

go to → *pages 12–15 to refresh your ideas on knowing the market*

On a very practical note, any product that is produced must be financially viable. When businesses look at new products or at updating existing products, the finance department always has a role to play. A product may work very well and look wonderful but if it can't be sold at a price that customers are prepared to pay, it isn't viable. There are, of course, legal requirements for many products. Safety has to be at the top of the agenda and standards have been laid down for almost everything.

Critical thinking

1 If you are developing a marketing strategy for a product, you need to consider different factors for different products. What factors are important in marketing trainers, a small car, a fridge, an apple, a hairdresser, a garden centre and a theme park?

2 Why is it important to make sure that the product is financially viable? Why not just charge a higher price?

Next steps

1 Look carefully at some adverts and decide on the nature of the tangible and intangible benefit that are determining the advertising strategy.

2 Choose a business that you know and look at its product range. Work out where each product is in its life cycle and position them in the product portfolio. What makes the products different from each other?

KEY TERMS

Intangible benefits relate to the feel of the product and the image it is trying to give.

Tangible benefits relate to practical aspects of the product.

Developing products

Product
development

starSTUDY

On track

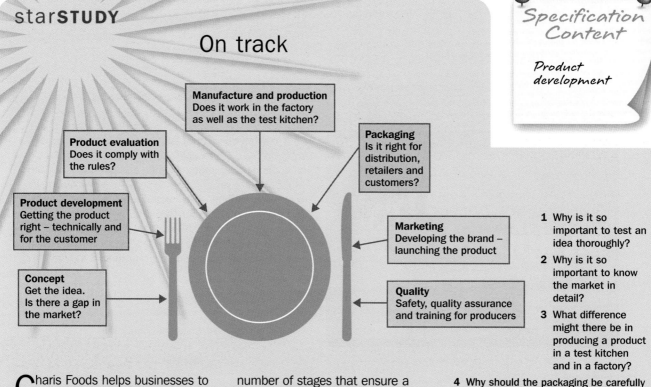

Manufacture and production
Does it work in the factory
as well as the test kitchen?

Product evaluation
Does it comply with
the rules?

Packaging
Is it right for
distribution,
retailers and
customers?

Product development
Getting the product
right – technically and
for the customer

Marketing
Developing the brand –
launching the product

Concept
Get the idea.
Is there a gap in
the market?

Quality
Safety, quality assurance
and training for producers

Specification
Content

Charis Foods helps businesses to develop new products. It has developed Food Track, a programme designed to guide small and medium-sized enterprises (SMEs) through the process. The development work involves a number of stages that ensure a product meets everyone's needs. A business might also use part of it to develop an existing product. It has been put to work to help companies produce a wide range of new food products or extend the life of others.

1 Why is it so important to test an idea thoroughly?

2 Why is it so important to know the market in detail?

3 What difference might there be in producing a product in a test kitchen and in a factory?

4 Why should the packaging be carefully evaluated?

5 How might a business use stages of the process to update existing products? Can you think of some examples of products that have been updated or remodelled?

Why develop products?

New products almost always attract attention. New cars are reviewed on the television and in newspapers and motoring magazines. New food products often get coverage in a similar way. The launch of a product provides an opportunity for businesses to let the market know what they are doing. It also adds products to a business's portfolio to keep a healthy mix of old and new.

Existing products must not be forgotten. Keeping the product portfolio up to date is important otherwise other businesses will take advantage and a reputation for being behind the times might develop. A steady stream of product development also helps to differentiate one business's products from another. It is, however, important to ensure that the money spent on development is recouped through more sales or the customer's willingness to pay a higher price. As with new products, making modifications to existing ones can elicit media attention.

Innovation also gives a business competitive advantage because customers recognise that it is at the forefront of the market.

Next steps

Choose a range of products and work out how they might be developed in future. Be realistic because lavish expense on change will probably not be recouped if the price can't rise.

KEY TERMS

Small and medium-sized enterprises are independent businesses, managed by their owners or part-owners and having a small market share.

New product development

FINDING A NICHE

FINDING A NICHE for a new product means researching both the market and customers while thinking 'out of the box'. A business must try to identify a product that

- makes the most of new technology
- appeals to customers
- will make a profit
- is not under development in another company.

The decision that a new product can be sold at a realistic price is critical to future development. It is easy to dream up a product that everyone would like but if it costs so much that no one will be prepared to pay the price, it's a non-starter.

DEVELOPMENT OF THE PRODUCT

involves many people in the business:

- Technical people make sure that it works
- Designers make sure it both looks good and functions
- Marketing people check the product against known customer habits
- Finance people keep an eye on costs.

TESTING THE MARKET

TESTING THE MARKET is important with a new product. The marketing department will try to find an area that is similar to the market they expect to sell into and put the product to the test. This is often combined with local television advertising to draw attention to the new product. While this happens, the market research continues and the findings will offer guidance on the launch of the final product.

LAUNCHING THE PRODUCT

LAUNCHING THE PRODUCT once it has proved itself is a major challenge and can cost millions. A careful combination of marketing activities will be used to get the message to the public. Free samples of new food products are often handed out in supermarkets to entice the public to buy. Sachets of shampoo and samples of perfume are frequently to be found in magazines. New cars are often launched at motor shows with much hype and special events are organised for journalists to encourage them to write flattering articles. Drug companies have sometimes come in for criticism for inviting doctors on expenses-paid trips to exotic places to find out about a new drug.

A star, cash cow, dog or problem child?

go to → Review the Boston Matrix on page 24

Letting people try the product first often encourages them to buy.

Every business would like to see its new product become a star. Having a large share of a growing market is a very desirable situation. Inevitably, few products achieve this quickly. Some will become problem children because they have taken a small share of a high growth market. Products like this will need further development or different marketing to win more market share or be dropped as a lost cause.

A new product is unlikely to become a cash cow quickly because cash cows are usually found in mature markets. A dog would lead to despair. The food industry often has low growth markets, simply because there is a limit on how much we can eat. A new product would aim to have an impact and steal market share from others. A dog would fail to do this.

The Boston Matrix can be put to work like this in order to analyse the position of products in the portfolio of a business. Decisions can then be made about future activities.

Critical thinking

1 Look out for the launch of a new product.
2 How is the product different from others?
3 Work out who the target market is.
4 Does the product appeal to that market? Why?
5 What promotional techniques are being used?
6 How successful do you think the launch is? Explain your answer.
7 Try to find out from the media or the Internet whether it has been successful.

Prices and people

Specification Content

Calculation and interpretation for decision making of price elasticity

starSTUDY

1 What happens to bus company revenue when fares go up? Why?

2 What would happen to revenue if either restaurant put its prices up? Why?

3 Why do makers of electrical products have to think hard before they raise prices?

4 Why does the customer go on buying chewing gum even when the price goes up?

5 Draw up a chart showing
  a things that people buy even if the price goes up
  b things that people cut back on a bit if the price goes up
  c things that people stop buying when the price goes up.
  Work out what each category has in common.

6 If you ran a business, which sort of product would you prefer to supply? Why?

7 Many businesses try to make their products a little bit special so that people really want them. What are they trying to do?

When prices change ...

People's buying habits are influenced by price but they do not react in the same way in all their purchases. The different responses are measured by **price elasticity of demand**. The examples above show these different responses.

If a business knows how people will react, it can plan its pricing strategy more accurately. Many people in business deny all knowledge of the elasticity for their products but in fact they know just what will happen if they put the price up.

Using price elasticity

IN THE KNOW

Knowing about the price elasticity of your products is clearly invaluable to people running businesses.

SETTING PRICES

Elasticity provides the basic information for decision making. It must be used with other information about the costs and feasibility of changing the scale of production. If a price cut leads to a large increase in demand, can the business cope? McDonald's had a 2 for the price of

1 offer and couldn't meet the demand. The strategy was viewed both as a failure and success. There were some angry customers who couldn't get the cheap burgers but many others stayed and bought something else!

CHANGING THE PATTERN

Elastic demand is not good news for businesses that want to put prices up. Many work hard to try to change people's perceptions or reduce competition in order to make demand more inelastic.

• **Differentiating the product** works by creating a product that is distinct from its competitors.

Price and demand

If a business wants to put prices up, it helps to know just what will happen to sales and revenue. It might generate more revenue, stay about the same or even fall – so it is worth thinking about.

Price elasticity of demand helps to provide an answer. The formula below gives a figure that shows the outcome.

$$\text{Price elasticity} = \frac{\%\ \text{change in quantity demanded}}{\%\ \text{change in price}}$$

If the price goes up by 10% and sales fall by 15%, the formula will look like this:

$$\frac{-15\%}{+10\%} = -1.5$$

This means that a price rise will reduce revenue, therefore it is not a good strategy. Demand for most products is elastic so businesses have to think carefully before putting up the price. If the price of a Solero ice cream goes up, customers will look at the alternatives.

If, on the other hand, a 10% rise led to a 5% fall in sales, the story would be different.

$$\frac{-5\%}{+10\%} = -0.5$$

This means that revenue doesn't fall when the price goes up. It rises. Most business can't do this forever because customers will become more price sensitive as the price rises. Designer labels can put prices up considerably before demand starts to fall but, eventually, even the most fashion conscious person wonders if it is worth it.

Products like gas, electricity and petrol are more price inelastic because they are products which we can't do without. Season tickets for buses and trains fall into the same category. We have to travel to work, come what may.

You will have noticed that all these figures are negative. An elasticity figure is always negative so the minus sign is often ignored.

TO SUM UP ...

Elastic demand
Value of more than 1   Revenue falls when price rises

Inelastic demand
Value between 0 and 1   Revenue rises when price rises

Buying habits change with income too

As people earn more, they spend more on some things but less on others. This is known as **income elasticity of demand**. They don't buy much more milk, but they will buy a more expensive car and long-haul holidays. Demand for some products actually falls. People move from own-brand products to brand names. From a business point of view selling luxury products has great advantages but sales are very sensitive to recessions.

Critical thinking

1 How elastic or inelastic is demand for the products in the Star Study? Explain your answers.

2 Choose a range of products that you know and work out how sensitive they are to price changes. Select one with elastic demand and another with inelastic demand and draw up a spider diagram for each one, showing the factors a business would have to consider before changing the price.

Designer clothing companies do this all the time.

- **Merging with the rivals** reduces competition so there are fewer substitutes and customers have less choice.

- **Price fixing** among businesses reduces competition. If airlines decided that they would all charge the same price for a flight to Paris, customers would have to pay up. It is illegal.

KEY TERMS

Price elasticity of demand measures the responsiveness of customers to a change in price.

Income elasticity of demand measures the responsiveness of customers to a change in income.

Next steps

Walk round a supermarket or other large store and look at the pricing strategies that are being used. How is price being used to persuade customers to buy? Is it being successful? Why do you think the business is doing it?

Setting the price

starSTUDY

Want to go to Malaga?

Planning to fly to Malaga on a Tuesday in October? There's plenty of choice. It all depends on what you are prepared to pay.

Flight 3711

departs London Stansted at 07:45

web fare 16.49 GBP (phone fare 21.49 GBP)

Flight 3713

departs London Stansted at 11:35

web fare 26.49 GBP (phone fare 31.49 GBP)

Flight 3715

departs London Stansted at 21:15

web fare 21.49 GBP (phone fare 26.49 GBP)

Not including taxes
Fly from Stansted airport. No seat allocation.
Food and drinks available to buy.

Economy

Depart London Stansted at 8.25
£139.30 including taxes
Depart London Stansted at 14.45
£139.30 including taxes
Depart London Stansted at 18.30
£139.30 including taxes

Fly from Stansted. Seats allocated before departure. Food and drink provided.

Club Class

Depart London Stansted at 8.25
£526.30 including taxes
Depart London Stansted at 14.25
£526.30 including taxes
Depart London Stansted at 19.30
£526.30 including taxes

Fly from Stansted. Wider seats allocated before departure. Better quality food and drink provided.

 AIR PARTNER PLC

Air Partners
An executive jet for 6 people from any location, at any time.
£8,000

Specification Content

Price: based on cost, competition, customer

1. How do these four products vary?
2. Do these variations in price reflect the different costs of providing the service?
3. Are the prices presented in the same way?
4. Why do you think the prices are set at these levels?
5. Look at the information on the rest of these two pages and work out which pricing strategies are being used by each business.

What price?

Businesses set prices with the aim of making as much profit as possible – immediately or in the longer run. An understanding of the elasticity of demand helps because it informs decision makers about the likely effect of a change. Before setting the price, they need to ask:

• How fierce is the competition?

If there are many competitors in the market, people will look around for a good deal. On the other hand, the bus company may be able to raise fares because there are no direct competitors. Some businesses will keep the price higher in order to differentiate their brand from others, giving it snob appeal.

• Will consumers buy if the price is high?

It all depends on the product and the customer. Those with high incomes might spend £39.50 on an Italian orange squeezer, when you can buy a perfectly good one for £4.99.

Snob appeal?

• Is there much of the product available?

A shortage is always popular because a business can charge more. When Christmas comes and the favourite toy is in short supply, parents will pay anything to get hold of one! Later on, when supplies are restored to normal, they will be much more careful about looking for a good deal.

KEY TERMS

Discount is a reduction on the price. It is generally expressed as a percentage.

Pricing methods

Businesses use a variety of approaches to pricing. They may be based on cost, competition or customers – the 3Cs.

COST-BASED PRICING

Pricing strategy	How it works	Comments
Cost plus or mark up	Add a certain percentage to costs. e.g. 50% on £50 = £75. This is often done on items bought by retailers from wholesalers.	This is often done by tradition in some industries but isn't very sensitive to market conditions.
Target	A business knows how much return it expects and works out the price of the product to provide it.	The target must be set with market conditions in mind. A business will quickly get into trouble if unrealistic targets are set.
Contribution	Contribution pricing is based on variable costs. If the variable costs are £10, any price above that will make a contribution to the fixed cost of the business. If fixed costs are £50,000 and the price is set at £12, the first 25,000 sales will cover the costs and the 25,001st sale will start making a profit.	The mark up needs to be set in the context of the market. Is demand strong enough to pay the price? A business can compare the effectiveness of a product by looking at the contribution it is making.

go to → Find out more about variable and fixed costs on page 45

COMPETITION-BASED PRICING

- Price leadership occurs when there is one dominant business that sets the price. Price takers follow.

- When businesses charge the same price, they are often trying to avoid a price war because this means cutting profit margins.

- Predatory pricing happens when a business deliberately sets its prices very low to force competitors out of the market. Prices usually rise once the competition has gone.

CONSUMER-BASED PRICING

Penetration pricing is used for new products. A business might aim to get in quickly and set a low price. A new gym will often give a discount when it opens in order to attract members.

Price skimming is a different strategy for a new product. A very trendy gym might decide to charge a premium because it wants to be viewed as elite.

Price discrimination is used when people can be divided into separate markets for a product. Commuters have to travel at a particular time of day, therefore they can be charged a higher price.

Which strategy?

Many businesses use more than one strategy because they keep an eye on the market and aim to make the most of prevailing conditions. Cost plus pricing is the most frequent method but others are used to make extra profit. A business might give a **discount** to attract a big customer.

What tactics?

Loss leaders have low prices, even below costs. The aim is to get customers through the shop door so they buy other things.

Special offers also tempt us into shops. Supermarkets often offer 'buy one get one free' or try to tempt you to buy two complementary products.

A psychological price is one set at £19.99, for example – not quite £20.

Critical thinking

1. Which pricing strategy would you use if you set up a new sandwich bar? Why?

2. What effect would a business hope to have if it went for predatory pricing? Think of an example of this happening.

3. Why is it important to keep an eye on the market?

4. How might a business which offers financial advice aim to develop its pricing strategy?

5. How does price elasticity of demand affect the decision that a business makes on pricing?

Next steps

Have a look at some businesses in the high street or the web and work out how they are setting their prices.

Promoting the product

starSTUDY

What a week of wizardry!

 £1 million spent on a book launch by a publisher

 A character becomes a brand

 Tantalising snips of information leaked from time to time

 £1 million webcast of the author

 £200,000 movie premiere style party

 £100,000 to turn a bookshop into a theme party

 Author has an audience with 4000 readers in the Albert Hall

 Competitions on Blue Peter and MTV

 Book covers for children – another one for adults

 200 products to be found on Amazon

 Media coverage of every step

 200 million copies sold in 47 languages

 Read by 1 in 3 adults and innumerable children

What else could it be but Harry Potter? Promotion for J.K. Rowling's books and films has outstripped everything else in the children's entertainment market. The books were released on the stroke of midnight. Children celebrated in bookshops up and down the country. At exactly the same time in New York's Times Square, Potter lookalikes gave away stickers and badges at the same moment as the book cover flashed up on the billboards. Not really surprising for a product that is worth £3 billion a year!

1 Which market segments are Harry Potter books aimed at?

2 Do they sell beyond the intended segments? Why?

3 What is the objective of promotion of this sort?

4 Why is becoming a brand a key to marketing success?

5 How did the marketing strategy achieve even more promotion than the businesses organised?

6 What promotional strategies has the Potter brand used? Why?

Specification Content

Promotion: above and below the line

Marketing magic

Harry Potter is a phenomenon. A simple story that turns into a major brand is very unusual. The first book caught the public imagination and then the marketers had a major opportunity and made the most of it. The marketing departments at Bloomsbury, the publishers, and Warner, which makes the films, have used a wide range of promotional activities to make the most of this opportunity.

Promotion

IN THE KNOW

The objective of all promotional techniques is to get a message across to customers and persuade them to buy the product. It should be informative, persuasive or reassuring. Everyone thinks of advertising, which is known as an **above the line** method, but there are many other strategies as well. They are generally called **below the line** techniques.

ADVERTISING comes in many different forms and in many different places. It is on television and radio, in the papers and magazines and on hoardings, racing cars and anywhere that there is a little space. Product placement means seeing James Bond drive an Aston Martin or a football star wearing a particular designer's outfits. It is a discreet way of having a product associated with famous names and visible to many.

PERSONAL SELLING also happens in many different ways. It involves direct contact with the customer, so it ranges from selling in a car showroom to knocking on doors or holding marketing parties. Personal selling in general is expensive because of the cost of recruiting, training and motivating staff. Telesales has become increasingly important as it is a cheaper way to get to customers.

DIRECT MARKETING involves using mailshots and catalogues that go straight to the customer.

POINT OF SALE promotion is used where the product is being sold. It can take the form of posters, leaflets, stickers, etc.

SALES PROMOTION often involves incentives such as loyalty cards, vouchers for money off your shopping in coming weeks or two for the price of one, etc. It also includes getting the branding and packaging right.

PUBLIC RELATIONS tries to put positive messages about a product or a business in the public eye. It uses press releases and contacts to persuade newspapers to write articles about the benefits of a product. It may involve sponsoring an event or competition in order to draw attention to a business or brand name.

How to decide?

There are so many ways of promoting a product that a business might be lost for choice – until it looks at the cost. A thirty-second spot on national, peak time television costs so much that it is only an option for the biggest advertisers. It is, therefore, only an option for big name businesses. Before making decisions, a business must consider the nature of the product, the size of the market and the costs. A mail order company needs to send out a catalogue, put it on the web – or both. The local takeaway might put leaflets through people's doors or perhaps have a short advert at the local cinema. If a product appeals to a specialist market, a specialist magazine or website may be the answer.

The types of promotion that are selected will have been informed by market research. You can often look at adverts and see how they are trying to change people's perceptions. Cruise companies, for example, try to persuade people that their holidays are not just for the elderly.

The marketing department will have been allocated a budget and will have to make choices within its limitations.

Critical thinking

1 Make a note of all the promotional activities that you come across in a day. Why do you think the businesses have chosen each strategy?

2 Who is the target market?

3 Can you spot the messages from market research that have informed the promotion?

4 Do you know of other things that each business does to attract customers? How do you think the mix works?

5 Which business's strategy is most effective? Why? Try to take the amount of money spent into account in your decision.

KEY TERMS

Above the line promotion includes all direct advertising.

Below the line promotion includes all other forms including sales promotion, personal selling, etc.

Next steps

You have been asked to promote a new bar/restaurant that is aimed at young people in your area. What would you do?

Placing the product

starSTUDY

Right place – right time

On the day that another Harry Potter book hit the market, 2 million books had to be in the right place at the right time. It was to be found in 6,200 bookshops, supermarkets and even petrol stations in the UK and around the world. Amazon already had 350,000 orders for the book and many orders had been placed on the publisher's website.

After all the hype, failing to meet the deadlines would have been a disaster. The image of disappointed children without their Harry Potter books was not the message that Bloomsbury, the publisher, wanted to see. Routes of distribution to retailers and e-commerce companies were critical, especially in a business that isn't used to working on this scale.

Specification Content

Place: channels of distribution

1 Why do you think the book was available in unusual places like petrol stations?

2 Why was it important to make sure the books were in the right place?

3 Do you think retailers needed to be persuaded to stock the book? Why?

4 What sort of products might a retailer have to be persuaded to stock?

5 All sorts of products are now available through a bigger range of outlets. Give some examples.

6 Why do you think producers
   a welcome this change
   b are less enthusiastic about it?

Right product – right place

Different sorts of products are to be found in different places. Chocolate bars are probably the most widespread product. They are to be found in supermarkets, corner shops, newsagents, petrol stations, vending machines, pubs and many more. A producer of a new chocolate bar, however, might have to work hard to persuade retailers to stock it. Space on the shelves is valuable because a shop depends on rapid stock turnover to keep profit levels up. The best place varies from product to product. Levi, for example, didn't want Tesco to stock its jeans. One reason was that it felt that its image would be tarnished by being associated with Tesco. The second reason was that Tesco wanted to cut the price.

The place where a product is sold is often used to influence the image of the product. When Coca-Cola wanted to relaunch Cherry Coke with a more risqué image, it ran events in clubs across the country.

Harry Potter books don't provide a problem as retailers know that they will sell very quickly, but many products are more of a problem. A retailer will want to know about the promotional activities associated with a product. Will there be television or newspaper advertising? Is there point-of-sale advertising material? Are there any introductory offers on the product?

Getting the product to the retailer also has to be thought about carefully. When shops run out of stocks, customers may buy another product and never come back. Getting it right is critical to keeping and gaining customers.

Channels of distribution

TRADITIONAL ROUTE

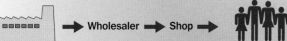

Wholesalers buy stock from manufacturers and sell them on to shops. This is a helpful process for small shops, which cannot deal with the large quantities at one go. Many small shopkeepers go to cash-and-carry warehouses, which are the equivalent of the traditional wholesaler. The process might even involve an agent who is authorised to sell the product in bulk to wholesalers. The traditional route is also known as a long channel route.

MODERN ROUTE

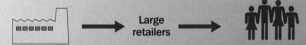

Supermarket chains no longer use wholesalers. They buy direct from the producers. The scale of purchase is so great that the supermarkets make deals directly with suppliers. This process is criticised because of the power that these large buyers have over the price. Most producers cannot afford to be ignored by the major supermarket chains, therefore they are prepared to accept lower margins.

Some supermarkets have taken things a stage further. Waitrose, for example, has its own farm which supplies produce direct to the shops.

Food is not the only business that works directly with the suppliers. PC World buys computers direct from the manufacturer. It also has models made specifically for it to give it a cost advantage over other stores.

This is a short channel route.

DIRECT

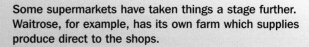

An increasing number of producers sell direct to the customer. The Internet has assisted this process. Harry Potter books can be bought straight from the publisher just like most other books. Some businesses, like Dell computers, have based their whole system on direct selling. The great advantage is that it cuts costs. If a Harry Potter book is sold to a bookshop, the price has to be set so the shop can make a profit on the selling price. The telephone and text messages are also used by direct sales businesses. Cutting costs can mean lower prices, so customers are increasingly tempted to buy direct.

This is a short channel route.

Mushrooms from Waitrose's Leckford Farm on sale in the supermarket

Critical thinking

A business is launching a new model of personal stereo with lots of up-to-the-minute features. Work out where it should want to place the product and how it should persuade shops or other outlets to stock it. Can you think of any other distribution strategies? Explain why you think they would work.

Next steps

1 Have a look at Dell's website, www.dell.co.uk. Find out the price of one of its computers.

2 Have a look in a high street store and compare the price of a computer with a similar specification.

3 How much cheaper is Dell?

4 What are the advantages and disadvantages of buying from Dell and a high street store?

KEY TERMS

Short channel routes include direct and modern channels of distribution. They cut out wholesalers and agents.

Long channel routes are distribution methods that include wholesalers or agents.

Chester Zoo

Chester Zoo is a zoo without bars. You watch the animals by just strolling through the zoo's complex, but it is more comfortable to board the monorail or tour by boat. Highlights are the glass-sided penguin-pool, the Twilight Zone bat cave, the orang-utan breeding centre and the crocodiles in the Tropical Realms.

Chester Zoo is a charity run on firm business lines. The zoo's marketing budget of £670,000 was spent on advertising and promotion to attract more visitors, raise funds and raise public awareness. Average spend per visitor continues to rise and last year reached £12.39. This is in addition to the rise in visitor numbers to 1,050,000 for the year. All good news because the extra revenue is essential if the zoo is to achieve its objective of supporting and promoting conservation.

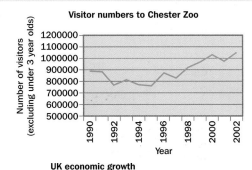

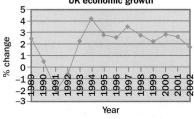

Year	Inflation Index
1991	100
1992	105.0
1993	108.6
1994	110.5
1995	112.3

Year	Visitors
1990	890,000
1991	880,000
1992	770,000
1993	810,000
1994	770,000
1995	760,000
1996	870,000
1997	830,000
1998	920,000
1999	970,000
2000	1,020,000
2001	975,000
2002	1,050,000

Chester Zoo has five simple and clear marketing objectives:

- To encourage customers to come back through new exhibits and promotions, memberships and adoptions.
- To get new visitors through promotion activities and ticket pricing.
- To spread the visitors more evenly over the whole season through special events.
- To raise awareness of the zoo's work in conservation.
- To sell more food, drink and souvenirs.

To meet these marketing objectives the zoo must monitor and evaluate its marketing plan.

The marketing department wants to continue developing its nationally recognised brand, explore and trial commercial enterprises and events, and develop cost effective promotional techniques.

The zoo believes it offers its customers high standards of care and high quality visitor facilities that cater for all ages. It wants to be sure that its facilities meet the top tourist attraction standards. It won the Zoo of the Year award in 2002, but it needs to be sure it understands what its customers think.

The zoo pays a specialist market research business to make up a questionnaire and analyse the results. The information collected has a 96% confidence level.

Until recently the main method of collecting information was to:

- Undertake yearly visitor surveys carried out by the zoo staff or during the summer months by staff specially employed for the task.
- Read existing published information.
- Encourage all the staff to observe and listen to customers.
- Monitor voucher returns in newspapers.

Chester Zoo groups the questions into three broad areas.

1. Questions about their customers. The zoo wants to know their ages, why they decided to visit the zoo, how long they spent there, when they arrived, how they got there and where they came from.
2. How effective is its promotion?
3. Views or opinions of their customers including likes and dislikes plus how the zoo could be improved.

The marketing team will use the market research information to produce a report or a marketing plan. This will be presented to senior managers from other functional areas who will discuss its implications for their area. For example, the marketing department at the zoo recognised a need to improve catering, but this has an effect on human resources and the finance departments.

From the website:

'Chester Zoo offers a fun and stimulating day out for everyone, no matter what age or ability. As well as our 500 different species of animals and award-winning gardens, we offer first class facilities that ensure your day out really is as enjoyable as possible.

'The Zoo is completely wheelchair and pushchair accessible, and all of our toilet facilities have disabled access, as well as plenty of Parent and Baby changing rooms. And parents will be delighted to know that our new Fun Ark adventure play area, near the Ark Restaurant, is a great place for children of all ages to let off steam!

'There is a wide range of shops, cafes and ice-cream kiosks located around the Zoo; which cater for all tastes and budgets. At our Fountain Shop a fun and professional face-painting service is available during peak periods.'

- Bring the family along for a Halloween disco, supper and other creepy happenings. £14.00 per adult £9.00 per child
- Visit Santa in December

Up until now we have put the price up by 50p each year! We are currently doing a price audit to look at how we can manage the pricing structure more scientifically over the next few years. We have changed our discounting structure this summer from £5 to 10% off, which has put an extra £25,000 on our net ticket sales.

Socio-economic groups of visitors	
Group	
A+B	14%
C1	35%
C2	35%
D+E	16%

WEDDINGS

CORPORATE & PRIVATE FUNCTIONS

SAFARI EVENINGS WHEN THE ZOO IS CLOSED TO THE GENERAL PUBLIC, WE INVITE YOU TO BRING A PRIVATE PARTY OF 30 PEOPLE OR MORE FOR A UNIQUE EVENING'S ENTERTAINMENT.

BIRTHDAY PARTIES

Monthly attendance

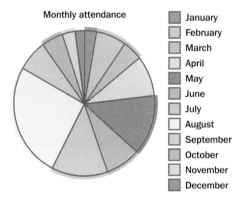

- January
- February
- March
- April
- May
- June
- July
- August
- September
- October
- November
- December

Age group of visitors	
Age in years	%
0-3	12.5
4-6	7.5
6-7	6
8-10	3
10-12	5
12-15	6
16-19	1
20-24	5
25-34	20
35-54	20
55+	11

Visitors returning to the zoo	
	Re-visits
This year	13%
last year	30%
2-3 years ago	19%
4-5 years ago	13%
6-10 years ago	7%
Over 10 years ago	18%

Advertising seen by visitors

- TV
- Posters
- Radio
- Leaflets
- Press
- Other

Overall, how good value would you say the admission charge for here was?	
• Extremely good	10% (results given)
• Very good	58%
• Fairly good	30%
• Not very good	1%
• Not at all	0%

54% of visitors have heard or seen advertising about the zoo recently

Most visitors are within a 45 minute drive time

assessment questions

1 In what ways does the zoo's marketing objectives help support its overall objectives? **(4 marks)**

 This requires you to make the simple link showing how marketing supports the zoo in its main objectives.

2 How does Chester Zoo go about adding value? **(4 marks)**

 You will need to define added value and relate this to the activities undertaken by the zoo.

3 Discuss two promotional methods and strategies that might be suitable for the zoo to use to encourage new customers. What methods might be suitable to encourage repeat customers? **(8 marks)**

 A simple example of above and below the line promotional methods that might be used by the zoo to attract the two types of customers. Try to justify which might be more cost effective.

4 What is market segmentation? How and why might the zoo segment its market? **(4 marks)**

 Straightforward definition followed by two examples using evidence from the case study.

5 Explain two internal and two external factors that have influenced the rate of growth of customers to the zoo. **(6 marks)**

 Internal means talking about what the zoo has done to attract more customers and external wants you to write about influences beyond the control of the organisation.

6 Assume a new marketing campaign costs £20,000 and manages to bring in an extra 3000 adults. Would it be regarded as successful? **(4 marks)**

This requires a calculation of the extra revenue that will come in minus the campaign costs. Will there be other costs? Think about how the zoo is adding value.

7 Why is market research important to the zoo? **(4 marks)**

 Straightforward asking you to comment on how it informs decision-making and can be used to make forecasts.

8 How might it best carry out its research? **(6 marks)**

 Mention primary and secondary examples and how this may be best gathered. There is plenty of evidence within the case study.

9 Analyse the results of past market research. **(8 marks)**

 This requires you to extract information from the data, but don't forget to comment where the data is insufficient. What more would you want?

10 Why has the zoo been able to raise its prices regularly over the past 12 years? **(10 marks)**

 This is a tricky question. First, think carefully about the concepts that lie behind such a question. Changes in income elasticity of demand and price elasticity of demand come to mind. Use the data on zoo visitors, zoo prices and the economy to help make some calculations.

11 Produce and justify a marketing plan to increase customers who might be attracted to events outside normal zoo hours. How might such a plan be monitored? **(10 marks)**

 There are plenty of examples to choose from in the case study. Choose from Santa, safari evenings, Halloween, children's parties, weddings and corporate functions. You could then comment on the make up of the marketing mix to your example.

Why keep accounts?

starSTUDY

The collapse of energy giant Enron is the largest bankruptcy in US corporate history. In just over 15 years, Enron grew into one of the US's largest companies. However the company's success was based on artificially inflated profits, dubious accounting practices, and – some say – fraud.

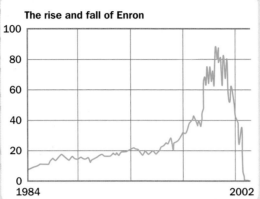

The rise and fall of Enron

Enron share price

- The energy giant – once the US's seventh largest firm – paid no income tax between 1996 and 1999.

- Enron executives bribed tax officials in order to fabricate accounts.

- Share price rose steadily as the profits appeared to grow.

Specification Content

Accounts help a business keep records, monitor and control performance; financial accounts are used by stakeholders to assess performance

1 Why might the executive directors of Enron have tried to cover up the company's real performance?

2 When do you think the problems of Enron's financial records started to be uncovered?

3 Make a list of the stakeholders who are hurt from accounting errors or bad practice and performance described in the examples above and below.

- Shareholders and directors sacked Jean-Marie Messier, boss at France's media giant Vivendi Universal. In two years shareholders have watched the value of their investments drop from $120 a share to about $20 a share. At the same time, debt has risen sharply.

- Two former top executives at bankrupt telecommunications firm WorldCom have been arrested and charged with fraud. 'Corporate executives who cheat investors, steal savings and squander pensions will meet the judgement they fear and the punishment they deserve.' (US Attorney General John Ashcroft)

- A Scottish breast cancer charity has its bank accounts frozen after a judge hears that only a small amount of the millions it raised went on good causes.

- A Devon health trust calls in outside accountants after finding mistakes in its accounts for the last financial year. It found it had an extra £1m debt.

Keeping accurate records

IN THE KNOW

Accurate records are essential to help a business check for errors and monitor how well it is doing by providing the evidence for the accounts. The information can assist managers in making decisions. It can also be used to help support businesses wanting to raise money since it will improve investors' confidence. Lastly, transparent records add to the trust between buyer and seller.

Accurate records are legally needed for the Companies Acts and Partnership Agreements and provide information for the assessment of taxes.

Different stakeholders are interested in different financial documents. For example:

- The tax authorities want to calculate how much tax is due from a business

- Investors want information on how profitable the company is

- Suppliers want to be sure they will receive the money owed to them

- Banks will need to assess the risk of getting back their loan

- Business managers need the data to help them control, monitor and plan

- Unions representing workers will want to know how much the business can really afford in wage increases

- Workers will want to know if their pensions are safe.

What's recorded?

Paperwork in a business is really all about keeping accurate records of its:

• expenditure – or everything it buys

• income – or everything it sells.

Although it is referred to as 'bookkeeping' most businesses now keep their records on the computer. Specialist software makes sure the data entered from a source document automatically updates other financial documents, including the interim final accounts. This allows the business to check the accuracy of its records easily. It is also easy to search the data to bring up exactly the information required, for example overdue payments. What is more, the data can be put into graphs to provide an easier way of looking at how well the business is performing. In this way the software functions as a management information system (MIS) to help monitor and control performance, and predict and plan for the future. This area of accounting is called **management accounting**. It includes budgets and cash flows. It is mostly used internally by the business.

The information tells a business about:

• how its money is being spent

• the cost of producing each item

• when the costs will be covered

• if employees are working effectively.

Accurate financial records must be published annually for all companies.

The final accounts, often known as **financial accounts**, include the profit and loss account and the balance sheet. Shareholders will be able to use these final accounts to make judgements on a company's performance. The final accounts are the public face of the business and help people to judge its success during the previous year.

There is no excuse for managers and directors being unaware of what is going on in their company. If they can't or don't keep close control of their business or they try to cover up problems then they deserve to get into trouble. They will be letting down the stakeholders in their business.

Critical thinking

1 Who are the main internal and external users of financial information?

2 Why should accounts be both reliable and honest?

3 Accounts must represent a true and fair view of a limited company's performance. Accounts are verified by auditors before being signed by the directors and filed with the Registrar of Companies. How, given this system, do things sometimes go wrong?

4 The UK accounting system is based on principles such as honesty, consistency and accuracy, but should it be based more on law?

KEY TERMS

Management accounts describe financial information that is used to monitor, control and plan.

Financial accounts provide users of these accounts with an accurate guide to the financial performance of the business.

Next steps

1 Search through the BBC news website for news about accounts: http://newssearch.bbc.co.uk

What are the costs?

Specification Content

Fixed and variable, direct and indirect overheads and total costs

starSTUDY

Amy runs trips to see big bands in the NEC from the south-west. She can purchase tickets for, on average, £20. She spends about £200 promoting the trips through her internet site, by e-mailing past customers, advertising in the local papers and putting up posters. Other costs include the hire of a fifty-seater coach for £200.

Liz Brook is a Product Manager for International Services (roaming), which looks after calling and texting to and from the UK. At the time, Virgin Mobile was charging 55p per minute for all calls to the UK. Within the EU, the roaming partners charge different amounts for rerouting the call. Virgin Mobile averages this out and part of the 55p charge reflects this.

The marketing department at Virgin Mobile is called Brand. It is responsible for promoting the brand of all Virgin Mobile services including international calls.

Source: Virgin Mobile.

1 Identify the costs to each business.
2 Which of these change when there are more customers or calls?
3 Which of these stay the same irrespective of the number of customers or calls being made?
4 Why is it useful for a business to know how its costs change when sales increase?

Business costs

Businesses of all sizes have costs which fall into similar patterns. Some vary according to how much is produced. Others stay the same whether the business is producing nothing or is at full capacity.

The balance between the different sorts of costs will affect the decisions that are made about which products to produce, how many of them and whether to go on producing, so it is important to know what is happening.

Why collect the information?

Managers must have a clear picture of how much products cost to make. Without this information a business has little chance of success, as it is important information for pricing.

go to → *Go to page 32 for a reminder on pricing*

Costs are also important when a business wants to monitor progress. Once a budget has been set and targets allocated, knowing how costs are changing is important. The decisions on future plans will depend on the financial information that is coming in.

Although it seems an easy exercise to work out what things cost, it is a little more difficult because allocating overhead costs to a particular item is tricky. Spreading the costs of running the office, for example, is not easy.

What sort of costs?

It is useful for businesses to break down costs into categories in order to understand performance and aid plans.

ONE METHOD OF LOOKING AT COSTS ...

- **Fixed costs** are those that remain the same no matter what output is, within a short-run period. They include items like rent and management salaries.

- **Variable costs** change with output and include costs such as buying components or materials.

Adding the fixed costs to the total variable costs gives the **total costs**. The variable costs are not always constant. For example, buying in bulk will often reduce the price paid for components and this will be reflected in a reduction in the average variable cost as output increases.

Sometimes costs cannot be easily separated into fixed and variable and are called semi-variable costs. For example, a vehicle delivering stock has to pay a fixed level of insurance and road tax, but the more it is used the greater the fuel bill and maintenance cost.

ANOTHER WAY OF LOOKING AT COSTS ...

- **Direct costs** involve all the costs that can be directly related to the product or service or a cost centre. An example of this would be the food, chefs and waiting staff for a restaurant cost centre within a hotel.

- **Indirect costs** are those that cannot be directly allocated to a specific product or service. This might be the hotel's promotional expenditure or the cost of cleaning, which cannot normally be allocated to just one product or service. Indirect costs are often known as **overheads**. When we add the direct and indirect costs together we get the total costs for the product or service.

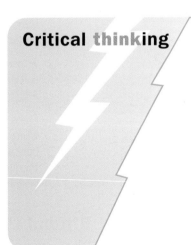

Critical thinking

1 Make a list of all the costs you can think of associated with your school. Identify the
   a direct or indirect costs
   b fixed or variable costs.
   Explain your decisions.
2 Draw up a table showing the various types of cost. Complete the table with the costs in each category for the following businesses:
   a a hairdresser
   b a website developer working from home
   c a car factory
   d a childminder.

KEY TERMS

The **short run** is the period of time when the scale of the operation cannot be changed easily. Any increase in output comes from using spare capacity.

In the **long run** the output can be increased by investing in a new factory.

Variable costs, such as raw materials, change with output.

Fixed costs, such as rent, remain the same irrespective of output.

Direct costs are those that can be allocated to a particular product or cost centre.

Indirect costs or **overheads** are usually connected with a number of products or cost centres.

Total costs are calculated by adding fixed, variable and semi-variable costs or direct and indirect costs together.

Making a profit

starSTUDY

Amazon stacks up first non-Christmas profit

Unilever gives profit warning

Sony's profits dip leads to job cuts

Businesses aim to make a profit but it's not always easy and change has knock-on effects.

1 Explain the change in each of these examples.

2 What might have caused each one?

3 What effect might it have on the businesses?

4 What must a business aim to do to keep out of trouble on the finance front?

First Choice Holidays bounces back after strong summer

Leeds United makes football's biggest loss ever

From costs to profit

Businesses need profit to survive. It is calculated by deducting all the costs of making and selling products from the revenue that is received from sales. Profits are then used in a variety of ways to keep stakeholders happy.

What is revenue?

Revenue is calculated by multiplying the number of goods sold by the average selling price.

Sales revenue = volume of goods sold × average selling price

Average price is used because when a business sells its products to retailers, the price may vary according to the size of the sale. Large purchasers expect a lower price.

Revenue therefore depends on the price that is charged. The price will in turn affect how many are sold.

- If demand is elastic, a high price may deter customers who will buy from competitors instead.

- If demand is inelastic, customers are happy to buy even at a high price. This is often true of the latest, high-tech equipment.

What sort of revenue?

The revenue a business is looking for will depend on the nature of the market for its products.

Businesses in niche markets often run a high price–low sales policy effectively. They know that they won't sell vast quantities but people are prepared to pay a high price.

A low price–high sales strategy is often used to sell products in very competitive markets such as food retailing.

Costs, revenue and profits are clearly interrelated. Every business would like low costs and high prices but this isn't often achievable. Market research is therefore important if a business is to work out the best strategy to keep profits as high as possible.

Critical thinking

Jo's Diner has increased profits this year after a series of years when they had been less than expected. Jo opened the Diner four years ago and thought she was onto a winner. There was nothing like it in the area but trade wasn't as good as expected. This year she had cut her prices and found trade picked up. There was also a new housing development nearby and she had invested in a large sign on the main road. During the summer, she'd bought some tables and chairs so people could eat outside. Profits had also been boosted by the sale of the old jukebox, which she'd taken out to make room for another table. A big office down the road has just relocated further out of town so Jo doesn't know if the customers from there will travel from their new site.

What will happen to Jo's profits next year? What would you advise her to do with her profits this year?

Why make a profit?

Profit is calculated by deducting total costs from total revenue.

Profit = Total revenue – total cost

Businesses need a profit for several reasons:

- **TO KEEP SHAREHOLDERS HAPPY.** They have invested money in the business and expect a return – known as a **dividend.** If dividends fall, they may sell their shares and weaken the public's perception of the business. If they rise, new shareholders will be attracted to the business.

- **FOR GROWTH.** Profits can be reinvested in the business. They might be spent on new machinery, opening new shops, developing new products or other ways that lead to expansion.

- **AS A MEASURE OF SUCCESS.** The size of the profit in relation to the size of the business shows how well resources are being used.

A business with low profits may end up contracting and even disappearing. Decisions about the future always have to be made in the context of the current economic climate. If people are not buying things because there is high unemployment and people fear that they might lose their jobs, the business has to look ahead and consider how it might adapt to fit the market if there doesn't seem to be any change ahead.

The decision about the use of profits will be affected by plans for the future. There is a trade-off between distributing profits to shareholders and retaining them for future growth. **Profit utilisation** therefore has to be thought about carefully if it is to be in the best interest of the business.

ACCOUNTING FOR THE PROFIT

Profit is counted at various points in the accounting process. The information that is available as a result of the process can help a business to make decisions because it is explaining the stage at which profits are being created.

GROSS PROFIT is revenue less cost of sales, which are mainly the direct costs of production, such as materials and wages.

OPERATING PROFIT is gross profit less overheads. These are the things that do not change as production levels change, such as the rent.

PRE-TAX PROFITS are operating profits less any one of items such as relocation to a new site.

PROFIT AFTER TAX deducts tax from pre-tax profits. This is what the business has left at the end to distribute to shareholders or reinvest.

What sort of profit?

Making a profit sounds good but there are questions to be asked before deciding just how good it is.

- **How does it compare with last year?** Most businesses aim to increase profits on last year but it doesn't always work out that way. Exploring the reasons for higher or lower profits is therefore important for future planning.

- **How does it compare with the plans?** Is it higher or lower? If so, why?

- **Are they high quality profits?** If the profits have been made from activities that are likely to continue, they are high quality. It they are from a one-off source such as selling a site and moving to a cheaper one, they are not.

- **How does it compare with the amount invested in the business?** A company with masses of resources in the business should expect to make a good profit or it is failing to use them effectively.

- **How are other businesses doing?** If other businesses in the same field are doing better,

then questions must be asked about the efficiency of the company. If they are doing worse, it is probably time to give everyone a pat on the back.

The media often gives big businesses that make high profits a hard time but the relationship between the size of the business and the size of the profit should be taken into account. If a little local business is making the same amount of profit as a major multinational, the latter's shareholders should be asking questions!

Next steps

Have a look at the business section of a series of papers. Find a story about a business and its profits. Are they low or high? Why? What effect is this having on the business? What effect is it likely to have on other businesses? What plans does the business have for the future in light of its profits?

If you track the story over a few days, you may find a range of ideas about what is happening.

KEY TERMS

Dividends are paid to shareholders in return for buying a share of a company.

Profit utilisation is how the company uses the profits that are left after tax.

Profit quality depends on whether they come from a source that will continue in the future.

Making a contribution

Specification Content

Contribution, its calculation and uses

starSTUDY

The Rondo Theatre is a small provincial theatre in the south-west. In fact it has just 200 seats. It is hiring a comedian for a one-night show. The costs include:

- Publicity   £100
- Paying the comedian   £500
- Overheads such as rent and rates   £100
- Theatre employees booked in advance for the night   £100
- Tickets are sold through an agency that charges   £2 per ticket sold
- The seats are priced at   £10.

The Rondo Theatre is a simple business with just one product – a ticket for the show – so it is quite easy to work out the costs associated with each sale and the contribution that each item sold makes to costs. In other businesses with more products it is more complex but contribution costing is a strategy which makes it more straightforward.

1 Which of the costs would have to be paid even if no tickets were sold?

2 Which of the costs are directly dependent on each ticket sold?

3 What is the extra cost of selling one more ticket?

4 If 100 seats were sold what would be the total costs and what would be the total revenue?

5 What would be the profit if all seats were sold?

6 How much does each ticket sold contribute to the costs?

7 How many tickets must be sold before the business starts to make a profit?

IN THE KNOW

Contribution and profit

The contribution a product makes is the revenue gained less its variable cost.

For the Rondo Theatre the contribution is the sales price of £10 less the variable cost of £2 giving a value of £8. It means every ticket sold contributes £8 towards covering the costs of the show.

Total contribution is sales revenue less variable costs. So for Rondo it is:
Contribution = Sales – Variable costs
             = £2000 – £400
             = £1600

To work out the profit, just deduct the fixed costs from the total contribution.
Profit = Contribution – Fixed costs
       = £1600 – £800
       = £800

The term 'contribution' is used because that is exactly what each item sold is doing. Because variable costs have been deducted already, the extra cost of making the item has been covered. Every £ of 'contribution' goes directly to covering the fixed or overhead costs. Once enough has been sold to cover overhead costs, the business starts to make a profit.

Critical thinking

	Glimmer £	Sparkle £	Starry nights £
Variable costs			
Materials	10	9	14
Labour	8	20	24
Selling price	40	22	60

1 A candle business produces three product ranges. It sells them to retailers in boxes of 25. The figures shown are for one box. Overhead costs are £80,000.

a How much does each box of candles contribute?

b What is the total contribution if 2000 of each line are sold?

c How much profit or loss is being made?

d Which product is most successful?

e What recommendation would you make to the business on the basis of current profits and losses?

2 Why might the level of spare capacity influence pricing decisions for an airline?

Contribution costing

Even a small business has a range of overheads which are hard to share out among the different products or services that are sold. If a beauty salon does manicures, massages and a wide range of other treatments, how do you allocate the rent, coffee, marketing, etc. to each service sold? Contribution costing avoids the need to do this because it looks at the contribution that each product sold makes to these overhead costs.

Total contribution is £36,000.

The fixed costs of running the salon are £20,000.

Profit is therefore £16,000.

The great advantage of contribution costing is that it does not attempt to share out overhead costs, which is always difficult, so errors are not built into the decision-making process.

	Manicures	Massages	Make up	Slimming treatments
Sales revenue	10,000	15,000	4,000	20,000
Variable costs	(2,000)	(5,000)	(2,000)	(4,000)
Contribution	8,000	10,000	2,000	16,000

Is it contributing?

Contribution is a useful idea because it shows whether items that are being produced are beneficial to the business. If there is no contribution because the variable cost of each item is not being covered, questions should be asked. It may be because it is a new product that is getting established and needs some time to make its mark. If no reasons can be found, a business should stop production.

Contribution can tell a business whether it is worth selling something at below full cost. Many businesses will cut prices when demand is low.

In January, newspapers are full of vouchers for low price meals at smart restaurants because everyone has overeaten at Christmas and has stopped eating out. If diners are covering the variable costs of their meal and making a small contribution to overheads, it is better than an empty restaurant.

This strategy avoids upsetting existing customers who are paying full price and the restaurant doesn't lose its exclusive status because this is clearly a special offer for a limited period. These are both problems which affect other businesses when they try to sell spare capacity at lower prices. Many businesses use contribution costing in markets that can be differentiated. 'Off peak' is a concept often used to do this. It can apply to trains, gym membership, flights and other products.

Making decisions

Contribution helps a business to take an overall view of what is going on. Being able to see the contribution of each product in the context of the whole business makes planning and decision-making more accurate.

Better information leads to better decisions but there are some questions that should be asked first.

- Will cutting prices mean that total contribution will never cover the overheads?

- Will cutting prices now make it hard to go back to the old price level?

- Can fixed and variable costs be clearly distinguished?

- Have changes that have taken place in costs been considered?

Remember that contribution can only be looked at in the short run. When fixed costs change, costings will change.

Most important of all – remember that contribution is not all profit. It only becomes profit when all the fixed costs have been paid. Break-even on the following page will make this clear.

KEY TERMS

Contribution is sales revenue minus variable cost. Contribution minus fixed costs is profit.

Specification Content

Break-even analysis to support decision making

Break even?

starSTUDY
'What ifs' at the Rondo Theatre

Price	£10.00
Average variable costs	£2.00
Contribution	£8.00

When the Rondo Theatre is planning an event, the management ask all sorts of questions. Try to answer them. You could use a spreadsheet package to help you.

What if output was?	0	50	100	150	200
Fixed costs	£800	£800	£800	£800	£800
Variable costs	£0	£100	£200	£300	£400
Total costs	£800	£900	£1,000	£1,100	£1,200
Total revenue	£0	£500	£1,000	£1,500	£2,000
Profit/loss	−£800	−£400	£0	£400	£800

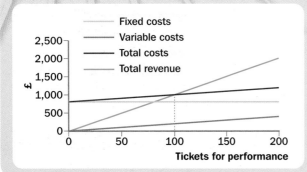

Rondo Theatre's break-even chart

1 How many seats have to be sold to cover all the costs?
2 How much profit will be made if all 200 seats are sold?
3 What would happen if the agent decided to charge £3 to sell a ticket?
4 What would happen if the comedian's fee went up to £600?
5 What would happen if the ticket price was £12?
6 What is the relationship between contribution and the break-even point?

Breaking even at the Rondo Theatre

At the Rondo Theatre the contribution is the sales price of £10 less the variable cost of £2 giving a value of £8. It means every ticket sold contributes £8 towards covering the fixed costs. The fixed costs are those not dependent on customers buying seats. They include paying the performer and theatre employees as well as the rent and the publicity making a grand total of £800. If only 10 tickets were sold then some £80 of the fixed costs would be covered by the contribution and the loss would be £720. To calculate the break-even point, the fixed costs need to be divided by the contribution. For the Rondo, this would be £800 divided by £8 meaning 100 tickets would need to be sold to exactly cover costs. Each ticket sold above that adds £8 towards profit. If the Rondo sold out it would make a profit of £800 as the contribution from the first 100 tickets exactly covers the costs and so the contribution from the last 100 tickets is all profit.

KEY TERMS

Break even is the level of sales at which there is no profit or loss.

Margin of safety is the level of output beyond the break-even point.

Next steps

1 Try to get hold of the figures for a recent school event such as a disco, concert or play. Did it break even? What was the contribution of each ticket sale?

2 How much profit did it make? What advice would you give about pricing to the organisers of the next event?

When will we break even?

Working out when a business will **break even** is a simple matter once the numbers have been established. You need the following information.

- Fixed costs

- Variable costs

Together, these two tell you

- Total costs

And, finally,

- Sales revenue.

When a business sells its products, it creates revenues that allow it to cover its costs and eventually start to make a profit. The level of sales required so that the total contribution exactly covers the fixed costs is called the break-even point.

To calculate the break-even point a business will often assume that:

- The selling price remains the same whatever amount is sold
  - Fixed costs also remain the same regardless of output
  - Variable costs vary in direct proportion to output.

The **margin of safety** is the amount by which sales exceed the break-even point. It informs a business of the amount by which demand can drop before it makes a loss. For example, assuming the break-even level of sales for a particular airline flight is 130 tickets and the average sales for Thursday flights has been 150 seats, then the margin of safety would be 20. For Saturday flights past data indicates the average sales rise to 200 giving a higher margin of safety of 70. This information is likely to be extremely useful when deciding ticket prices.

Using break even

The advantage of using break even is that it provides information to managers on the profit or loss that can be achieved. It is easy to see the effect of a change in costs or price especially when using a spreadsheet. The main advantages are that it is simple, quick and cheap.

It does have some downsides (below) and needs to be used wisely with allowances made for the assumptions.

The downsides

It assumes that fixed and variable costs are clearly distinguishable.	Employees, for example, are considered a fixed cost but the Rondo might need more for some events.
It assumes that costs increase constantly.	Economies of scale make bulk buying cheaper.
It assumes that everything will be sold.	It doesn't allow for fashion and changing tastes.
It cannot tell what actual sales will be.	Will you reach break even? It's hard to tell.
It assumes that the price of every item will be the same.	Many businesses give discounts for bulk buys.
It assumes that sales revenue will increase when the price goes up.	An increase in price may lead to a fall in demand. It all depends on elasticity.

Critical thinking

A low cost airline needs to fill about two-thirds of its seats to cover its costs which include:

- Telesales staff
- Advertising
- Crew
- Ground handling
- Insurance and airport landing fees
- Air traffic control fees
- Fuel
- Aircraft ownership costs
- Maintenance

1 Once a plane is scheduled to fly what cost headings will be included in calculating the variable costs for low cost airlines?

2 Why is the variable cost much lower for low cost airlines compared with normal airlines?

3 Does the variable cost help explain ticket prices for these airlines? What other costs are important?

Keeping the cash flowing

Specification Content

Importance of cash flow; calculating cash flow and interpretation of cash flow forecast

starSTUDY

Just Bangers is a new business that makes sausages for sale to restaurants and delicatessens. After spending £8000 on new equipment and a second-hand vehicle, its owner, Jay, has £7000 in the bank. Jay starts making, selling and delivering sausages in March. Since Jay relies on credit sales, his customers have 28 days to pay. This means the sausages sold in March will be paid for in April. Similarly, Jay receives 28 days credit from his suppliers, so the meat he receives in March he pays for in April. Jay makes a cash flow forecast.

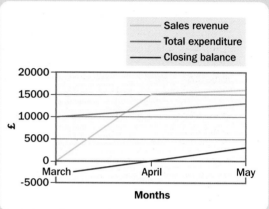

Cash flow forecast

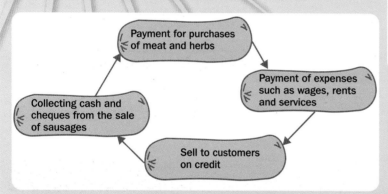

Cash Flow Forecast	March	April	May
Income			
Sales revenue		15,000	16,000
Total income	**0**	**15,000**	**16,000**
Expenditure			
Rent	1,500	1,500	1,500
Services such as power, water			1,000
Purchases of meat and herbs	0	2,200	2,500
Wages/salaries	5,500	5,500	5,500
Motor expenses	1,500	1,500	1,500
Insurance	300	300	300
Other (including marketing)	1,200	1,000	700
Total expenditure	**10,000**	**12,000**	**13,000**
Opening bank balance	**7,000**	**-3,000**	**0**
Balance of cash in and cash out each month	**–10,000**	**3,000**	**3,000**
Closing balance	**–3,000**	**0**	**3,000**

1 Why was no sales revenue forecast in March?

2 What money flows out of Jay's business in March?

3 How short of cash will Jay be in March should his forecast be correct?

4 Suggest how he might meet that shortfall.

5 Why is it important for Jay to be certain that cash flows in before he has to pay the bills?

KEY TERMS

Cash flow measures the actual money received by a business in a time period set against the expenditure of the business.

Cash flow forecast tries to be realistic and predict the cash flowing into and out of the business.

Creditors are organisations that the business owes cash to.

Cash flow

Cash flow measures the money flowing in and out of the business. Money must come in from sales revenue or the business is in real trouble. The business may also receive income from interest earned and from one-off sources such as loans, grants or selling assets.

The cash budget is the expenditure on the day-to-day running of the business. It is also known as revenue spending. Money flows out of the business to pay wages and bills. These bills come from suppliers who usually expect to be paid 28 days after the delivery of the goods. The supplier becomes a **creditor**.

Sometimes money flows out of the business to pay for fixed assets like property, vehicles or new equipment. This is called capital expenditure because it is spent on long-term operations. The assets purchased will be used for several years to make the product.

Controlling cash flow is essential for business survival. Cash flow problems can lead to business failure. If more money goes out than comes in during a time period, a business may be unable to pay suppliers who may be reluctant to continue to sell to the business.

A business will make a **cash flow forecast** to predict cash needs and prepare for shortages, for example by getting an overdraft.

A budget is the plan for the future that the business wants to achieve. The cash flow forecast is a prediction of what might happen. They interact because the business tries out its plans by feeding 'what ifs' into the cash flow forecast.

These might include:

- If we accept that order can we pay the suppliers?
- If we accept that order will we need to employ more and what will this cost us?

These are estimates, so it is important to make them as realistic as possible.

If a decision is taken to go ahead, the business needs to record actual income and expenditure on the cash flow spreadsheet. It then needs to look at the variance.

The process

Budget feeds into cash flow forecast.

↓

Needs recognised and fed back into budget.

↓

Decisions made whether to go ahead or not and how to meet any shortfall.

↓

Actual cash flow recorded and compared with forecast to produce variance.

Why worry?

Cash flow problems are responsible for causing over 70% of businesses to fail within their first year. Symptoms of a poor cash flow include:

- wages not paid
- increased overdraft
- later and later payments to creditors
- stocks build up because sales are less than forecasted.

Jay would need to be confident that his forecast is realistic. Jay also needs to make sure there is enough cash to pay the bills. If Jay failed to obtain a loan Just Bangers would be lacking in cash even though it was profitable.

On the other hand, a sound cash flow doesn't always guarantee success. A business could have a positive cash flow but still be unprofitable. For example, the business may have sold off a lot of old stock cheaply. This would raise money from the sales but produce little, if any, profit.

Critical thinking

1 Just Bangers has been asked to consider a contract from a supermarket that would provide an additional £15,000 revenue a month. Some costs remain the same but others would increase. From the evidence in the Star Study identify both these groups of costs and then make a cash flow forecast for June. What cash would Jay need to find before accepting the order? What might be the attitude of the bank if asked for a loan?

2 What are the limitations of cash flow forecasts?

Controlling the flow

starSTUDY

Just Bangers cash flow and variance after three months trading ('variance' figures in brackets are negative)

Cash flow	March forecast	March actual	March variance	April forecast	April actual	April variance	May forecast	May actual	May variance
Income									
Sales	0	0	0	15,000	13,000	(2,000)	16,000	17,000	1,000
Total expenditure	**0**	**0**	**0**	**15,000**	**13,000**	**(2,000)**	**16,000**	**17,000**	**1,000**
Rent	1,500	1,500	0	1,500	1,500	0	1,500	1,500	0
Services such as power, water	0	0	0	0	0	0	1,000	1,100	(100)
Purchases	0	0	0	2,200	2,000	200	2,500	2,700	(200)
Wages/salaries	5,500	5,500	0	5,500	5,500	0	5,500	5,500	0
Motor expenses	1,500	1,200	300	1,500	1,600	(100)	1,500	1,600	(100)
Insurance	300	300	0	300	300	0	300	300	0
Other (including marketing)	1,200	1,300	(100)	1,000	1,000	0	700	600	100
Total	**10,000**	**9,800**	**200**	**12,000**	**11,900**	**100**	**13,000**	**13,300**	**(300)**
Opening bank balance	7,000	7,000	0	(3,000)	(2,800)	(200)	0	(200)	200
Balance of cash in and cash out each month	(10,000)	(9,800)	(200)	3,000	1,100	1,900	3,000	(1,100)	4,100
Closing balance	(3,000)	(2,800)	(200)	0	(1,700)	1,700	3,000	(1,300)	4,300

1 What actually happened to the total sales for the three months when compared to the forecast?

2 What happened to the total costs for the first three months compared with the forecast?

3 Which items were accurately forecast?

4 Which part of the cash flow forecast was the poorest prediction?

5 Although the sales from March would only show up in the April figures, Jay would know in advance what the figure would be as he had sent out invoices. Jay had badly underestimated the sales level. What can be done?

Sometimes things go wrong

BAD PAYERS

Customers who buy things from a business on credit become **debtors**. When customers fail to pay at the agreed time, it can have a major impact on the cash flow. You may need to raise more finance to compensate for the delay in payment. If people don't pay up, the business may not be able to pay its bills because there is not enough **working capital** in the business.

A business must keep control of its debtors and follow up immediately if payments are late.

DO YOU REALLY NEED ALL THOSE ASSETS?

Buying too many assets can mean increased borrowing and more interest payments. The loans may have to be secured against business assets or even your personal possessions. You may not be able to meet payments.

Buying in bulk can seem beneficial at the time, but holding excessive amounts of stock ties up money in unproductive assets, particularly if the stock is not sold on quickly. Effective stock control is a key to controlling cash flow.

go to → Find out about stock control on page 113

PREDICTING DEMAND

Sales may rise or fall unpredictably. A change in demand may be impossible to forecast, but sound market research and effective marketing may help a business to predict the change and reduce the effects.

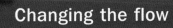

KEY TERMS

Debtors are organisations that owe the business cash. They are usually customers.

Overdraft is an arrangement with the bank to overdraw on the account up to an agreed sum.

Working capital is used to carry out the day-to-day running of a business. It pays for the process of turning stock into products, despatching them to customers and waiting for customers to pay.

Total forecast	Actual total	Total variance
31,000	30,000	(1,000)
31,000	**30,000**	**(1,000)**
4,500	4,500	0
1,000	1,100	(100)
4,700	4,700	0
16,500	16,500	0
4,500	4,400	100
900	900	0
2,900	2,900	0
35,000	**35,000**	**0**

Next steps

1 Find out about current cost of borrowing and the overdraft rates from a bank.

2 Ask your teacher about the credit periods given for book orders.

Changing the flow

To manage cash flow, a business needs to delay and reduce outflows of cash and speed up inflows of cash to the business. Doing this increases the amount of working capital in the business.

Increase inflows:

Action	Good points	Bad points
Give customers a shorter credit period	You will receive your payments earlier	Your customers may get a better deal elsewhere
Use a factoring company to chase up unpaid bills	You will spend less time chasing unpaid bills	You will have to pay the factoring business a cut of the money they bring in
General good credit management	Once a system is set up, it leads to good habits	People may need training to run the system so there is a cost

Delay outflows:

Action	Good points	Bad points
Ask suppliers for a longer credit period	Delays payments for supplies already received	Supplier may be worried about your business performance and may not want to risk selling to you
Buy stock only when needed	Less storage and less waste	Need to be sure that suppliers can deliver on time
Lease equipment instead of buying it	Spreads the payments over a period of time	It's not yours to keep
Cut costs through increased efficiency	This reduces outflows	This may reduce motivation and quality

If it all goes pear shaped ...

Many small and even medium-sized businesses go under because they underestimate the importance of cash flow. A business that can't pay its bills is insolvent. Many try to borrow to overcome a problem but sometimes banks will refuse to lend or allow a business an **overdraft** because they are worried about repayments being made. It has been known for businesses with full order books to become insolvent because they have tried to grow too fast.

starSTUDY

Yes ... but ...

'Orders make us profits so why can't we accept this order from France? It's for £280,000.'

'You have estimated the job will cost £80,000 for components, £20,000 power and £100,000 for production plus £50,000 towards cover rent.'

'Yes, exactly my point. We can make £30,000 on this deal.'

'Fine, but hold on, we won't get the money until one month after delivery. That's four months' time. Yet we have to pay out wages, fuel bills and buy in the components. Have you seen our bank balance?'

1 What problem is there in accepting the order?

2 How might the business attempt to overcome this problem?

3 What might happen to the business if it takes the order but can't pay its bills?

What is finance for?

Specification Content

Sources of finance – internal

starSTUDY

Finance matters

Harriet Kessie always wanted to run her own hairdressing salon. She knew just what she wanted to do. The plans for her hair salon were clear but she had one major problem to surmount. Getting the money together was a challenge.

Harriet had £10,000 in savings and managed to borrow £8,000 through the Business Link scheme, a government organisation that supports local businesses. Lloyds TSB lent her another £8,500, which meant she had enough to turn her ideas into reality. Her dream came true when she opened Harriet Kessie Hairdressing in Edmonton, London.

1   What did Harriet have to pay for before she started her business?

2   What does Harriet have to pay for once the business is running?

3   Why do you think it can be difficult for new businesses to raise money?

4   Why was it easier to borrow money from Lloyds TSB once Business Link had agreed to help her?

5   Why might Harriet need finance for her business in future?

Finance for business

Running your own business gives lots of people a buzz of excitement but often the financial aspects cause sleepless nights. Learning to manage the money is often critical to the success of a new venture.

Harriet needed to raise money because she didn't have enough to get going on her own. She had to be able to pay to set up the salon and then run it. Any business is in the same boat.

Raising finance for a new business can be difficult because people who lend want to be convinced that they will get their money back. As a new business has no track record, lenders have to have confidence in the person and his or her plans. They have to see that the money is going to be put to good use.

Big businesses need to organise finance as well if they are going to develop or grow. Few businesses can afford to stand still or they will be overtaken by more dynamic competitors.

Why raise finance?

SETTING UP THE BUSINESS

To buy equipment and lease a shop, office or factory.

RUNNING THE BUSINESS ON A DAY-TO-DAY BASIS

To pay the bills for everything the business needs, from stock to employees. A shop will need heating and lighting. A business nearly always needs marketing if people are to know about it. The accountant has to be paid. Working capital is the term used to describe this aspect of a business's finances. A business should aim to cover these costs from revenue but when starting up or in difficult times, it may need to raise finance to pay the bills.

EXPANDING

To cover the costs of setting up a new shop or office. Expansion often means increasing the working capital as well. A bigger business will be buying and spending more. It may also mean taking over another business so finance will be needed to buy out the owners.

DEVELOPING

To create new product lines or move into a new market. Getting new products right takes time and money. A business that decides to export its products for the first time will have to explore the market where it plans to sell.

EMERGENCIES

To protect the business in difficult times. Sales might fall if there are economic problems. A new product line might not have sold as much as expected. Bad debts might be mounting.

Finding finance

Harriet found some of the funds she required from her own resources but she had to look outside the business for the rest. Most businesses work in this way. Once up and running, a business aims to make a profit and some of this can be used to fund developments or help out if things get difficult. Finance from inside the business is known as **internal finance**. If it is from other people or organisations, it is **external finance**.

go to → (Find out more on page 58)

There is a range of sources for both types of finance. A business needs to choose carefully depending on the circumstances.

Internal finance

IN THE KNOW

RETAINED PROFIT

If a business wants to develop it often ploughs back part of its profit. It is a secure way of growing because the business is not borrowing, and is therefore not dependent on anyone else.

SALE OF ASSETS

A business might sell assets that it no longer uses to raise money.

It might also decide to focus on one aspect of its business – as Sainsbury's did when it sold Homebase to raise finance to develop the supermarket chain. Businesses can sell an asset to raise cash, and then lease it back. Some football clubs have done this with their grounds in order to pay current debts.

WORKING CAPITAL

A business that is in need of cash may cut its stocks or give customers less time to pay. It will then have more money to use for other things.

Critical thinking

1 Why might a business that is in difficulties need finance?

2 Why might a lender be unwilling to help?

3 What other options are possible?

4 Why do you think a business must plan carefully when in this situation?

KEY TERMS

External finance comes from sources outside the business.

Internal finance comes from within the business.

Next steps

Look at some newspapers or search the Internet for stories about businesses that are expanding. What do you think they will need finance for as they develop?

Where does the money come from?

starSTUDY

Harriet Kessie Hairdressing 2015

Harriet's business flourished. She had obviously found a gap in the market. As the years went by, she opened more and more salons across the country. Soon after opening her first shop, Harriet set up a private limited company. As the business grew Harriet Kessie Hairdressing became a public company.

1 What does Harriet have to pay for as she opens each shop?

2 What advantages are there in becoming
a a private company
b a public company?

3 Harriet had to raise a lot of money to develop a high street chain. Use the

information on internal and external sources of finance to work out where it might come from. Explain why.

4 Draw up a table of the different sources of finance with a column to show how Harriet could use each type.

Raising finance

Any business wanting to raise finance must select the right type for the purpose. If Harriet wants to refurbish a shop, she will have to decide whether to use retained profit or borrow money to pay for it. She will need to ask some questions before making up her mind.

• How long is the finance required for?

• How much is needed?

• What will it cost?

• Will it affect control of the business?

• What is the current financial state of the business?

• Will the use of finance add to revenue?

Critical thinking

1 If a business wants a photocopier, what finance would you suggest it used?

2 What about
a opening a new shop?
b designing a new product?
c building a new factory?
d starting to export a company's products?

Sources of finance – external

The type of external finance a business chooses to use depends on how long it wants the money for and what it wants to do.

Short term

Bank overdrafts	Trade credit	Debt factoring
A bank allows a business to spend more than is in its account. It is a cheap way of borrowing because you only pay for the amount borrowed on any day. The limit must always be agreed and it can be risky because a bank can 'call in' the debt if it is worried that it might not get the money back. This often results in the business going under.	A business can increase the amount of cash it holds by delaying payment of bills. This often has a cost because early payment often means a discount.	Most businesses trade on credit so customers have time to pay. If cash is needed more quickly, the debts can be sold to a debt factor. This is another business, which buys the debt at a discount and waits for payment to be made by the original customer.

Medium term

Leasing or hire purchase	Medium-term bank loans
Many businesses lease equipment because it avoids tying up cash which they can use for other things. It often comes with a service agreement so they know it will be looked after. There is usually the option to buy at the end of the contract but as technology changes so fast, many firms just replace an old model with a new one. Hire purchase has the same effect but extends payments over a period of time. At the end of the contract the item of equipment belongs to the business.	Businesses borrow from the bank for a fixed time at an interest rate that may be fixed or flexible. It is more expensive than an overdraft because the loan is for a fixed amount of money.

Long term

Long-term bank loans	Debentures	Selling shares	Venture capital
Long-term borrowing works in the same way as medium-term borrowing. Banks may be unwilling to lend to small or new businesses unless they feel quite sure that they will get their money back. Business Link, the government agency which helps small and medium-sized businesses, can help to organise guarantees which make it easier for businesses to borrow.	Debentures are loans made to companies. They are for a fixed period and some can be sold to other investors during that time.	All companies sell shares when the business starts. Owning a share means ownership of part of the company. If a business wants to raise further funds, it can issue more shares. Most of these shares are known as ordinary shares. A private company will sell shares to people after the agreement of existing shareholders. Once a public company has sold shares they can be traded on the Stock Exchange. The Alternative Investment Market deals in the shares of smaller companies. It is part of the Stock Exchange but has less stringent rules.	Some organisations and individuals specialise in providing venture capital for young businesses. They will take a share in the company and hope to sell when their investment has shown a gain.

Selling shares versus borrowing

Many businesses use a mix of debt and equity, or shares, to fund activities. It can be hard to decide which to use and will depend on whether the owners want to give up some control and whether a business can borrow enough to carry out its plans. Money from shares is known as share capital. Money from loans is called loan capital.

	Advantages	Disadvantages
Sell shares	You don't have to pay it back	Shareholders own part of the company, have a vote and expect a return on their investment in the form of a dividend
Borrow	Ownership of the business doesn't change	Interest has to be paid on the debt even if the company makes a loss

KEY TERMS

Leasing is renting a resource needed by the business. The resource can be bought, if desired, at the end of the lease.

Hire purchase is a type of medium-term credit to buy by instalments after paying a deposit.

Debentures are long-term loans from investors.

Why budget?

Specification Content

The nature and purpose of budgets as an aid to decision-making and control; comparison of budget and actual achievement

starSTUDY

The Eden Project is a charity whose objectives are:

- To educate without being like a school

- To hold conversations that might just go somewhere

- To research and share this with anybody

- To provide a sanctuary.

This is why they built the centre and this is where the money has gone.

£86 million may sound like a lot of money but, far from being rich, the Eden Project has actually been a lean machine in order to stretch the resources to cover its basic needs.

	£Million
Buying a large and unusual site and car park with roads and paths to get there	10
Reshaping the ground to make it safe, useful and dry	8
A couple of decent greenhouses	25
40 acres of plants, some tall	3
50,000 m² of soil to grow them in	1.5
A nursery to practise in and grow some unusual plants	1
Buildings and contents for visitors and our team	10
Services to keep it all running	7
Paying the team to run it over 5 years	2.5
Exhibits to entertain visitors	2
Advice on doing bits we couldn't do ourselves (including designing and engineering the world's biggest greenhouse)	9
Bits we needed to add to the plan to keep us going in the future	7
Total	86

Source: Eden Project

1 In what ways did the Eden Project's budget plans fit in with the objectives of the project?

2 Why did the charity set aside £7 million as a contingency?

3 What problems would the charity have encountered if it didn't have a financial plan?

4 Why might the charity need to review its plans given the unexpected popularity of the centre?

5 Which budget area has a clear time period?

Planning ahead

The initial objectives of the Eden Project required it to build a centre costing up to £86 million. It was financed by a number of sponsors including the Millennium Commission. The charity employs a number of managers who are budget holders and whose job it is to make sure that the charity works within its budget. The objectives of the Eden Project will need continual review. Visitor numbers were higher in the first year so this meant more revenue, but inadequate facilities. Future plans had to be adjusted to take account of this.

Next steps

Find out something about your school or college budget.

1 What is the total budget?

2 How much goes on staffing and how much on maintenance and repairs?

3 What is the Business Studies budget for the year and how is this monitored?

Decision-making

A **budget** is a financial plan that looks at costs and revenues. Budgets are usually linked to the objectives of a business and show how the strategy will be followed in order to achieve those objectives. Business objectives set out what the managers hope to achieve. They can be both short term and long term. A short-term objective might be the introduction of a new product line or the refitting of a shop. Long-term objectives are

concerned with where the business aims to be in a few years' time. For example, Innogy's (the electricity company) strategy to diversify might involve it requiring budgets to take over other businesses.

All types of organisation need to have budgets, whether they are governments, charities or businesses. They are needed so that it is clear whether financial plans are working.

ADVANTAGES AND DISADVANTAGES OF BUDGETING

Advantages

- **Monitoring the business's financial position.** Once budgets are set for the business and its departments, it is easy to see which are working effectively and which need closer inspection. When all the budgets are integrated into the computer systems, monitoring becomes even easier. The effects can be seen instantaneously and tracked back to show where things are going wrong.

- **Delegation motivates.** When departments run their own budgets people have authority to make decisions to achieve the targets. Increasing sales or keeping within cost targets has a motivational effect on staff, especially when the decisions have been within their control.

Disadvantages

- **Not always right.** Things are always changing in business so budgeting cannot always be accurate. If costs rise unexpectedly or demand falls, a department can find it difficult to keep to the budget. Unless there is flexibility, motivation may fade if targets seem unachievable. Some managers may have more power and get bigger budgets than they really need and others may not have enough to make the most of opportunities.

- **Short-term achievement.** Staying within a budget can sometimes mean harming future prospects. If managers are offered bonuses for achieving targets, they may be prepared to cut corners at the expense of their customers. If staff on help lines are only allowed two minutes per customer, people may decide to buy elsewhere next time.

Planning budgets

Budgets are often set for the following year, so it is not an easy task as things can be expected to change. Costs may rise or sales may fall, so they must be treated flexibly. Last year's budget is generally used as the basis for the following year but this may not take changes into account. Some businesses use **zero budgeting** to overcome this. Every year starts with a clean sheet and people have to justify spending from scratch. Although this means that money is used effectively, it can be very expensive to run because a great deal of management time is

spent in creating the budget. These managers could be spending their time more creatively.

Good budgeting means:

- Having clear links to the organisation's objectives so that money is allocated on the basis of the strategy.

- Having open processes for decision making so that powerful managers don't get more than their fair share.

- Having inputs from people who are affected to increase motivation on achieving targets.

Critical thinking

1 If a business doesn't have a budget, what can go wrong?
2 Why are people likely to respond more effectively if they feel they have been involved in setting budgets?
3 How should budgets be determined? Think about your school budget.

KEY TERMS

Budget is a financial plan linked to an organisation's objectives.

Zero budgeting means that every department has to justify spending from scratch every year.

Is the budget working?

starSTUDY

The target for the first year was 0.75 million visitors. There were 2 million.

Specification Content

Interpreting variances; calculation and interpretation of favourable and adverse variances

1 What happened to the Eden Project's revenue?
2 What effect would this have on the business?
3 If the Project had planned for up to one million visitors a year, how might its expenditure need to change?
4 What effect would this have on its budget?
5 Why is flexibility in budgeting important?

Accounting for change

The Eden Project's staff were delighted by the public's enthusiasm, but they had to make some changes as a result. The figures in the budget flagged up what was happening. Any differences between what is actually happening and the budget are known as a **variance**. When it is good news, the variance is **favourable**. Bad news is an **adverse** variance. Businesses should monitor their budgets carefully to make sure they are staying on the right track.

Critical thinking

A garment manufacturer produces clothes for all sectors of the market. Here is the budget statement for September:

		September budget	September actual
Men's Clothing	Revenue	€ 80,000	€ 78,500
	Cost	€ 70,000	€ 71,000
	Profit	€ 10,000	€ 7,500
Ladies' Clothing	Revenue	€ 120,000	€ 125,000
	Cost	€ 100,000	€ 110,000
	Profit	€ 20,000	€ 15,000
Children's Clothing	Revenue	€ 60,000	€ 61,000
	Cost	€ 45,000	€ 46,000
	Profit	€ 15,000	€ 15,000
Total	Revenue	€ 260,000	€ 264,500
	Cost	€ 215,000	€ 227,000
	Profit	€ 45,000	€ 37,500

1 Work out the variances for September.
2 Which items are causing concern? Why?
3 What might be causing the problems?
4 Suggest solutions.

KEY TERMS

Adverse variance is a difference between budgeted and actual figures which means profits will be less than predicted.

Favourable variance is a difference between budgeted and actual figures which means profits will be more than predicted.

Management by exception means that people only receive the information that they need and are involved in decisions that need to be taken at their level.

Variance analysis looks for reasons and proposes solutions for difference between the budget and actual figures.

Variances

IN THE KNOW

WHAT IS A VARIANCE?

In any business someone needs to take responsibility for each budget area and the budget as a whole. Each person involved will need to monitor both spending and revenues to check whether they are more or less than was expected. The difference between the budget and the actual amount is called the variance. A favourable variance occurs where the actual figures are better than those in the budget. This will happen if costs are lower or revenue is higher than expected. An adverse variance means either revenue is lower or costs higher than the budget. The table shows how it works.

	Budget (£)	Actual (£)	Variance (£)	
Sales	500	600	100	Favourable
Materials	350	390	40	Adverse
Other direct costs	150	140	10	Favourable
Overheads	100	110	10	Adverse

HOW CAN BUDGETS GO WRONG?

Budgets must be as realistic as possible, but there are difficulties.

- Budgeting for something for the first time is going to be more hit and miss than if you have done it before, since you will not have had the experience of past budgets to incorporate into current ones.

- Keeping close control is another problem. It is important to note and react to variances as they happen so you can attempt to correct them.

- Sometimes the variance can be beyond your control. For example, good weather can make building projects completed within time and within their budget and a prolonged spell of bad weather can have the opposite effect. The latest fashionable diet might affect a food manufacturer.

To overcome such problems a business should ensure that regular statements are produced and monitored for variances. To avoid an overload, IT systems can be set up just to produce the budget for areas with variances rather than deluging people with endless, unnecessary paper. This is known as **management by exception**.

Analysing variances

Once a variance has been spotted, the reason for it must be found, so there are some questions to ask.

- Is it a quirky month?
- Is the market changing?
- Have suppliers' prices risen?
- Is the sales force up to strength?

- Is it best equipped and motivated to sell?
- Is marketing working?
- Are costs being watched?
- Is quality being watched?

There are many more possibilities and they will vary according to which figures are different from those in the budget.

Budgetary control can be used in a business as a means of control or a method of encouraging team working. The attitude to budgets will depend on the culture of the business. A boss who wants to be in charge of everything may use them as a weapon whereas one who wants people to be involved in decision making will be more open and encourage discussion about what should happen next.

Critical thinking

- The Channel Tunnel train company revealed that its passenger numbers had fallen for a fifth consecutive quarter, declining by 3.3%.

- England's Arts Council has been criticised after 13 of its 15 major projects went over budget, costing £94 million.

- Most building projects under the controversial Private Finance Initiative are being delivered on time and under budget, according to the public spending watchdog.

1 Is the variance positive or negative in each of the examples?

2 How might the first two organisations mentioned react to their budget variance?

go to → *Find out more about leadership on page 90*

Cost centres and profit centres

Specification Content

Cost centres and profit centres; elementary management accounts focusing upon the value of delegated power over budgets; accounting, organisational and motivational purposes of cost centres and profit centres

star**STUDY**

Future Publishing produces over 80 magazines for enthusiasts with a wide range of interests. Each magazine has to show that it is making a profit, so the system is set up to show how each one is doing.

1 Why should Future Publishing want to know the cost of producing each magazine and whether it is making a profit?

2 How should it go about it?

3 How might the information affect decisions made by the business?

4 How might the following businesses organise their cost or profit centres? You may have more than one suggestion for each business: Sainsbury's, Sony, Toni and Guy, the AA, BMW and WH Smiths.

Being in the know

A business with a range of products wants to know the cost of producing each one so that it can make decisions. These decisions are not just about money but about how the business works. A cost or profit centre is responsible for its product so each one is like a business within a business. People behave as if they are running a small business rather than just being a small cog in a large wheel.

Cost centres

Cost centres are parts of a business in which the costs are identified and fed into the accounting process. A budget will have been set up for the cost centre so that everyone can see how costs are being allocated. As the months pass, the financial performance of the cost centre is monitored. Is spending within the budget? If not, the people responsible for the cost centre will be asked to explain. There may be a good reason. If, for example, output has increased, costs will probably have risen. If there isn't a good reason, careful monitoring will be necessary and adjustments will have to be made.

Businesses identify cost centres in different ways:

• A business might use its departments such as marketing or finance.

• A retail business might use each outlet.

• A supermarket chain might use its food sections.

• A car manufacturer might use each model.

• A factory might use a group of machines.

• A manufacturing business might use each factory.

• A business might use the sales team or individual sales people.

PROFIT CENTRES

Profit centres work on just the same principles as cost centres. The key difference is that costs and revenue are monitored to work out the profit that is made by each centre. This gives more information but it can be hard to work out how overhead costs should be allocated.

Why run cost and profit centres?

IN THE KNOW

MAKING DECISIONS

go to → Go to page 43 for a reminder on management accounts

Management accounting aims to give people within the business information about how things are going so that they can plan ahead. Cost and profit centres mean that this information can be collected at a more detailed level and therefore helps the decision-making process. If Future Publishing found that one of its magazines was making a loss, it would have to work out whether it needed changing so that more people would buy it, or perhaps the market for it had shrunk to a size that made it no longer viable.

Management accounts include cashflow forecasts, break-even analysis and budgets. Any of these can be drawn up for a cost or profit centre and help a business to ask 'What if …?' questions.

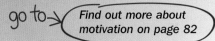

ORGANISING THE BUSINESS

When managers have financial information from cost and profit centres, they can see which parts of a business are working well and which need more support or direction. If one shop is doing badly, a decision might have to be made about whether to close it, increase marketing in the area or change the range of products it sells, for example.

MOTIVATING PEOPLE

People who run their own businesses are often highly motivated. They really want to make a success of it. Setting up cost and profit centres can have a similar effect within a business. The people responsible for them probably want them to work well because it is a measure of their personal success. It is much easier to make a small team work together effectively than individuals who do not feel that they belong to a team.

go to → Find out more about motivation on page 82

But …

Allocating costs can be tricky. All businesses have overheads which are hard to share out between cost or profit centres. Who should pay for the costs of running the head office? Should it be shared according to the cost or profit in each centre?

Time consuming data collection is necessary to produce the financial information needed. People could be used more effectively on other activities.

Competition within the business can increase efficiency but may also lead to one department putting its own objectives above that of the company.

Success or failure may be caused by factors beyond the control of the cost or profit centre. If the cost of oil has risen, the plastics used to make a personal stereo will rise. The production team will resent being blamed for not meeting their targets, so motivation may decline.

Critical thinking

Tec–tables makes desks for computers. The models range from a simple desk with a sliding shelf for the keyboard, to a foldaway cupboard with drawers, shelves and lots of gadgets. Each product is a profit centre.

	Tec 1	Tec 2	Tec 3
Price	£50	£100	£200
Quantity	2000	1200	1000
Direct costs	£50000	£110000	£120000
Overhead allocation	£25000	£25000	£25000

1 Which products make a profit or loss?
2 Suggest another way of allocating overheads.
3 How much profit or loss would be made with this re-allocation?
4 What advice would you give the management of the business about changes that need to be made?

KEY TERMS

Cost centres are parts of a business which collect and record their costs.

Profit centres are parts of a business which collect and record their profits.

testing–testing

Finance – assessment

The Carpet Barn

Part A

Murray and Ellen had recently set up The Carpet Barn, selling and fitting carpets. They worked out start-up costs. One early decision they made was to buy in a computer system with specialist software. It would save time invoicing and the orders would automatically go through to the suppliers.

The complete system would set them back £4000, but save the business £3000 in reduced staffing in the first year. Fitting out the shop would come to £3000 and another £2000 was needed to buy a second-hand van.

They found two suppliers that would provide 28 days' credit and deliver within 5 working days. With this and information from other research Murray was able to produce a cash flow forecast to predict the first 6 months cash in and out. He took this to the local bank and arranged a £7000 loan with an overdraft facility for £4000 to help cover the first few months. Murray and Ellen invested £12,000 from their savings.

They estimated that the average sale for purchasing and fitting a carpet would be £500. The cost of materials comprising the carpet itself, the underlay and gripper board would be half this price, and the fitting charge would come to 25 per cent of the sales price. Murray was the main fitter, but he had a friend who he could hire if work was busy. Murray would also receive a salary of £1000 a month for his role as finance manager. Ellen's salary would be £1800 a month. These salaries and other expenses would make up estimated overheads of £6250 a month. With all this information they constructed a break-even chart.

Output	0	20	40	60	80
Fixed costs	£6,250	£6,250	£6,250	£6,250	£6,250
Variable costs	£0	£7,500	£15,000	£22,500	£30,000
Total costs	£6,250	£13,750	£21,250	£28,750	£36,250
Total revenue	£0	£10,000	£20,000	£30,000	£40,000
Profit/loss	-£6,250	-£3,750	-£1,250	£1,250	£3,750

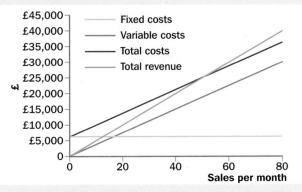

Murray and Ellen reckoned The Carpet Barn would make around 60 sales each month and bring in a profit of £7500 in the first 6 months. They had a marketing budget of £1200 to help them reach their sales target, which worked out at £200 a month. This was included in their overheads figures.

If things went well they would supplement their pay by drawing out a reasonable sum from the profits. It would still allow some profits to be invested back into the business. If orders went above 80 a month they would need to take on more staff in the shop and their overheads would rise.

Part B

The Carpet Barn's cash flow forecast for the first 6 months of trading

	May	June	July	August	September	October	6 month forecast
Owners' funds	12,000						12,000
Bank loan	7,000						7,000
Sales revenue (turnover)	0	30,000	30,000	30,000	30,000	30,000	150,000
Total income	19,000	30,000	30,000	30,000	30,000	30,000	169,000
Start-up costs	9,000						9,000
Purchases	0	15,000	15,000	15,000	15,000	15,000	75,000
Direct costs	7,500	7,500	7,500	7,500	7,500	7,500	45,000
Overheads	6,250	6,250	6,250	6,250	6,250	6,250	37,500
Total payments	22,750	28,750	28,750	28,750	28,750	28,750	166,500
Net cash flow	–3,750	1,250	1,250	1,250	1,250	1,250	
Opening balance	0	–3,750	–2,500	–1,250	0	1,250	
Closing balance	–3,750	–2,500	–1,250	0	1,250	2,500	

The first 6 months of trading was disappointing, turning in £2000 loss instead of the targeted £7500 profit. DIY programmes on television meant that house owners were buying more laminate flooring as people tried creating the minimalist look featured in magazines and on DIY television shows. As a consequence sales of carpets nationally were falling.

The Carpet Barn's actual cash flow for the first 6 months of trading

	May	June	July	August	September	October	6 months actual
Owners' funds	12,000						12,000
Bank loan	7,000						7,000
Sales revenue (turnover)	0	26,000	2,5000	2,4000	23,000	22,000	120,000
Total income	19,000	26,000	2,5000	2,4000	23,000	22,000	139,000
Capital budget	9,000						9,000
Purchases	0	13,000	1,2500	1,2000	11,500	11,000	60,000
Direct costs	6,500	6,250	6000	5750	5,500	5,500	35,500
Overheads	6,250	6,250	6250	6250	6,250	6,250	37,500
Total payments	21,750	25,500	2,4750	2,4000	23,250	22,750	142,000
Net cash flow	−2,750	500	250	0	−250	−750	
Opening balance		−2,750	−2250	−2000	−2,000	−2,250	
Closing balance	−2,750	−2,250	−2000	−2000	−2,250	−3,000	

Murray and Ellen looked closely at the actual cash flow and compared it with their forecast. After a heated discussion they decided the business needed to diversify into laminate flooring. Murray decided to set up two profit centres so that he could monitor performance of the carpet and the laminate flooring sales. They seemed happy and confident once again. Of course the shop would require refitting to take on the laminate side of the business and stocks of laminate flooring would need to be ordered and old bills still had to be paid. The Carpet Barn was now very short of finance. Murray made a revised cash flow forecast using the experience of the first 6 months of trading. Although overheads would rise to £8000 a month Murray set a new profit target of £8250 for the second 6 months of trading. Murray, ever the negotiator, went along to the bank to arrange an overdraft or an additional loan to cover the shortfall. Murray knew that any loan would be secured against his and Ellen's personal possessions, but he was confident that his updated plan would persuade the financial adviser at the bank. However, the bank was more cautious and limited the amount it would lend. This meant that Murray needed to rethink his financial plans and look closely at reducing expenditure. He and Ellen were still convinced about their overall strategy and so with adjustments they went ahead with what Ellen called "plan two".

Within two months a major employer in the town announced redundancies and Murray knew that his forecasts were again wrong.

The second 6 months of trading for each profit centre was as follows:

	6 months forecast	6 months actual
Owners' funds	12,000	12,000
Bank loan	7,000	7,000
Turnover	150,000	120,000
Total income	169,000	139,000
Start-up costs	9,000	9,000
Purchases	75,000	60,000
Direct costs	45,000	35,500
Overheads	37,500	37,500
Total payments	166,500	142,000

		Second 6 months of trading in £s	
		Budget	Actual
Carpets	Revenue	150,000	130,000
	Direct cost	112,500	97,500
	Overhead allocation	24,000	25,000
	Profit	13,500	7,500
Laminate flooring	Revenue	75,000	90,000
	Direct cost	56,250	67,500
	Overhead allocation	24,000	25,000
	Profit	−5,250	−2,500
Total	Revenue	225,000	220,000
	Direct cost	168,750	165,000
	Overhead allocation	48,000	50,000
	Profit	8,250	5,000

testing–testing

assessment questions

(Many of the questions have been designed to make you look more closely at the data.)

Part A

1 What is the purpose of budgets? How might The Carpet Barn have reduced the budget for start up? **(6 marks)**

 The first part requires a straightforward explanation and the second part requires some simple analysis of the start-up budget. You may consider the following approach. What was the amount, what was its purpose, could it be reduced, what were the alternative sources?

2 Name two variable costs for this business. **(2 marks)**

 Straightforward.

3 Explain two types of fixed costs faced by The Carpet Barn. **(2 marks)**

 State two fixed costs and comment on why they are fixed.

4 What is the contribution made by each sale? What is the relationship between contribution and profit? **(4 marks)**

 Define contribution and show your working.

5 Calculate the break-even point. **(4 marks)**

 Define how to calculate break-even and show your working.

6 What was the forecast margin of safety? **(2 marks)**

 Briefly state what the margin of safety is and use your answer to question 5 along with the predicted monthly sales figure.

7 What would be the average overhead if sales were 40, 50 and 60 a month? **(2 marks)**

 Simple calculation assuming expenses = monthly overhead.

8 Use the forecast data in the case study to explain the difference between profit and cash flow. **(6 marks)**

 The forecast profit is given in the text and the cash flow forecast shows that early on more cash is paid out than is coming in.

Part B

1 In which months did The Carpet Barn need to draw on its overdraft facility? **(2 marks)**

 You should look at where the closing balance is negative.

2 What happened to the overall budgets on expenditure and revenue over the first
6 months of trading? What might have caused the difference between the budget
forecast and the actual performance? **(6 marks)**

 You need to refer to total figures for the 6 months forecast and actual.
Use variances in the actual figures or percentage changes.

3 Evaluate various options open to Murray and Ellen when the bank refused to give
them the entire loan they required. **(10 marks)**

 There is a lot you can consider here. Obviously they could stop trading,
but are there costs to this? If they carry on should they change strategy
and how can they reduce their cash needs?

4 The decision Murray and Ellen needed to make after 6 months was whether or
not to cease trading. Comment on their decision to carry on. **(12 marks)**

 There is some overlap between this and the last question. In a real exam
you wouldn't get such similar questions. Consider their performance, who
they owe money to and what they stand to lose if they give up. What are
the risks and rewards for carrying on?

5 Why was it useful to divide the business into two profit centres? **(2 marks)**

Straightforward.

6 Complete the variance table. State what was favourable and what was adverse. **(6 marks)**

The table should be straightforward, but then looking at it suggests
that sales of laminate flooring are much poorer than carpets. This may
be due to it being a new product, but more likely it is because the way
overheads have been allocated.

End of Module 1 assessment

What to do first when opening your exam paper?

It helps to highlight key terms and make sure you understand these. You should look at each sentence to see if you can relate it to a concept or issue. For example in the first paragraph in the case study below you might think about the idea of

a market segment and product life cycle.

Another idea is to highlight any numerical data that lies within the text.

You should highlight the key terms in the questions and use a different colour to mark the command words or instructions. Look at the marks available for each question to help you judge how much detail you need to provide.

You may not have to use what you have highlighted, annotated and thought about because the questions simply may not require it. However, going through this process will help your thinking and sharpen your mind so that you are more likely to be able to draw in the relevant concepts and ideas behind each question.

AQA Business Studies Unit 1

Summer 2003

- Time allowed 1 hour

Question 1

Study the information and answer all parts of the question that follows.

In poor health

Penman Ltd publishes twenty magazine titles each month, mainly on sport. Each of the company's magazines operates as a separate profit centre. Penman's financial position has been weak for some years. Profits have been low and the company has had problems with working capital. In an attempt to improve its financial position, Penman launched a new magazine, called Vitality, in June 2002 aimed at people who want a healthier lifestyle.

market segment and product life cycle

Vitality contains regular articles on diet, exercise programmes and learning new sports. The magazine was aimed at all ages, and not merely younger age groups. At its launch Vitality faced fierce competition from similar magazines produced by large publishers. Penman Ltd spent heavily on promotion and offered reduced price memberships for health clubs for readers taking out a year's subscription to Vitality.

product and how value is added

economies of scale

repeat customers

However, Vitality had a disappointing first year. The magazine fell short of its sales budgets and exceeded forecast costs. In its first year, the magazine recorded a loss of £400,000. The cash flow position of Vitality was also poor, partly due to high start-up costs.

adverse variance of budget forecasts

Despite this poor start, Penman Ltd's management team decided to continue with the publication, as sales had improved towards the end of the magazine's first year. The team agreed to approach the company's bankers for a loan to support the development of Vitality. Tough budgets were set for Vitality's second year. The managing director insisted that a cash flow forecast should be an important part of the financial planning for Vitality's second year.

Forecast costs, revenue and profits for Vitality July 2003–June 2004	
Item	£
Sales revenue	1,250,000
Fixed costs	602,000
Variable costs	550,000
Total costs	1,152,000
Profit	98,000

Answer all questions.

a What is meant by the term 'budget' (line 00)? (**2 marks**)

b (i) How many copies of Vitality would have to be sold in the year from July 2003 for the magazine to break even? (**5 marks**)

   (ii) If sales in the year from July 2003 were actually 600 000, what level of profit would Vitality earn? [Assume that fixed costs and variable costs per unit are unchanged.] (**3 marks**)

c Analyse one reason why Penman Ltd should draw up a cash flow forecast for Vitality for next year. (**6 marks**)

d Discuss the case for and against Penman Ltd's management team deciding to publish Vitality for a second year. (**9 marks**)

(**Total 25 marks**)

Question 2

Study the information and answer all parts of the question that follows.

Mars faces tough times

extension of product range

Mars bars have been around a long time. The Mars Company launched the chocolate bar in Britain in 1932. It has changed little since, despite the launch of related products such as Mars bar ice cream. However, reports suggest sales fell significantly from a figure of two billion in 2000. Mars bars are seen as an old fashioned product and are struggling to compete in a demanding market.

maturity on product life cycle, cash cow

The UK market for confectionery such as Mars bars is mature, meaning that market size is unlikely to alter much. Mars has a market share of about 19%, similar to Nestlé, but behind market leader Cadbury's. Mars' competitors have recognised that a way to compete when market growth is low is to launch new products. Cadbury's and Nestlé have enjoyed increased sales from new products such as Fuse and Chunky KitKats.

Promotion is important too. Over two-thirds of all chocolate snack purchases are impulse buys where decisions are made in the shop. The big chocolate manufacturers spent over £100 million each on promotion in 2001.

change in strategy

Mars has taken decisive action in the light of the heavy fall in sales for one of its major products. The company is adopting a more contemporary look for the product's packaging. The familiar red, gold and black colours remain, but the lettering will be more modern and the bar will be slightly slimmer. However, the company has taken the decision to keep the price at 29 pence, although the 'new' Mars bar will be 2.5g smaller.

slim bars more appealing to this market segment

The company is looking to attract more female purchasers. Most chocolate products attract more female than male consumers; market research shows this is not the case with Mars bars. The company intends to win more female customers.

Source: adapted from www.guardianunlimited.co.uk, 18 March 2002 and www.news.bbc.co.uk, 17 March 2002

Answer all questions.

a Distinguish between 'market share' and 'market size'. (**4 marks**)

b Mars bars have been a cash cow for many years. Explain one benefit the company may have received as a result of this. (**3 marks**)

c Examine two problems Mars might have faced as a result of the large fall in sales of Mars bars in 2001. (**8 marks**)

d Mars decided not to reduce prices as part of the new marketing strategy for Mars bars. Evaluate the case for and against this decision. (**10 marks**)

(**Total 25 marks**)

People in organisations

Module 2

People and operations mangement

What structure?

Specification Content

Principles of structure, span of control, hierarchy

starSTUDY

What shape and why?

The business had grown since it was set up. Production was still under Jim's control as this was how the company began. In the early days, he'd done everything – even the books. There were eight people working in production and he knew them all well. He'd taken on a bookkeeper and that had worked for a while but things were very different now.

He'd appointed managers for marketing and finance and several people now worked in each department.

It was getting a bit too big for him to manage the whole business as well as looking after production but it was a hard decision for him to take. He wanted to run the business but it was the shop floor he really loved. Sitting in an office all day was not really his cup of tea but there was probably little option if he wanted to keep an eye on everything that was going on.

1 Draw diagrams to show the business organisation
   a when it was first set up
   b when the two managers were appointed
   c in the future.
   Use the information on these pages to help if you get stuck.
2 Why does a business need to bring in experts like this as it grows?
3 Why is it important for Jim to delegate responsibility?
4 Why do you think it is important to have clear lines of responsibility in a business?
5 What problems do you think might arise if you get too many levels in the hierarchy?
6 What conflict is Jim facing as his business gets bigger? How might this affect his motivation?

Organisations and structures

All organisations, from the Brownies to BP, have a structure. Getting the organisation right, so that it achieves the tasks intended, is not always easy. Different structures have different benefits and work most effectively with different sorts of people and different outcomes. Jim's business is developing a hierarchical structure – which many do as they grow. He can bring in experts but he must learn to delegate responsibility.

A simple hierarchy

Critical thinking

1 Use the terms included in 'Understanding organisations' to explain the workings of the business in the large chart.

2 Explain how motivation is affected positively or negatively by the structure of an organisation.

KEY TERMS

Culture of a business reflects the attitude of the staff and the way in which they perform their roles.

Productivity is a measure of efficiency. It can be capital productivity, which measures output against capital invested, or labour productivity, which is measured against the number of people employed.

Next steps

Draw up an organisation chart for your school, college or an organisation that you know. Explain how it works. Does it reflect what actually happens?

Formal organisations

An organisation chart shows the roles and responsibilities of people in a business. In a small business it will be very simple. In a multinational, it will provide an outline of the structure.

UNDERSTANDING ORGANISATIONS

- All organisations have a HIERARCHY. Tall organisations have many layers. Flat organisations have few.

- Tall hierarchies have long CHAINS OF COMMAND because there are many people between the chief executive and the operators on the factory floor. Flat organisations have short chains.

- SPAN OF CONTROL shows the number of subordinaters under the control of a boss. A narrow span gives more control. A wider span means more delegation and can increase motivation. It is likely to be greater in a flat organisation. It has been suggested that span should not be more than five if a business is to run efficiently.

- CENTRALISATION leads to decision making being kept to the top layers of an organisation. This gives tight control and focused strategy, especially when finance, marketing and other key functions are organised from head office. On the other hand, it can lead other parts of the organisation to feel that they cannot make decisions about factors that affect them first hand.

- ROLE defines what an employee should do. It is set out in the job description. A poorly defined role can lead to inefficiency.

- AUTHORITY comes from an individual's position in the hierarchy. The Finance Director has authority over the Finance Manager and the Accounts Manager.

- A subordinate is ACCOUNTABLE to a superior. A superior is RESPONSIBLE for people directly beneath them in the hierarchy. This can be a positive experience or it can appear to be a threat if mishandled.

Is it manageable?

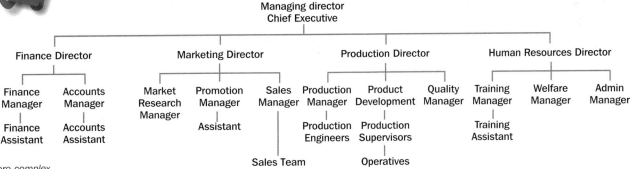

A more complex hierarchy

A formal structure works best when roles are the key factor in an organisation. Marketing, for example, is clearly in the hands of the marketing department rather than being spread through product groupings. It also provides clear lines of communication and procedures for dealing with problems.

Much is dependent on the quality of leadership from the top and at different levels. The match of leadership to the organisation is critical to the success of the structure. The ability to delegate is also important. A boss who can't let people get on without interfering will demotivate employees because they are not allowed to take responsibility.

People do not always behave as a structure implies. They may create other groupings within an

organisation which may affect how people's roles work. If this happens it can cause difficulties because their objectives may conflict with those of the whole organisation.

There is not, of course, one structure which perfectly suits all organisations – or even all parts of one organisation. The finance department might need a formal structure with a clear chain of command but the design department might work in a very different way. This may be because of the **culture** which exists in different areas. A whole business may have a culture of its own but within departments of a big organisation there may be local cultures. This can be reflected in the organisational structure, and the way people dress and address each other.

Why is organisation important?

Getting the structure of an organisation right affects **productivity** – the amount that is produced by each person or other resources in the business. If people are

working in a structure which doesn't suit them, their output is likely to be low.

go to →
Find out more about productivity on page 104

Structure and purpose

starSTUDY

Future Publishing: getting the right shape

Future Publishing produces 52 magazines on computing, computer games, hobbies and sports from their offices in Bath. Each magazine has a team that is responsible for putting it together and getting it to the newsagents. Within the business, there are other teams that specialise in marketing, production, distribution, finance and the other functions needed to get magazines to customers.

The magazine team is responsible for the content and design of each edition. Members of this team are also responsible for liaising with

the other teams to keep everything running smoothly and ensure that each edition reaches the news-stands on time.

Specification Content

Organisational design: functional versus matrix management

1 What drives Future Publishing?

2 Why is it more efficient to have specialist teams involved in marketing, finance, production, etc. rather than having specialists in every magazine team?

3 Are there likely to be more or fewer layers of hierarchy in this sort of structure? Why?

4 Is the organisation likely to be more or less flexible? Why?

5 Why are people likely to be more motivated when working in this type of structure rather than a hierarchical one?

6 Why might senior managers feel threatened in such an organisation?

Making a match

Future Publishing has developed a structure that meets its needs. The creative people who organise and write the content for the magazines need a flexible environment in which to work. Getting the products printed and distributed to the shops requires a different sort of approach.

The formal hierarchical structure doesn't fit the bill for many organisations because of the nature of the work and the people involved. As a result, a range of alternative structures has developed. They are often more decentralised and flexible.

Right business – right structure

One size does not fit all. Devising a structure and making it work is a challenge for many organisations. Some spend millions on reorganising only to find that there are unexpected effects.

A formal hierarchy is unlikely to be effective in a business which must respond quickly to change or where people are expected to work creatively. It can be frustrating when decisions have to be made much higher up the ladder as it often takes time and the people involved may not have been party to earlier discussions.

It can also be frustrating for people who want to take responsibility quickly and are full of good

ideas. They may have to wait until others have moved up the ranks before them.

Some businesses do need this formal structure because of their size or the need for safety. Rules and regulations mean that things are done correctly. A multinational, for example, must have very clear lines of command if corporate objectives are to be achieved.

Many organisations are a mix of several cultures. They may develop because of the type of people in different areas of the business. This is probably a good solution providing they can all communicate with each other and understand that corporate objectives have to be achieved.

Shapes for a purpose

MATRIX

A matrix structure combines functional departments with task-focused groups. Such businesses generally have a flattish hierarchy and a wide span of control. Someone working in marketing will be answerable both to the head of marketing and the magazine team leader. This may be of concern to people who are used to clear chains of command but it has been found to save time because it shortens lines of communication – which run between groups rather than up to the top and down again. People often succeed in such organisations because they work effectively rather than climbing the hierarchical ladder.

The group focus is often the product. The scale of a group can vary. Many hotels work as a group but refer to head office for setting objectives, financial management and marketing, etc. Businesses that run a cell structure will generally be a matrix organisation.

BUT ...

The matrix structure can lead to problems if project groups have to fight for the attention of the functional departments. In a business where project groups depend on the IT department for programming time, deadlines can put pressure on relationships between groups when one feels it is getting more attention than another.

	Finance	Production	Marketing	Distribution
Playstation 2	✓	✓	✓	✓
PC Answers	✓	✓	✓	✓
What Guitar?	✓	✓	✓	✓
Official Xbox Magazine	✓	✓	✓	✓

Senior management can find the structure unnerving because power lies quite low down in the structure. They have to balance the challenge of less power with the ability of groups to achieve their outcomes quickly and flexibly.

WEB STRUCTURE

At the centre of a web culture is a powerful leader. It is often the person who set up the business. Decisions are made at the centre and people often try to second-guess the outcome. A business built on this structure is often quite flat because there is no role for middle managers.

BUT ...

The culture will depend greatly on the boss.
If the leadership style gives people freedom once decisions have been made, staff will find it motivating. If they feel scrutinised all the time, they will be less so.

PERSON CULTURE

Some small organisations revolve round a group of stars. They are often people who are renowned in the field and work within an organisation that is designed to support them as effectively as possible. Many are creative organisations like advertising agencies or architects.

Such organisations are generally very flexible and can initiate or respond to new circumstances very quickly.

BUT ...

A bunch of stars can be hard to control. They tend to spend money beyond budget because they consider the outcome to be more important.

Critical thinking

Two major pharmaceutical companies were planning to merge but failed because the culture and organisation of the businesses were very different. Why do you think it was such a big stumbling block? Can you suggest any ways of motivating staff to adapt to a new environment?

Next steps

1 Do any of these structures match an organisation that you know?

2 Does the organisation match the objectives and nature of the business?

Effective management

1 What is the objective of this business?

2 What is the focus of attention for these managers?

3 What are they missing?

4 Why does this put the business at risk?

5 How might the objectives have been set?

6 What benefits are there in having clear objectives?

Specification Content

Management by objectives: purpose, method and implications of this approach; distinction between aims (or mission) and objectives

What do managers do?

Managers have an important role in medium and large businesses because they are too large to be controlled by one person. They have areas of responsibility depending on the structure of the organisation. It might be a department, a product or a shop, for example.

Managers must …

> **Forecast and plan** the work of the department in order to achieve the business's objectives

> **Organise** the department's resources to achieve the objectives

> **Command** people below them in the hierarchy

> **Co-ordinate** the people and resources in their area of responsibility

> **Control** activities so they can check that objectives are being achieved

Managers are responsible for making the part of the business under their control work effectively. They clearly need to know what is going on and use their interpersonal skills to encourage people to work together. They are also an excellent source of information because they see the day-to-day workings of their section of the business. Their leadership skills often determine success in achieving objectives.

Management by objectives

The idea of **management by objectives** was formalised by Peter Drucker in 1973. He was convinced that a clear line of objectives for all levels of a business should stem from the aims in the **mission statement**.

The development of the objectives should involve everyone at every stage. It means that each employee can see why they are doing what they are doing – and how it all fits together.

Large organisations can become inefficient because they suffer from diseconomies of scale.

 go to → *Find out more about economies of scale on page 106*

Management by objectives (or MBO) helps such businesses to stay on track because the activities of each part of the organisation result from careful planning and relate to the corporate mission.

Individual objectives
Team objectives
Department objectives
Corporate objectives
Mission

Benefits	Problems
Motivation is greater because people are involved in setting objectives.	**Time consuming** meetings have to be held to set objectives.
Priorities are clear so people should be able to decide what tasks are most important.	**External factors** can make targets impossible to achieve. Changing targets frequently is expensive because it takes time.
Benchmarking results from setting objectives. Everyone knows what the targets are and aims to achieve them. If things are not going according to plan, changes can be made.	**Inflexible targets** do not allow for a changing market. Managers may not use their initiative because they are obsessed with targets and unaware of changes in technology or other products that might affect them.
Targets are realistic because they are agreed together and people in the organisation understand why they have been set.	**Traditional organisations** may find it hard to work this way. People have to be trained for a different approach.

Good objectives motivate people. They should be:

CLEAR so managers can see exactly what they are expected to achieve

QUANTIFIABLE so that achievement can be measured

AGREED so people don't feel that targets have been foisted on them

ACHIEVABLE so people don't feel that they are being asked to achieve the impossible.

go to → *Find out more on motivation on page 82*

Using MBO

In an organisation which uses MBO, effective **delegation** is important to the success of the organisation. Setting objectives involves input from different layers in the hierarchy and gives people responsibility for their part of the business. They have to feel that they are trusted and that their contribution counts.

MBO is one technique used to make a business work. People are aware of the problems that it can cause but any business needs objectives if it is to meet targets. Today, businesses often draw on the strengths of MBO but use other strategies that encourage greater flexibility and more creative thinking.

go to → *Find out more about delegation on page 81*

Critical thinking

Find some business objectives or mission statements from company websites. How do they fit with the activities of the business?

KEY TERMS

Management by objectives is a way of organising a business in which the setting and achievement of objectives is used to run and control the activities.

Mission statement sets out the aims of the business.

Delegation is the handing over of authority to someone else to carry out specific tasks.

Delegate and consult

starSTUDY

Specification Content

Delegation and consultation: purpose of each and difference between them; relationship with leadership styles and structures such as quality circles and kaizen groups

1 The people in the circle are involved in making personal stereos. Output has been a bit slow and they are working out how to improve things. Why do you think this approach might be effective?

2 What sort of management strategies might be less effective? Why?

3 How might people be encouraged to look for ways of improving things rather than letting them slip?

Managing

Whether a business uses management by objectives or a more informal method, managers need to be able to organise themselves and other people.

This will include **consulting** others to find out how things are working and gathering views on plans for the future.

Once the objectives have been put in place, managers must plan, organise, lead and control.

In anything other than a very small organisation, they can't do all this by themselves so must learn to delegate. The owner of a small but growing business often finds this very hard to do. Having organised everything and made all the decisions, handing over responsibility can be a challenge.

Consultation

IN THE KNOW

Managers have to make decisions. Gathering information from subordinates in the organisation generally means that better decisions are made because they are based on accurate facts. It also motivates people because being consulted gives people a greater sense of involvement in the process of planning and decision making. Being a good manager means knowing whom to ask for information and how to consult effectively at all stages of decision making.

Critical thinking

1 Why can it be difficult for someone running a small business to delegate as the business grows?

2 Why is it important for people running a business to delegate tasks to others?

3 Why does effective consultation and delegation motivate people?

4 How can the structure and leadership of a business affect people's ability to delegate?

KEY TERMS

Consultation means that managers request information from subordinates before making a decision.

Quality circles are small groups of workers who meet at regular intervals to talk about maintaining and improving quality.

Kaizen is a practice that involves everyone looking for continuous improvement in the product and processes. It originated in Japan.

Delegation

In businesses large and small, **delegation** has to take place if everything is to get done. The owner or manager does not lose responsibility for the business but must be prepared to hand over authority so that the individuals concerned can carry out their tasks effectively. Once the marketing manager has worked with the team to develop a plan, the team members must be allowed to make their own decisions about the best way to carry out the tasks. They should be able to spend money, as long as it is within the budget and can be clearly seen to be helping to meet the targets.

RULES OF DELEGATION

Is the task clear to both sides?
Is the timing clear?
Are other people involved clear about the task?
Can the members of staff carry out the task? Do they need training?
Have the persons concerned got enough authority – either themselves or through the business structure?
Do they and others know the limitations of their authority?
Are reporting requirements clear?
Do they know where to go for help?
Is everyone involved kept informed?
Does everyone know that the manager is still accountable?

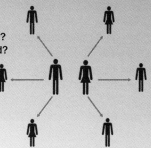

What makes delegation difficult?

Sometimes delegation just won't work.

- A business may be too small to allow delegation.
- An autocratic leader may not allow it to happen.
- Customers may want to see the boss, not the person responsible.
- Work might be confidential.
- Staff may not have the necessary skills.

Sometimes delegating can take more time and be more expensive than carrying out a task single-handed. This may work in the short run but if it continues, it can mean that resources are not being used effectively. Spending some time training people will mean that they can do the work in future so the manager can concentrate on other things. The pressure of targets and deadlines can mean that this doesn't happen.

Keeping people in the loop

Delegation can leave people feeling out on a limb, which can mean that they do not feel involved with the targets set. Consultation is therefore critical to success. Managers lead in different ways. Some consult and delegate effectively but others want to keep all control for themselves.

go to → *Find out more about leadership on page 90*

The culture of the business is affected by and affects both consultation and delegation. An open culture means that people are consulted, feel involved and therefore participate more effectively. Because they have been consulted, they understand why targets have been set and therefore are more likely to strive to achieve them.

Quality circles and **Kaizen** are both techniques which are used to involve people in this way.

Quality circles bring people together to discuss a problem or issue. It might be the team involved in producing an item or a cross-business group, which draws on different aspects of production.

go to → *Find out more about quality circles on page 123*

Kaizen, or continuous improvement, underpins the way a business works. Everyone is responsible for quality and looking out for ways of improving all aspects of the business. It motivates people in the business so they feel that they should work hard to achieve objectives and find ways of doing things even more effectively.

go to → *Find out more about Kaizen on page 123*

Next steps

1 Who is consulted in your school, college or a business that you know?

2 How is authority delegated in your school?

3 Are the managers good at letting others take responsibility for carrying out their tasks – or do they interfere?

The science and psychology of motivation

Specification Content

Motivation theory, Taylor, Mayo

starSTUDY

Jethro's is a fast food fish restaurant operating in a busy Cornish seaside resort. Customers demand to be served quickly and they want to eat in a clean environment. Jethro knows what's best and he wants to maximise his profits. Jethro gives each employee straightforward tasks to do. At busy times two employees have the job of taking orders, another two clear the tables, one makes sure the litter bins are empty and that the floors are clean. Two cook the fish and two cook the chips. Lastly, one employee is responsible for the drinks. He has separate fryers for the fish and chips and has a specialist machine that dispenses hot and cold drinks. Most of his employees are part-time and staff turnover can be high. However, because the tasks are straightforward it is not costly to train them and by concentrating on one task they quickly become proficient. He only employs two full-time staff and these are trained to complete a number of tasks when the restaurant is less busy. Although wages are at a given rate per hour, Jethro gives a bonus related to the turnover generated in each shift.

Future Publishing produces a range of specialist magazines including those devoted to computer games, mountain biking and music. Each magazine has a specialist team of writers whose task is to produce a thoroughly accurate, well-written magazine within the time allowed. The production editor organises the team and ensures everything runs smoothly. There's also a deputy editor who takes responsibility for what goes into the magazine. Lastly, there are two writers. The writers are encouraged to be creative and are delegated tasks. The editor encourages teamwork both through regular meetings and getting the team to support each other. The most important meetings are those at the beginning and end of the publishing cycle. The first meeting decides what is to go into the magazine and the post-publication meeting allows the team to review what went well and what could be improved. Employees are paid a salary.

1 How do these businesses differ in their attitude to their employees?

2 Which business offers its staff greater responsibility and allows more initiative? Why do you think this is so?

3 Which business instructs its staff to undertake simple repetitive tasks? Why might this seem an appropriate method?

4 Can they both claim to encourage teamwork?

5 What effect do the different approaches have on the staff?

Critical thinking

1 To what extent do you agree with this statement: 'A motivated worker will be more productive'?

2 How would the fish and chip business and its staff in the Star Study benefit if Jethro knew about Mayo's ideas?

3 How do you think Future Publishing uses Mayo's ideas?

4 How much are you motivated by your current studies? What would help to motivate you more?

Next steps

Consider two businesses in your area and investigate how they organise their employees.

Taylor: scientific management

IN THE KNOW

Around 100 years ago an American engineer, F.W. Taylor, carried out scientific investigations on how to make workers more efficient. He undertook a series of observations looking closely at time and motion. He believed his results showed that with repeated tasks and the proper equipment each worker would become more efficient and productive. He advocated the division of labour and de-skilling of the workforce. Managers needed to keep tight control and provide the workers with clear-cut instructions. The workers' job was to do what they were told. Henry Ford used these principles to mass produce cars by providing workers with discrete, uncomplicated, repeated tasks using purpose-built equipment. Many other businesses followed.

Taylor believed that the incentive to work hard was to link pay to the amount produced. This piece-rate paid workers more per unit after a threshold was reached. Those who did more work would receive more pay. This scientific approach seemed to treat workers more like machines than people, and factories adopting his approach saw a big increase in union membership because this approach alienated the workers.

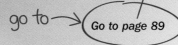

go to → Go to page 89

Mayo: human relations management

IN THE KNOW

Elton Mayo, a follower of Taylor, conducted research in which the conditions of a group of women workers at a factory at Hawthorne near Chicago was varied every few months. The results were discussed with the group. Each change, such as work layout, rest break times, refreshments and varied bonuses, led to an increase in productivity. Productivity even improved when the group went back to the original conditions, suggesting that the causes of change could not wholly be explained by scientific management, but was based on human relations management.

MAYO'S FINDINGS

- Group felt more of a team and wanted to contribute to the experiment.
- Workers were pleased that the managers showed an interest in them.
- Women gained satisfaction from making decisions themselves.
- Workers' expectations of each other might be influenced by informal relationships rather than the formal ones.
- Communications between people on the same level and between them and managers had an influence on morale and production.

His findings had a huge impact on business thinking. Businesses organised themselves in a different way. Personnel or human resources departments were established and the organisational structures were designed to take account of formal groups with an appointed leader and clear objectives.

Which method?

KEY TERMS

Motivation is the willingness to work because you enjoy it.

The scientific approach uses technical research to help establish how to achieve the highest output per worker.

The human relations approach uses psychological and social ideas to help improve motivation.

Different businesses organise their employees in different ways. There is no right or wrong method. Jethro's approach is more scientific as he instructs his employees to undertake tasks in order to increase efficiency. The staff can perform their tasks well, but may find the jobs narrow and boring. He tries to reward them through bonus payments. He could allow them to decide how to operate the business. This would provide them with increased responsibility.

Members of the writing teams working for Future Publishing have individual and group responsibility for their magazine although the ultimate accountability for the quality of the magazine and the meeting of the deadlines falls to the publishing editor. He or she must have confidence in the quality of the team to deliver the goods. The publishing editor would still need to provide clear instructions but the team has an opportunity to propose amendments which will be considered. Giving the writers responsibility helps to motivate them and fosters a good team spirit. Frequent communications, both formally at meetings and informally across the office or by e-mail, help to boost morale. Future Publishing firmly believes in human relations management as put forward by Herzberg.

go to → Find out more about Herzberg on page 85

Work needs, satisfaction and dissatisfaction

Specification Content

Motivation theory: Maslow and Herzberg

starSTUDY

Terry didn't do too well at school but he was good at practical things and could work with numbers. He related well to others and had a streak of determination. He became an apprentice engineer at 16 learning how to convert specialist vehicles. He was promoted to supervisor and was well respected and trusted by his fellow workers. He was promoted to sales manager because of his experience, knowledge and negotiation skills. Things were going well and he felt proud of his achievements, especially given his limited academic qualifications. However, when the firm started to suffer Terry was made redundant.

Terry and a colleague used their redundancy money to set up in business. A nice house, BMWs and great holidays followed. Terry sold to his partner and set up on his own. Success followed until competition became so fierce that Terry had to close down. He felt he'd let down his workers.

What do you think was Terry's most important need when he
- started his career
- became a supervisor
- became a sales manager
- was worried about being made redundant
- worked with his colleague to set up a new business
- sold the business to his partner
- saw his business fold?

Maslow: hierarchy of needs

IN THE KNOW

Elton Mayo had introduced psychology to the field of business management and Abraham Maslow, an American psychologist, subsequently developed the hierarchy of needs.

He wanted to know why people worked. He came up with a hierarchy of five groups of needs. It is a 'hierarchy' because once they have totally achieved a lower order need they may wish to achieve the next order up in order to maintain their motivation. Not everyone will achieve all the needs, even though they may strive to do so. For example, a threat of redundancy may change an individual's focus back to a lower level.

Maslow's hierarchy of needs

Highest order need 5
4
3
2
Lowest order need 1

Maslow's levels of need	For employees to reach the level a business should
Self-actualisation means you have achieved your target and reached your potential	Encourage employees to meet new and demanding challenges
Esteem needs include status, recognition and self-respect	Recognise achievement and provide promotion prospects and responsibility
Social needs such as the desire for friendship and a sense of belonging	Have good social facilities, promote effective communication
Safety needs – security and a stable and safe environment	Offer of job security, a clear job role, and safety at work
Physical or basic needs include food and shelter	Reward employees with adequate pay

Critical thinking

1 How does Terry's story relate to the hierarchy of needs proposed by Maslow?

2 How might a business go about ensuring hygiene factors are in place and providing for motivators?

3 To what extent does Terry's story fit in with the two-factor theory?

Business managers use Maslow's ideas to improve motivation. For example, Terry's potential for leadership was recognised by his employer and he was promoted. Such people can be singled out for extra training especially if they are likely to stay loyal to the business.

Today, many businesses use employees on a part-time basis. These will be on the lower level of needs. If Maslow is correct such businesses will find it hard to get their workers to take on responsibility since they have not reached the safety needs.

Herzberg: hygiene or motivation?

Frederick Herzberg was an American psychologist whose research in the 1950s led to his two-factor theory. They are factors which lead to

- job dissatisfaction – known as hygiene factors

- job satisfaction – known as motivation factors.

Both of these are equally important for businesses. Managers can reduce dissatisfaction by addressing hygiene factors, but they must provide opportunities for motivators to increase the level of satisfaction. Not providing motivators does not lead to dissatisfaction.

He made an interesting distinction between motivation and movement. The latter persuades people to go to work but has nothing to do with how they work once they get there. Pay will persuade you to work and therefore is a hygiene factor. Giving a bonus would just make the worker do enough to achieve that bonus but not their best. To achieve this there must be motivators.

Hygiene or maintenance factors	Motivators
Culture and ethos of the business	Achievement
Level of supervision	Recognition of your efforts
Pay (wages and salaries)	Work itself
Relations with others	Responsibility
Working conditions	Advancement

WHAT HAPPENS IF HYGIENE FACTORS DECLINE?

A dissatisfied worker may show:

- Greater reluctance to respond to change

- Increase in lateness

- More absence

- Work becomes poorer

- Increase in industrial disputes.

WHAT HAPPENS IF MOTIVATORS ARE PUT IN PLACE?

Businesses must react to success by finding new challenges and new methods. They should foster innovation and motivate employees so:

- There will be a greater desire to meet the firm's objectives

- Employees adopt a more positive approach to change

- Employees show greater initiative

- Employees care more about the quality of their work.

Critical thinking

1 Does Maslow's theory work for all people? If not why not?

2 What do Maslow's and Herzberg's theories have in common?

3 Why do you think Herzberg was against piece rates as a means for motivating workers?

4 Look back at the Star Study on page 82. How do Maslow and Hertzberg's theories apply? How could they be used to improve things?

Next steps

1 Find someone who really likes his or her job and explore the reasons why.

2 Now find someone who is dissatisfied with his or her work and ask for the reasons.

3 How well do their explanations fit in with Herzberg's ideas?

Working better

Specification Content

Motivation in practice: job enrichment, job enlargement, empowerment, team working

star**STUDY**
Working together

Canon makes printers, copiers, digital and film cameras and video camcorders. The production staff now work in small groups instead of on conveyor-belt production lines. Each group or cell is made up of multi-skilled workers, who are supervised by Experts; employees who have mastered every facet of the production process. These initiatives encourage employees to improve their skills. The new way of working has put creativity back in the hands of real people, rather than machines and systems.

1 Work out why the staff at Canon are better motivated from the move to cell production.

2 Why does being 'multi-skilled' encourage people to work more effectively?

3 How might being regarded as an 'expert' affect the way people work?

4 Which motivation theories explain the change?

5 What effect do you think the change has had on production at Canon?

Involving people

Many businesses have taken on Herzberg's ideas and moved away from the traditional assembly line. Canon has shifted from mass production using conveyor belts to cell production, which involves **team working**. By involving people in what they are doing, motivation tends to rise and has beneficial effects on production, quality and profits. There are various approaches to involving people but they generally give people more responsibility and greater powers to make decisions.

Getting it right

Like in most things, there are horses for courses. A manager has to decide how best to encourage staff to do their best. If people really don't want responsibility, giving them more may be disastrous. Equally, people often don't know whether they like something until they've tried it. Consultation can be both motivating and a key to bringing about change. A business that wants to introduce plans to empower its staff must look carefully at the process. Within one business, departments may work in different ways. It is not always appropriate for everyone to work in the same way. The creative staff in an advertising agency may expect to be very self-directed whereas others may need more careful monitoring.

Critical thinking

1 How does Canon's move to cell production fit in with the ideas of job enrichment and empowerment?

2 What implication does this change have for the human resources department?

3 Canon's ethos is 'Living and working together for the common good'. How does the change to cell production help improve this for the employee?

4 In a business you know, how are staff motivated? Which theories back up the strategies used? What effect does it have on the staff?

KEY TERMS

Empowerment means giving staff greater responsibility for their actions and more power to make decisions.

Job enrichment involves giving staff more challenging activities in order to make life more interesting and increase their motivation.

Job enlargement means widening the range of tasks that are performed.

Team working occurs when the workforce is organised so groups take responsibility for defined parts of production.

Motivation strategies

TEAM WORKING

Working in teams can give people:

- more responsibility
- power to make decisions
- more variety in their work
- mutual support
- more satisfaction from achieving targets.

In businesses that use Kaizen, or continuous improvement, staff are expected to be on the alert all the time, looking out for ways in which the product and production processes can be improved. This again raises the sense of involvement in their work.

 Find out more about Kaizen on page 123

Team working isn't successful for everyone because of their own personality or the way the business is run.

Some people are:

- individualists who thrive on their own
- bossy and want everyone to see things their way.

Some businesses:

- don't structure jobs to make teams effective. Competition needs to be between teams not individual team members.
- don't support teams by providing communication systems or support staff.

JOB ENRICHMENT

Job enrichment was Herzberg's main recommendation for improving motivation. It allows people to use their ability by giving employees responsibility and stretching them in their current role. It means offering a range of tasks and challenges, some of which are beyond the employee's current experience.

> The task should be a complete, meaningful unit of work, not just a small section.

> People should be able to develop relationships with people within and outside the business because such interaction aids motivation and provides feedback.

> People may need training to deal with vertical loading which means the extension of their skills.

> The employee should receive direct, regular feedback in the form of appraisal to identify successes and training needs.

This view opposes that of Taylor who said tasks should be simple and repetitive. Much depends on the nature of the workforce. People in manual jobs often question such strategies because they feel they are being asked to do more for the same pay. It is generally more applicable to white collar workers.

Although Herzberg's research used a limited sample of accountants and engineers, business leaders have successfully adopted it. Its advantage over Maslow's hierarchy of needs is that it offers a practical approach to improving motivation. Although the term is heard less today, the ideas have been incorporated into other motivation techniques.

JOB ENLARGEMENT

Job enlargement is a general term used to describe anything that expands the range of the job. This is known as horizontal loading, as there is no more responsibility but a wider range of things to do. It is one aspect of job enrichment.

JOB ROTATION

Job rotation means an employee changes activity regularly in order to make the job more interesting.

It does not increase responsibility, but does increase flexibility and people become multi-skilled so that they can cover for each other. In an office this might involve spending some time each day answering the phone, filing, word processing and photocopying. Developing a range of skills means that a process doesn't grind to a halt if one person is absent. In a car plant, this is critical because output can be lost if people are unable to swap roles.

As with many strategies, there are trade-offs. To achieve job enlargement, people will need training to develop new skills. It may be more time consuming as people move from one job to another and they may never become completely adept at all the jobs.

EMPOWERMENT

Empowerment means giving people more responsibility and authority over their working lives. Trust is the key to empowerment. If people are going to be given the power to make more decisions about how things are done, they have to be trusted. They also need help to make sensible decisions, so training has an important role. The sense that superiors no longer impose decisions – which may be right or wrong – increases job satisfaction, reduces stress and therefore improves motivation.

Rewards and motivation

Specification Content

Financial incentives: piecework, performance-related pay, profit share, share ownership, fringe benefits, salary

starSTUDY

Keeping the best

Microsoft has some of the best people working for it at its UK headquarters in Reading. The company spends a lot of money finding and training them and really wants to keep them. They do not pay the highest salaries but the rewards are wide ranging.

The Microsoft campus is spectacular, with a lake where charity rowing teams train, a forest and picnic tables.

There are wireless links throughout the campus so that people can open their laptops anywhere, mobile phones linked to the e-mail system, and broadband at home for everyone.

The Wellbeing Clinic offers everything from a mechanical massage chair to well-man clinics.

The 'bump' club helps pregnant women before their 18 weeks' fully paid leave. There are on-site nurses and a doctor, and even a facility to donate bone marrow. And more:

• a crèche

• four cafés

• a subsidised restaurant

• Xbox games terminals for entertainment

• £260,000 social budget for sports, outings to shows or trips abroad

• free private healthcare for 'life partners' and families

• a four-month sabbatical (unpaid) after four years

• a chance to buy days off.

Microsoft gave 9.6% of UK pre-tax profits to charity and matches fundraising by up to £7500 per person, per year.

1 Explain Microsoft's reward system in terms of motivation theory.

Just money?

Ask most people about why they work and they will place money at or near the top of their list. In fact, motivation theory suggests that money is not all we want. The range of possibilities is wide, although many industries and styles of work have traditions of particular types of reward.

KEY TERMS

Appraisal is a method used to assess the effectiveness of an employee's performance by comparing goals set with outcomes.

Critical thinking

1 It is not easy to isolate the effects of initiatives aimed at improving motivation, even using indicators such as lower labour turnover and reduced absenteeism. This is because other influences come into play. What might these other influences be?

2 A sceptical business will be worried that improving motivation will cost money and time and not prove worthwhile. What arguments could you use to persuade such a business that it could save money and increase turnover?

Ways to reward people

FINANCIAL REWARDS

SALARIES are usually paid to managers and professional staff. They do not usually receive overtime pay. Their annual pay is divided into monthly instalments.

TIME-BASED WAGES are calculated according to the number of hours worked. Overtime, night shifts and bank holidays are often paid above the basic hourly rate.

WAGES are the most common method of payment for production and unskilled workers.

COMMISSION is often paid to sales staff to encourage them to sell more. They may be paid a low basic rate, but receive a commission for each sale they make. Examples include people selling cars or furniture.

PIECEWORK is calculated according to the amount produced. It can boost productivity by encouraging people to work harder, but work may only be completed to an 'acceptable quality' and there may be more waste.

PERFORMANCE-RELATED PAY

provides an opportunity for employees to receive extra payments (usually less than 6% of their basic pay) for being good at their job. It encourages employees to work towards the company objectives. Great if you get it, but demotivating if you don't. Employees must reach agreed targets with their appraisers and review these at the end of the **appraisal** period. Many businesses complete this annually. To make it more acceptable, staff often receive training to improve performance in their weaker areas.

There are some strong arguments against rewarding individuals in this way, certainly if you believe Herzberg's ideas. Performance-related pay might damage team spirit as some staff might feel the system is unfair, with favouritism shown towards some individuals. Also the level of the award may not be significant enough to motivate people.

A more recent development is to encourage greater teamwork by organising groups of workers into cells. The members of each cell will receive bonuses if monthly targets are met.

go to → Go to page 118

Profit sharing gives employees a share of the annual profit as a bonus. This encourages employees to have a greater sense of being part of the business.

Shares are often given to employees as a reward. It is thought that they will work harder if they think the share value will rise. They may, however, sell them for fear that the price will fall.

Fringe benefits, such as company pension schemes, discounts and out of work social facilities, help to develop a sense of staff loyalty and reduce staff turnover.

NON-FINANCIAL MOTIVATORS

Herzberg's ideas were taken up by businesses. Job enrichment, job enlargement, job rotation and teamwork are all types of non-financial motivators. The ideas have been developed and taken further to include more delegation and the empowerment of workers.

Delegation means passing the authority down the levels of the hierarchy so that the delegated employee undertakes tasks. The boss must be able to trust the delegate to carry out the tasks and the delegate will want to be sure that the boss is not just handing down boring and time consuming tasks, otherwise resentment will build up. The boss is still accountable.

Empowerment is a step further than delegation and recognises that employees are often in the best position to make the decisions since they are the experts in their field. It allows freedom for employees to decide what to do and how to do it. For example, a manager of a travel agency might be allowed by head office to decide the best mix of holidays to sell since that manager will best know his or her customers.

Getting it right

A business will look for evidence that it is getting value from the measures it has taken to improve motivation. This may come in the form of positive appraisals, a reduction in absenteeism, lower labour turnover, an increase in productivity, a drop in complaints from customers, and an increase in customers.

What style of leadership?

starSTUDY

Specification Content

Leadership and management styles: authoritarian, paternalistic, democratic; McGregor's Theory X and Theory Y; team-based versus them and us, including issues relating to single status

1. How do you think the boss and the staff feel about their role in each picture?
2. Why is the style of leadership important in a business?
3. Think of a situation when the first type of boss is effective.
4. Think of a situation or type of business in which the second type of boss is effective.
5. What problems might the third type of boss have?

Leading people

Leaders – who may be the ultimate boss in a business or the leader of a team – can influence the way people work. The style of **leadership** is often a mix of an individual's personality, the culture of the business and the circumstances at the time. Some people are great in a crisis but not so good at the everyday things. Others might panic when problems arise.

KEY TERMS

Leadership is the process of influencing others to work effectively to help meet the organisation's goals.

Autocratic leaders make all decisions and expect obedience.

Democratic leaders consult staff and make decisions based on their advice.

Paternalistic leaders are autocratic but concerned about people's welfare.

Single status means that everyone in the business has the same rights and responsibilities. They use the same canteen and have the same rights to pensions and other benefits.

Team based management comes from the trend for people to work in teams and make decisions together.

Leadership styles

AUTOCRATIC LEADERS take an authoritarian approach. They tell people what to do and expect them to get on with it. They are not prepared to discuss their decisions and don't want any feedback. They 'know' what's best for the business and won't listen to anyone else.

Employees can find this undermining because their expertise isn't valued. It is unlikely to be effective in a creative environment where people like to share ideas and discuss the way forward. They will be demotivated because they want to share in the decision making and don't feel trusted. In a crisis or with people who need a lot of support, an autocratic style can be effective. People know what they have to do and get on with it.

DEMOCRATIC LEADERS expect staff to be involved in the decision-making process. Their contribution is valued and they are aware of it. This helps people to become more confident in their work and develop their abilities to the full. It provides a motivating environment in which responsibility is delegated and people are trusted.

PATERNALISTIC LEADERS often listen to people's points of view but then take little notice of them. They do show concern for people's welfare so employees may be very loyal.

LAISSEZ FAIRE LEADERS don't really lead at all. They wait for a crisis and then step in. They may be too busy to worry about what other people are doing or just too lazy. Some people thrive in such conditions because they love to manage themselves. Others are left feeling confused.

Theory X and Theory Y

Douglas McGregor in the 1950s analysed the way managers carried out their roles. He found two types, which he identified as Theory X and Theory Y.

Theory X managers assume	Theory Y managers assume
Workers need money to motivate them	Workers seek job satisfaction
They must be supervised to make sure they perform	Workers will respond to rewards and to recognition
Workers respect tough, decisive bosses	Low performance is the result of uninteresting work or poor management
Workers lack the ability to make decisions	Workers can work on their own
Workers avoid responsibility	Workers seek responsibility
Workers lack initiative and ambition	Workers can show initiative if trusted
So: a Theory X manager will be unwilling to delegate responsibility. As a result, people get bored and think more about pay than other rewards of the job. These managers tend to be autocratic.	So: a Theory Y manager will discuss issues and encourage people to contribute their ideas in a democratic environment. These managers tend to be democratic.

WHAT'S BEST?

It depends on the circumstances. A Theory Y manager is likely to get more out of the staff because they are happier and better motivated. A Theory X manager might be more effective in a crisis.

Is there a right answer?

Most successful businesses have good management teams. It is, however, hard to judge what is best because situations can be very different. It is also not always easy to train people to change their style. At best, managers should be able to adapt their style to match the situation. A crisis might need a quick, autocratic decision. A fall in sales might need a brainstorming session with staff to come up with some ideas in the light of the evidence. Using a range of expertise is likely to be more productive than one person's views.

The type of leadership which is appropriate on a particular occasion depends on a variety of factors. These include:

• The personality of the leader

• The skills of the leader

• The skills of the workforce

• The amount of risk involved

• The type of task

• The speed needed to get the task done

• How quickly things are changing.

Many employees expect to be treated in a more democratic way. The domineering boss may end up being neither liked nor respected, with a workforce which does not rise to the occasion when there is a crisis.

Team-based management has developed as empowerment has been used to motivate staff. Decisions are not made by a leader but by the team as a whole. In some businesses, the distinction between workers and management is disappearing. This leads to a **single status** approach in which every team member has the same conditions of employment, eats together in the same canteen and dresses in the same way. The manager still manages but from a different position in the organisation.

Critical thinking

If the appropriate leadership style varies according to the circumstances, how do you think a leader should manage the following situations:

1 An order has come in which is going to be difficult to produce in the time available.

2 The quality of output seems to be falling.

3 Customers have been complaining that the staff in the shop are not helpful enough.

4 The press has got hold of a negative story about the business which isn't true.

5 A member of staff has been sacked for dishonesty but some employees don't support the decision.

6 There's a flu epidemic and 25% of the staff are ill.

Human resource planning

Specification Content

The role of HRM in relation to effective planning and usage of staff as a major strategic resource. Workforce planning: assessing future labour needs (by type and number); ways of achieving labour targets

starSTUDY

People at Virgin Mobile

There are nine members of the human resources department at Virgin Mobile. Their role is to recruit, retain, reward and appraise. Others are responsible for training and development.

- Started in 1999 in Wiltshire, a location previously unused as a call centre market

- Needed to train people to meet our own needs

- Over 1200 employees on site mostly looking after customer care meet our own need

- Average age of employees is 30

- High turnover of younger staff means active recruitment

- Maximum of 800 on site on shifts with flexible working to cover 24 hours a day for 365 days a year

- An extra 40 employees a month are needed to meet the growth in demand for customer care

- We must provide enough staff to meet the changes in demand during the day and seasons

1. In what ways do the employees at Virgin Mobile add value?
2. What evidence is there that Virgin Mobile plans its human resource needs?
3. Why does the company take care to plan its human resource needs?
4. Which areas of human resources might the company be most concerned about and why?

starSTUDY

Building T5

Laing O'Rourke won the contract to build Terminal 5 at London's Heathrow airport. The contract says it must be completed on time. To guarantee the staff, some 3,000 building workers will be paid a 'ground breaking' salary of £55,000, following a deal struck between the contractors Laing O' Rourke and union leaders.

1. Why was it important for the contractors to reach a deal with the unions?
2. Why did the company decide to pay high salaries to staff working on the site?

Planning people

Employees add value to your business. That is why they are employed. To add the maximum value employees must be efficient at what they do and effective at meeting the business objectives. Employees must have the right skills and be fully aware of the business aims and objectives. There must also be a demand for their services. There is no point in employing too many because this would be a waste of money and tie up working capital. Employing too few is likely to result in a business failing to meet its objectives. Laing O'Rourke has a key objective to complete Terminal 5 on time. It helps to explain why it was prepared to pay such high wages.

Human resource planning

IN THE KNOW

Human resource planning means employing the right people at the right time. The human resources manager must communicate effectively with the departments within the business and understand their needs. The type of employees recruited must fit in with the culture of the business.

Most businesses find that change is constant and planning must predict what is going to happen.

CAUSES OF CHANGE

- Changes in business objectives and direction.

- Training needs resulting from new products or new technology.

- Changes in demand from new trends or seasonal changes.

- People leave through retirement, internal promotion and by just moving on.

- Trends in work patterns, such as **flexible working**, to allow for personal needs, for example caring for children or the elderly. More older people want to continue working to supplement their pension.

- New employment laws, for example health and safety, and the working hours' directive limiting the hours that can be worked by any one employee.

Getting it right

Employees at Virgin Mobile add value by providing customer service. One factor that contributes to its success is paying careful attention to **recruitment** and training. The human resources department

- regularly meets with the other departments to look at the present mix of employees and at what future requirements will be;

- needs to know when a vacancy arises through someone leaving or gaining promotion.

As well as call centre staff the company needs managers, computer technicians, statisticians for forecasting and planning, marketing experts, administration and maintenance staff. The call

centre needs staff 24 hours a day, every day of the year.

Getting the right staff in the right numbers hasn't been easy. Its Wiltshire call centre is not the best location to recruit 40 employees a month. The call centre is at its capacity and the number of customers is increasing. Potential employees are unwilling to commute long distances in this area especially with shift work. The company has looked at **homeworking**, but is reluctant to go down this line as it goes against the ethos of teamwork. It has decided not to expand in Wiltshire nor to relocate the call centre to Asia, but open up a second call centre in the north-east of England.

Critical thinking

1 Why is human resource planning difficult?

2 What things did Virgin Mobile take into account when deciding how best it could find staff to meet the expanding demand?

3 Look at the aims and objectives of Carphone Warehouse (page 186) and describe the most important elements of human resource planning for this company. To what extent would homeworking be a solution for this business?

Next steps

1 What type of people are required to keep your school or college functioning? How many employees left over the last two years? How much is spent on recruitment? How much of the school's budget is spent on paying its employees?

2 Find out the range of jobs available in a medium-sized business near you.

KEY TERMS

Recruitment involves identifying the need for a job and then attracting appropriate applicants for the position.

Homeworking means working from home.

Flexible working involves employing people who are part-time, full-time, temporary and permanent and on split shifts. It allows businesses to employ people in ways that keeps costs down.

Why worry about labour turnover?

starSTUDY

Why do they go?

'Working at a call centre isn't everyone's idea of a great job but we want to make sure that when people join us – they stay.'

'We recruit the best people in the country. It's an expensive process and we want to keep them.'

'There's a lot of demand for people in our business. We train them – then off they go to a business which pays more.'

'There are lots of people round here who would like to work but child care is always a problem.'

1 Why do businesses worry about a high staff turnover?

2 Why can a high turnover be expensive?

3 Why might the introduction of a crèche reduce labour turnover?

4 What questions might the company ask people who are leaving?

5 Why is this information important to the human resources department?

6 What do you think a business can do to reduce turnover?

'The turnover rate has been so high that we're having trouble getting orders out on time.'

'Everyone who leaves is given an exit interview.'

Critical thinking

1 Why is it important to compare labour turnover information over a period of time?

2 Why is it important for large businesses to break down labour turnover data into different departments, different skills levels, gender and different job roles?

3 Why might labour turnover data need to take into account the trends in the number of part-time employees compared with full-time employees? What might explain a high labour turnover in a specific department?

Next steps

1 Calculate the labour turnover in your school over the past academic year in terms of teaching and non-teaching staff.

2 How many of the staff moved on to new jobs and how many retired?

3 Why might either a low or high labour turnover over a few years be seen as a problem in a school?

Labour turnover

The attrition rate, or labour turnover, measures the percentage of people leaving an organisation over a time period. It is calculated by expressing the number of staff leaving the business in a year as a percentage of the average number of staff in the business.

Average number of employees   1000

Number leaving in the last year 250

Labour turnover   1000/250 × 100 = 25%

People leave for perfectly sensible reasons. For example, they might get promotion or they might retire. Students

may leave to concentrate on their studies. Sadly, others might be forced to leave through illness or they may die. Others might be dismissed. A big organisation will expect the percentage leaving to be stable on average. However, they will keep a close watch on comparisons with other similar industries and also look at the trends. Is labour turnover increasing or decreasing? If so, they will want to know why.

There are many causes of a high labour turnover.

Poor recruitment and selection means you may employ the wrong type of people who are not suitable and will not enjoy the job. Such people are not likely to stay long.

Poor induction and training means the recruits don't understand the business objectives and systems. New recruits are less likely to positively identify with the business.

Lower wage rates or poorer working conditions compared with local employers, especially if unemployment is low in the region.

Training can be too good and the employees gain transferable skills that are in demand elsewhere. For example, the RAF spends huge sums training pilots to a high standard. The RAF contracts these pilots for a set number of years to prevent them quickly moving into commercial airlines.

A lack of promotion opportunities within a business will force employees to look elsewhere.

Poor or ineffective leadership reduces the commitment of employees.

Low labour turnover can be viewed as being unhealthy because the business may lack new ideas and enthusiasm. Businesses can also recruit people who already come with the skills required and this would save on training staff within. A low labour turnover may result in a business looking to recruit externally rather than promote from within.

Why keep people?

Businesses generally want to attract the right employees and keep them. Recruitment and training are expensive processes, so costs rise every time they have to be repeated. More human resource staff are needed and time must be devoted to on the job and off the job training.

A high turnover also makes running the business more difficult. Experienced people guide a business –if they leave frequently, it can be hard to guarantee production, so orders may be late. This will annoy customers who may look elsewhere for future purchases.

The culture of the business can also be affected because people's commitment is reduced if they see others leaving frequently. It is difficult for management to sustain a positive environment when employees stay for only a few months.

Some jobs tend to have a higher turnover than others. More than one-fifth of call centres have a

staff turnover of over 40%. Many recruits leave within the first three months. The industry employs over 400,000 in the UK, but call centres are finding it increasingly difficult to recruit employees with the correct skills. Many companies are setting up new centres in India and South Africa.

A company may need to review its recruitment and selection process so that it presents a more realistic picture of what the job involves. The process might be part of a staff retention programme, which might investigate the pressures of the job, and how they could be reduced.

The human resources department can use more of its time and resources to improve the quality of the experience of the staff. Improving the conditions under which employees work includes providing more sociable shift patterns as well as providing an attractive working environment.

KEY TERMS

Labour turnover is the proportion of people who leave, as a percentage of the whole staff.

The recruitment process

starSTUDY

The recruitment challenge

Reproduced by permission of Virgin Mobile Telecoms Ltd.
© Virgin Mobile Telecoms Ltd 1999 – 2003.

1 Why might the Internet be a good place to reach potential employees?
2 Where else might a company like Virgin Mobile let potential employees know about vacancies?
3 What is the company looking for in its employees and how might it fit in with its image of 'being young at heart'?

Sainsbury's objective is to meet its customer needs effectively and thereby provide shareholders with good sustainable financial returns. It aims to ensure all colleagues have opportunities to develop their abilities and are well rewarded for their contribution to the success of the business.

Source: J Sainsbury's plc.

Could you manage your own Department?

Department Manager Fresh Foods

To join us you need a serious passion for retailing. We're not just talking a dull 9–5, this is a fast moving, demanding target driven industry.

We are looking for a self-motivated, enthusiastic team player to run our fresh foods department.

* To ensure that customer needs and values are met by developing and motivating the individuals in your team, so that they are fully equipped to contribute to the company's business goals.
* To ensure that current performance management processes are actively used to train, coach and develop the knowledge and skills of colleagues in the department.
* To manage the replenishment, merchandising and quality of goods in the department.
* To meet all statutory regulations regarding price control, health and safety and food safety.

All information © PeopleBank The Employment Network 2002.

1 Which part of the Sainsbury's advert tells you about the type of person the company is looking for?
2 Which part informs applicants of the types of tasks and responsibilities they will have to undertake?
3 How well do you think the advert will lead to employing someone who will contribute to meeting Sainsbury's objective?
4 How does the Department Manager for Fresh Foods add value to the company?

Critical thinking

1 What are the advantages and drawbacks of providing potential recruits with detailed information about the type of person the business is looking for?
2 In what ways could a business discriminate in its recruitment process?
3 What are the advantages and disadvantages of using phone interviews in the selection process?

Next steps

Look up two big companies on the Internet and find out about the types of vacancies on offer and how a potential recruit may go about applying for a post. In what ways are the two companies similar in their approach and in what ways are they different?

KEY TERMS

Aptitude tests measure how good an individual is at a particular skill.

Psychometric testing helps reveal the personality of candidates.

The initial recruitment stages

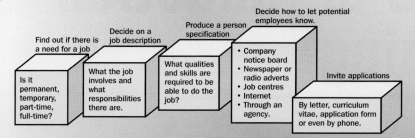

Find out if there is a need for a job
- Is it permanent, temporary, part-time, full-time?

Decide on a job description
- What the job involves and what responsibilities there are.

Produce a person specification
- What qualities and skills are required to be able to do the job?

Decide how to let potential employees know.
- Company notice board
- Newspaper or radio adverts
- Job centres
- Internet
- Through an agency.

Invite applications
- By letter, curriculum vitae, application form or even by phone.

The interview process is essential in testing out first hand whether the candidates have the qualifications, necessary experience and qualities that will support the business in achieving its objectives and goals. References from current or past employers are often called for to help verify the candidate's suitability.

A business will need to decide whether it wishes to promote internally or advertise outside the business to fill any identified vacancy. It is not a straightforward decision. The internal candidate will be familiar with the business and is already working towards fulfilling the business objectives, but the external candidate can bring in fresh ideas and use experiences gained in previous employment.

Another alternative is to use employment agencies. They will do the groundwork but charge a fee often related to a percentage of the employee's salary. Agencies are often used when a business needs to fill a position quickly and if the work is short term, usually associated with a timed project.

For some jobs, where communication skills are important, candidates may be asked to give presentations. Others might take **aptitude tests** to check on their skills levels. More senior posts may involve candidates undergoing **psychometric testing** to find out more about the attitude and personality of the candidates. This is useful in providing an insight as to whether the candidate is likely to fit in. For example, a business may want a recruit to be a team player or perhaps someone who questions actions rather than just accepting them. Psychometric tests will show up people who have the desired characteristics.

Some companies who recruit regularly are opting for phone interviews as a way of reducing the cost of recruitment.

THE SELECTION PROCESS

The selection process begins once the applications are in. The first stage is usually shortlisting, where a decision is made about which applicants to call for interview. Interviews can take a variety of forms, but the most common form is still face to face.

It is important not to discriminate during the recruitment process. Firstly, it is against the employment laws and, secondly, discrimination reduces the number available for the position and therefore the quality of the field. It doesn't make sense.

Methods of recruitment

Although 45% of the local working population has applied for a job at Virgin Mobile in Wiltshire, recruitment is still a difficult problem. Virgin Mobile uses a range of methods to advertise and then select for the posts on offer. Like many companies Virgin Mobile lists job vacancies on the Internet. It is cheap and can reach a large audience. The website gives a brief job description and informs potential recruits of qualifications and experience required. This acts as a filter for the business and some potential applicants may decide not to apply as they do not have the qualifications and experience or do not like the sound of the job.

Not all businesses provide a person specification, because some human resources managers feel it is easy for applicants to tailor their applications to this, thereby giving a false impression of themselves.

Virgin Mobile also uses its intranet to let people within the business know about vacancies. This helps provide equal opportunities for anyone within the company who wishes to seek promotion.

Virgin Mobile encourages applications through the Internet by completing a simple online form and attaching a CV before sending it off electronically. This has the advantage of saving time and the shortlisting can take place electronically. Its simplicity also encourages more people to apply. The human resources department may wish to follow this up with a phone interview before calling people in for final interviews.

The value of induction and training

MODULE 2: PEOPLE AND OPERATIONS MANAGEMENT

starSTUDY

To train or not to train?

'Our induction programme lasts five weeks and has been improved in the light of feedback from Customer Service Agents. It starts with a two-week programme of **hard and soft skills training**. The hard skills focus on using the equipment. The soft skills enable our recruits to get used to doing things the Virgin way. All this takes place in the training centre. The recruit is then attached to a team for a week to undertake simple tasks such as registering customers and working on the phones with an experienced CSA as a **mentor**. Then there's two more weeks in the training department.'

1 Why does Virgin Mobile bother with the soft skills training?
2 Why does the company allow trainees to operate with real customers half way through the induction period?
3 What different types of costs can you identify in the induction programme?

A survey by *Which?* researchers posing as customers revealed that one in eight gyms questioned had instructors who had not completed first aid training. This is despite the fact that many people who attend gyms have underlying health problems.

1 Why might some gyms be reluctant to provide adequate training in first aid?
2 What reasons would you provide to gyms to convince them that their staff should be fully trained?

Specification Content

Induction; on- and off-the-job training; potential for market failure (reluctance to train staff because of poaching)

IN THE KNOW

Induction

Induction is the first stage of preparing new recruits to reach the standard of performance expected of them. It is necessary because businesses need to ensure that new employees feel comfortable enough to want to stay and that they are well informed about the ethos and objectives of the business.

Elements of induction programmes	Benefits
Familiarisation with the work environment including how to use equipment, work in a secure way and follow health and safety procedures	Provides new recruits with basic skills and knowledge of how to work
Introduction to team members	Provides sense of belonging to the business and being part of a team
Introduction to amenities such as social facilities	Makes new recruits feel wanted
Awareness of the culture and objectives of the business	Ensures new recruits work in the way the business wants them
Administration arrangements such as what to do when ill, and who to contact if there is a problem	Helps ensure new recruits are aware of systems so that the business is run more efficiently
Attachment to a mentor	Helps recruits to settle in and any problems to be solved quickly

Preparing people

TRAINING helps employees carry out tasks necessary to perform effectively in their jobs. It is an ongoing process that applies to existing employees as well as new ones. It is necessary because of the continuous change in technology and the desire to improve processes. When a business changes its ethos and objectives it will need to set up training programmes. Training also develops individual skills and can be a motivating and rewarding experience.

ON THE JOB TRAINING is where employees learn how to carry out their tasks in the workplace. It may be demonstrated or a supervisor may coach the employee through it. Trainees will not be as efficient at their job as experienced employees and are often likely to make more errors. The trainee will be given simpler tasks and be under the eye of a mentor. On the job training is more likely to be job specific.

OFF THE JOB TRAINING refers to training that is not in the immediate workplace. It can take place on sites such as at special training centres or in conference rooms. Another alternative is to send employees away to specialist courses organised by experts in their fields. This can range from one-day courses at specialist training centres through to day release at colleges. Some courses result in qualifications that meet national standards. These courses are more likely to be skills-based training for general employees. Managers, however, might focus on more strategic issues and the latest business theories.

MULTI-SKILLED TRAINING involves making some employees able to undertake a number of tasks and means it is easier to cover for absent colleagues. Wider responsibilities also improve motivation.

Good training

Any training is an investment in human capital. Although induction and training are expensive it can be more expensive in the long run to cut back on training budgets. Big companies constantly monitor and evaluate their training programmes. Virgin Mobile's human resources department asks those who went through induction and training how to improve it and changes programmes in the light of this information. This brings a real sense of ownership and is likely to produce better results.

Poor or ineffective training can also result in a loss of income as customers go elsewhere. In a manufacturing business badly trained employees will produce poor quality work and there are costs involved in correcting mistakes, both in the extra time taken and in the waste of materials.

If training seems to bring such benefits why are many businesses poor at it?

- Training costs time and money. Training an employee on the job requires an expert supervisor who is therefore not working. The trainee usually carries out simpler tasks slowly.

- A business may train employees who then use their new skills and experience to get a job elsewhere, so other businesses benefit. Some businesses will therefore be choosy about the people they train and the level of training.

- Training budgets are often trimmed in a recession. Large businesses anticipate a decline in skills requirement and small businesses may need to cut costs just to stay alive.

Critical thinking

Businesses don't always want to spend money on training for fear of losing staff once they are trained. This doesn't help the economy and may make the UK less competitive than it should be. What should be the role of the government in terms of improving the skills level of the UK workforce?

Next steps

Find out about the training and induction programme in a local business. How is it monitored and evaluated? Do you work part time? What training and induction have you been given? Was it sufficient? How does it compare with full-time employees?

KEY TERMS

Soft skills training focuses on getting the employee to work towards the objectives of the business in the style the business wants.

Hard skills training is associated with the skills of using equipment such as computers and machines.

Mentor – someone in the business whom a new employee can turn to for advice. The mentor will keep comments in confidence.

testing–testing

People in organisations – assessment

More nurses needed

The Royal College of Nursing (RCN) represents many nurses and has warned that the NHS is in a 'race against time' to replace the 50,000 nurses who will retire over the next five years. The government needs to keep up their efforts to recruit more nurses, and to work even harder to retain those we already have.

On average, 10% of nurses on wards came from agencies or the staff bank, which leads to a lack of continuity.

The radical restructuring of pay, aimed at making sure that the most skilled nurses receive the highest pay, was welcomed by the RCN. However, many nurses leaving or considering leaving the profession do so because of poor morale, stress and a frustration that they could not meet all their patients' needs. Most of those leaving are the most senior staff leaving gaps that are difficult to fill.

Source: Caroline Ryan, BBC News Online
http/news.bbc.co.uk/1/hi/business/2389719.stm

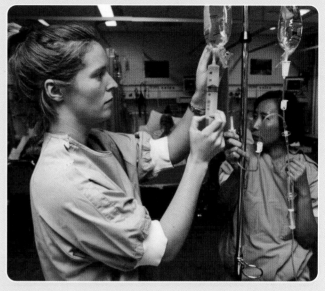

Student nurses 'left to cope alone'

assessment questions

1 What do you understand by the terms recruitment and retention?   **(2 marks)**

 Straightforward definitions testing knowledge.

2 What is workforce planning and why is it important in a large organisation like the NHS?   **(4 marks)**

 You will need to select evidence from the case study or from another
study to apply your knowledge about why workforce planning is important.

3 What might explain the high labour turnover in the past and what has been proposed
to reduce it? To what extent do you believe these proposals will be sufficient?   **(12 marks)**

This question requires knowledge, application, analysis and evaluation.
When you explain why something has happened you are analysing, but to
get high marks you will need to make sensible conclusions as to the
extent that the proposals work. Don't forget that you can state what
further information you would require to provide a more reliable answer.
Try to bring in key theories or ideas about motivation.

Amazon.co.uk

Amazon is recruiting for departments across the company. These include product areas like books, electronics and photos through to support systems like customer care, information technology, finance and marketing.
The company encourages online applications. Here is some of the information it provides for potential recruits.

Should I send samples of my work (writing, code, designs) with my application?

If you're selected for an interview, we may request samples of your work, so please do not send them with your initial application. However, if you have public copies of your work available that can be seen online, please include the link on your CV.

How long does it take you to decide whether I'll get an interview?

Our process is simple. We search the submitted CVs and then contact the people we'd like to learn more about (usually within 2–3 weeks after new CVs come in).

What is your interview process?

The process is variable. For some positions we begin with a phone interview. If there's interest on both sides, we invite you to an on-site interview, typically with the hiring manager and managers from other areas of the business. A candidate can expect to have two rounds of interviews and, depending on the role, some form of assessment or presentation to perform.

What are the benefits of working for Amazon?

- Shares in the company. All Amazon.co.uk employees are allocated a number of Amazon.com restricted stock units when they join. Additional performance-based annual stock is granted and depends on eligibility and start date.

- 22 days paid holiday (pro-rata) per year.

After successfully completing your probationary period of three months:

- Pension Plan

- Life Assurance

- Disability Insurance

- Private Medical Insurance through BUPA.

We operate in small working teams. As we grow, we continue to promote cross-functional teamwork, so it's possible that the people you work with will have all sorts of experience from other parts of our company. This team diversity encourages creativity, an open exchange of ideas across groups, and a respect for the challenges and trade-offs present across our business. Our hands-on approach to work is really demonstrated during peak selling times: no matter what your role, you will have the opportunity of spending time at our distribution centre ensuring that products get to our customers in time.

If you join us you'll be able to:

- **Learn** from smart, focused people who care about their work

- **Gain** from challenging, interesting projects that have a huge impact on our success

- **Work** in a casual but accountable environment in which hard work, initiative, and smart decisions are rewarded

- **Play** an important part in continuing our leadership in e-commerce by bringing new ideas to the table and launching new businesses

- **Be rewarded** by a great career opportunity and the chance to participate financially in the company's long-term success.

Source: Amazon website

assessment questions

1 Explain the stages in the recruitment process described by Amazon in the article above. **(4 marks)**

 This is best tackled by looking at the stages chronologically. You may come up with four or five stages.

2 What are the advantages of Amazon using this system? **(4 marks)**

 Straightforward analysis.

3 Recommend other methods Amazon might use to let potential applicants know about vacancies. **(6 marks)**

 This asks you to apply your knowledge in a logical way. There is a degree of analysis required for you to earn full marks.

4 How does Amazon structure the company? **(6 marks)**

 You must select from the evidence and apply your knowledge of relevant organisation structures.

5 Evaluate the methods Amazon uses to motivate its employees. **(10 marks)**

 Your evaluation must be underpinned by knowledge of motivation theories and business ideas such as enrichment. You could divide your answer into financial and non-financial motivators. Since this is an evaluation you should comment on the relative merits of the methods used and question what Amazon has in place to check up that its methods are motivating staff.

Co-operative Bank

Part of a Co-operative Bank advert on the Internet:

Okay what's it like working in a branch? It's fast paced, challenging, varied and with a great team spirit there's lots of support. One minute you could work behind the cash counter helping customers pay their bills, and the next you could be out in the banking hall helping customers with their enquiries. At all times you will be making sure that our customers know about the products and services we offer. As you can see, working in a branch is an excellent way to put your customer service skills to good use.

Because you are good at building rapport you will be able to talk to customers, helping them find the products and services they want. This is on a face-to-face basis finding out what your customers need, and then promoting our products and services in a positive and professional way. Your aim is to make sure that all our customers are always delighted with our service.

Interested, and want to learn more, then we are waiting to hear from you. Phone our recruitment line on 0800 587 0116, the lines are open Monday to Friday between 10:00 and 14:00. Come on, what have you got to lose, even the call is free.

We believe the Co-operative Bank is a great employer, and this has been reflected both in our staff surveys, and also through the various awards we've won.

The bank is an ethical bank supporting principles of human rights and not dealing with businesses that have links to oppressive regimes. It is committed to providing equality of opportunity for all potential employees and welcomes applications from all individuals for advertised jobs that match their skills and interests.

We believe our achievements are attributable to our way of working which is based on:

- Customer-focused teams and projects

- A flat organisation structure working across functions and

- A lot of hard work from focused and flexible people who can rise to a challenge.

We consult with managers and staff, to find out their opinions about the bank and their jobs within it. We are committed to carrying out this type of survey on a regular basis to ensure that we remain in touch with the views of our staff in everything we do.

Source: www.co-operativebank.co.uk

assessment questions

1 State one 'person specification' and one aspect of the 'job description' associated with this job. **(2 marks)**

 Extract this from the evidence.

2 Why might the bank be using the phone to shortlist rather than wait for written applications? **(4 marks)**

 Straightforward relating to saving costs and listening to the ability of the recruit to communicate effectively.

3 Define the terms flat organisation structure and flexible employee. **(4 marks)**

 Straightforward definitions testing your knowledge.

4 Evaluate the benefits and drawbacks of a flat structure to an organisation like the Co-operative Bank. **(12 marks)**

 You must consider the positive and negative aspects of having this type of structure. You should relate it to relevant motivational theory as well as the business ethos and culture. Has the business anything in place to reduce the impact of the negative effects? If not what would you recommend?

Being efficient

Specification Content
The study of operations management should focus on the way in which organisations use inputs to manage business processes efficiently in order to satisfy customers

star**STUDY**

1. Why are cars and wedding dresses made in different ways?
2. Which method produces more units per week?
3. What investment is needed before you set up a car plant and a wedding dress business?
4. How does this affect the return you expect?
5. How would you measure the effectiveness of the people working in the businesses?
6. How would you measure the effectiveness of the machinery and equipment used in the businesses?

Production or productivity?

Production is simply the amount that a business produces in a given period of time. There would be little point in comparing the production of a small wedding dress business with a major car plant.

A much more useful measure of output compares the relationship with the resources used and the output. This is known as **productivity**. It is one way of judging the efficiency of a business. Many businesses aim to achieve **productive efficiency**. This is the point at which average cost per unit is lowest. This is not as easy as it sounds because the operations manager has to be sure that all the raw materials are at the lowest price, the number of employees is exactly what is needed all the time, and that the technology used is up to the minute.

Measuring productivity

Productivity is important to a business because it has a direct impact on costs. Greater productivity makes a business more competitive as it can produce things at a lower unit cost.

Productivity can be measured in two ways:

- **LABOUR PRODUCTIVITY** compares output with the number of people employed. If 10 people are producing 500 items a week, costs will be lower per item than if they were making 300 items per week. If people become more efficient their productivity rises, and costs per item produced fall.

- **CAPITAL PRODUCTIVITY** compares output with the capital used in the business. Installing a new machine often increases productivity because more modern equipment is designed to be more efficient.

WHY IS PRODUCTIVITY IMPORTANT?

Businesses need to keep a close eye on productivity because competitors are always trying to get a step ahead. It is equally important to make sure that, in trying to achieve greater productivity, quality doesn't suffer. Just turning up the speed of a production line may mean that more is produced from the same resources but if there are faults as a result, customers will buy from somewhere else. If the faults are picked up and put right before leaving the factory, costs per item may rise rather than fall because such actions are expensive.

If a car company, for example, is wanting to close one of its plants, productivity often plays a key part in the decision. If looking for a location for a new plant, it will turn to national data on productivity because it will want to set up in a country where people work effectively. It is therefore important to watch both labour and capital productivity at both plant and company level.

Keeping ahead

In many industries, competition is cut-throat. The low cost airlines, for example, have been slashing ticket prices and the traditional airlines have been seeking ways to compete. When BA set about installing a staff management system it was perceived as a threat to staff because they assumed that the aim was to expect greater flexibility. The result was a strike, which stopped flights over the busiest weekend of the year. The company lost many millions that weekend. It shows how careful a business must be when it sets about increasing productivity.

IN THE KNOW

Being more productive

There are several ways in which a business may increase productivity. They involve making the production system more efficient by changes to equipment or people.

Whether in the primary, secondary or tertiary sector, businesses can use these strategies to become more productive.

Train people more effectively.
Businesses are sometimes reluctant because of the costs and if staff leave it is perceived as being wasted. It may, however, attract high quality staff who are looking for effective development.

Buy modern machinery.
New machinery is generally more productive but a business must be careful to make the right investment decisions. Markets can be fickle and the product people want today may be different tomorrow, so equipment needs to be flexible.

Motivate people.
Using strategies to encourage people to work more effectively can enhance productivity. If people are contented and feel well looked after, they are more likely to meet targets.

Manage the business efficiently.
Managers must watch both the production system and people constantly if productivity is to be improved. They can be more interested in production than productivity because of the way the business is organised. A system of continuous improvement encourages managers to be alert and spot strategies to improve productivity.

Making it work

Operations managers are responsible for making sure production works efficiently. They will be working to the operations objective and strategy, which have been developed with all the other corporate objectives.

Success will depend on their ability to maintain quality and flexibility.

go to → *Find out more about quality on page 116*

Much depends on the skills and attitude of people in the business. The operations department therefore has to work closely with human resources if targets are to be achieved. The corporate culture, leadership style and training will determine the attitude of staff to the importance of maintaining quality and the need for flexibility.

The finance department will also be involved because its objectives are usually to keep costs low.

The marketing department is also concerned about production because it needs to be certain that products are in the right place at the right time and meet the description that has been advertised.

KEY TERMS

Productivity is a measure of efficiency. It can be capital productivity, which measures output against capital invested, or labour productivity, which is measured against the number of people employed.

Production is the amount a business produces in a given time period.

Productive efficiency is the point at which the average cost of production is lowest.

Next steps

1 Choose two businesses that you know and identify ways in which they have improved productivity.

2 Can you suggest any ways in which they might improve productivity in future?

3 What might prevent them doing so?

Critical thinking

1 Why is productivity critical to a business?

2 Why can it be difficult to raise productivity in service industries? Which strategies might you use? How might these be the same or different from strategies used in manufacturing industries?

3 Spam e-mails are a nuisance and the number received by businesses is soaring. Why are businesses worried?

4 What aspects of motivation theory encourage staff to make high quality products in a flexible environment?

Is bigger better?

Specification Content

Economies and diseconomies of scale. Economies: technical, specialisation, purchasing; Diseconomies: co-ordination, communication, motivation. Distinguishing the quantifiable (mainly economies) from the qualitative (mainly diseconomies)

starSTUDY

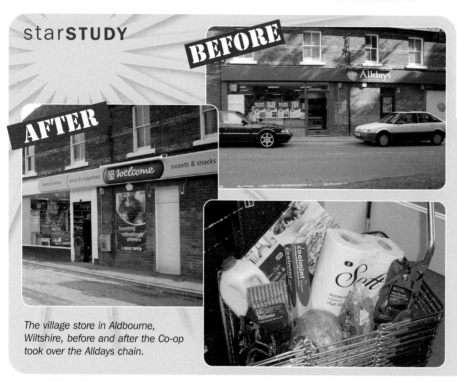

BEFORE

AFTER

The village store in Aldbourne, Wiltshire, before and after the Co-op took over the Alldays chain.

1 What effect did the takeover have on the number of outlets where Co-op products are sold?

2 What effect do you think this had on total sales of Co-op products?

3 Why do you think this led to an increase in efficiency for the Co-op?

4 What effect should an increase in efficiency have on the competitiveness of the business?

5 What effect do you think the takeover had on the management of the organisation?

6 How might the takeover affect capacity utilisation? How important do you think this was in the decision to go through with the takeover? Why?

Economies of scale

BUYING IN BULK works for bigger businesses because they order large quantities of raw materials for production or managing the organisation. A car producer will order millions of tyres in the course of a year and may need to install thousands of new computers in its offices. The larger the order, the greater the discount, so the lower the unit cost of the end product.

TECHNOLOGY can be used more effectively by larger businesses on many occasions. A firm that has very large orders will need equipment that allows it to produce cheaply and efficiently on a large scale. A smaller business will not be able to invest in such equipment because it probably hasn't got the financial resources and would have lots of spare capacity if it did so. The unit cost of each item would rise it the equipment wasn't used efficiently as the fixed costs would be spread over fewer items.

MANAGEMENT can specialise in a big business. In a small business, the entrepreneur often has to do everything – and may not be very good at it. Hiring experts for finance, marketing, human resources or production can lead to an increase in efficiency because they make better decisions and fewer mistakes.

MARKETING is an expensive process and it generally takes a considerable spend to be noticed. A big business will therefore benefit because it can spread the cost over more sales. Whether marketing involves television adverts, running a national sales team or any other type of promotion, the cost of selling 1 million items can be little different from 5 million.

FINANCE is often hard to raise for small and new businesses. Big, well-established businesses have a track record, so banks tend to lend them money more cheaply and easily. This all helps to keep unit costs low.

RISK is spread when a firm makes more than one product. Most big businesses, as they have grown, have diversified to sell a range of products. Some even make products which are safe in recession. We all continue to buy birthday cards whatever the state of the economy, so having them as part of a portfolio makes the business more secure.

Some economies of scale affect a whole industry. An industry which is concentrated in one area will develop local suppliers, a skilled labour force, as well as training and local government support. Information sources develop as an industry grows. These provide help for all businesses in the industry.

Many economies of scale have the advantage of being quantifiable so the operations department can measure changes. The greater the economies of scale, the closer to productive efficiency the business is likely to be.

The benefits of growing bigger

Businesses grow by expanding their activities or taking over other businesses. However it happens, it leads to a bigger scale activity. This may mean more shops, offices or factories – or larger shops, offices or factories. The objective of growth is often to become more efficient. This cuts costs and increases competitiveness. As it grows, the business benefits from **economies of scale** which lead to increased efficiency. They arise because the business can produce on a larger scale and can be managed more efficiently.

But can it get too big?

Being a big business obviously has many advantages but things can go wrong. People often find it hard to work in big organisations because they feel like a very small cog in a very big wheel. Unless a business works hard to avoid this feeling, people can become very disillusioned and demotivated. Once this happens, it is hard to restore a dynamic environment.

Diseconomies of scale

IN THE KNOW

WHAT CAN GO WRONG?

LACK OF MOTIVATION causes inefficiencies. People like to be treated like individuals and their contribution to be appreciated. The motivation theorists, Mayo and Herzberg, have written about the importance of valuing staff. In large organisations, it can seem hard to find the time to develop this sort of relationship between managers and staff. Once people lack motivation, their productivity falls and unit costs start to rise.

NO-ONE KNOWS WHAT IS HAPPENING in some

large businesses. If communication links are not developed productivity will suffer because people will feel alienated. In small businesses it is easier for people to talk to each other and explain what is happening. In bigger businesses things often have to be written down instead. Such messages often go unread and therefore the staff remain uninformed.

CO-ORDINATION of a big business is very time consuming. It takes meetings and planning to make sure that everyone knows what they should be doing. If information doesn't get through, poor decisions may be made on the basis of false assumptions.

SO REMEMBER THE PEOPLE ...

Spending money on enriching jobs and training people to manage an organisation better can seem to be an unnecessary expense. The shareholders of a public company are always looking for a good return on their investment and such training cuts into profits. However, a business is probably wise to look at the big picture and appreciate that profits are likely to be slight if the workforce is discontented. It is hard to quantify the effect before implementing change. Qualitative information is often harder to justify than information that can be turned into numbers.

Managers need to remember that there can be problems when growth is proposed. The economies of scale are often stressed in such proposals but the needs of the organisation are often forgotten. The profits may therefore be lower than expected.

Critical thinking

1 Work out which economies and diseconomies of scale might affect the Co-op in its takeover of Alldays.

2 How can motivation theory be used to overcome diseconomies of scale?

Next steps

Compare a large and small business that you know and work out how economies and diseconomies of scale affect them.

KEY TERMS

Economies of scale cause a fall in costs per unit as an organisation grows larger.

Diseconomies of scale cause unit costs to rise as the business grows larger.

How big?

Specification Content

Capacity utilisation. Impact of under-utilisation; ways of increasing usage including rationalisation and sub-contracting

starSTUDY

Under the Christmas tree

That's another order coming in.

But the factory is running at full capacity already. We even put on another shift and we still can't keep up.

If only we'd known we could have upped production for Christmas sooner.

At least its better than last year when we had all those stocks left over and we had to sell them off cheap.

Perhaps we should try to work out what's going to happen next year so we can make a better estimate of orders.

TOYS UNLIMITED

1 Why would a business want to meet all its orders?

2 What advantages are there for running a factory at full capacity?

3 What problems arise if the factory is running consistently below capacity?

4 Why is it difficult to deal with erratic demand?

5 What should it do to try to predict demand for next year?

6 Why can it be hard to predict demand for products like Christmas toys?

Too much or too little?

Businesses generally want to use all the capacity they have because it uses resources most effectively. A little bit of spare capacity is generally acceptable because it gives some flexibility. If a big order comes in from a customer who might become a regular, any business is going to want to be able to fulfil it quickly.

A little space also means that there is time to service the equipment and avoid breakdowns.

Over capacity means that expansion is possible provided that demand is likely to continue at the higher level. Problems arise when there is constant spare capacity.

Capacity utilisation

Capacity is the total amount that can be produced by a particular business. It will depend on the buildings, equipment and people employed. When all of these are used fully, the business is at full capacity. Providing it knows the total amount that can be produced, a business can work out current **capacity utilisation** using the following formula.

Whether a business produces tangible items or a service, the same applies. A hairdresser will know how many clients he or she can deal with in the course of a week and a bank will know how many staff it needs on the tills to keep the queues down.

The main reason for wanting to work as close as possible to full capacity is to spread fixed costs as widely as possible. Fixed costs do not change with capacity so if output is only half of the possible level, unit costs will rise.

$$\text{Capacity utilisation} = \frac{\text{Current output}}{\text{Maximum possible output}} \times 100$$

Toys Unlimited didn't manage to get it right from one year to the next. But it is in a business in which demand is notoriously hard to predict. Once a business has decided that there is a long-run problem with capacity, changes have to be made or competitiveness will be lost. If there is spare capacity, many firms will turn to the marketing department to try to sell more. It might mean making slight changes to the product to broaden the market – a waterproof version for swimmers

perhaps. If this fails there will be a need for a more severe solution – a cut in capacity.

If demand exceeds capacity, growth is required, but a business must be convinced that the increase in demand will be sustained. Many small businesses have expanded because of large orders from supermarkets. Trouble sets in when orders disappear after heavy investment has been made to increase capacity.

How to change capacity

IN THE KNOW

Capacity can be increased by changing working patterns. If it has been calculated initially on the basis of one shift per day, a second and third shift can raise capacity very quickly providing there are enough people with the right skills. Overtime can also help in the short run. Such a solution may be effective in service industries as well as production industries. A hairdresser with more customers than time may find that staying open in the evenings is a popular move especially with people who are at work all day.

Orang's salon is open from 10 a.m. to 10 p.m.

- **Outsourcing** is a solution if a supplier can be found to produce either semi-finished products or finished products of the right quality at the right time.

- Capacity can be changed by investment in new factories, offices or shops. This also involves training new employees, so there is considerable expense involved, but if demand is growing steadily, it is a sensible strategy.

- Capacity can be reduced by shutting down existing parts of the business – or **rationalisation**. This may mean that people have to be made redundant – skilled labour is therefore lost and motivation within the business will be affected. It is always difficult to manage a business that is contracting. Again the short- and long-run expectations must be taken into account when decisions are made.

Before any business makes a decision to change capacity there are some questions to be asked.

To grow …

- Is the business really at full capacity or could it be made more efficient within the existing capacity?

- Is an increased level of demand likely to be sustained?

- Is time critical? Will other businesses take your place if you can't meet orders?

- Can the business afford to borrow?

- Are there any activities that can be contracted out to avoid expansion?

To shrink …

- Will demand increase by itself?

- Why has demand fallen?

- Can demand be increased by attracting new customers with differentiated products?

- Can costs be cut to attract new customers?

KEY
TERMS

Capacity utilisation shows the extent to which existing capacity is being used.

Rationalisation usually involves cutting capacity in order to produce more efficiently.

Outsourcing involves contracting another business to carry out work for the business.

Critical thinking

Seasonal industries have to work on the basis of low capacity utilisation for much of the year. Draw a rough graph of how it might look for a seaside hotel. What might the hotel do to even up utilisation across the year and to keep costs under control?

Next steps

1 Are any businesses near you expanding or contracting?

2 How are they going about it?

3 Try to work out why it is happening.

How to produce?

Specification Content

Organising production: job, batch and flow

starSTUDY

Making products

A hoover manufacturer

Televisions – they are all just the same

When one batch is finished the machines are cleaned thoroughly before changing flavour

1 Explain why each product has to be made in a different way.

2 How is technology used in each example?

3 In which examples are labour costs a relatively low proportion of total costs? Why?

4 Which type of production gives employees most satisfaction? Why?

5 What problems do you think can arise with employees in the television plant?

6 What sort of production is easier for a small business to organise? Why?

7 Which types of production allow a business to spread its fixed costs furthest?

8 Can you think of an example of one-off products that are made using high technology?

Different product – different production

There are almost as many ways of making things as there are products but they can be divided into three main categories. The examples above show job, batch and flow production. A business needs to pick the most appropriate method for the product it wants to make because the cost implications are very different. In making the decision, it must consider whether the items are all the same or all different, how many the market wants, how much money is available to invest and the objectives of the owners.

Critical thinking

1 Draw up a chart which shows the advantages and disadvantages of each type of production.

2 How are the following items provided: a haircut, a personal stereo, a new garden wall, a croissant from a local baker, a croissant from a big bakery, a T-shirt from a high street retailer.

3 What steps must a business which uses flow production take to ensure that time is not lost because the line stops? How does this help to keep costs down?

KEY TERMS

Job production is used for one-off products.

Batch production is used when groups of items are made at the same time and move from stage to stage together.

Flow production is used to mass produce items by keeping them on a continuous process which moves them from stage to stage.

Job, batch or flow?

Job production is used to produce any one-off product. The size and shape is of no importance. It can range from a wedding dress to a spaceship to Mars. The one thing they all have in common is that they are specially made for the purpose.

It is an expensive process because it needs specialised staff who concentrate on the project. The outcomes are usually of high quality because the staff are highly motivated as each job is unique. They may use very little equipment, as in the case of the wedding dress, or masses of very specialised technology for a Mars probe. Unit costs are going to be high because each item takes a lot of time and, in some cases, investment.

Small businesses often use job production because they begin with the skills of the person who sets up the business. A window cleaner, for example, is using job production methods.

Batch production is the most effective way of working when products have similarities but are different. Yeo Valley's output is almost all of this kind. It produces yoghurt and other dairy products – but in different flavours.

It is flexible because if the supermarkets want more lemon yoghurt than strawberry, the machines are set up for a longer run. Printing works on a similar principle. The presses run for a long period every time a new Harry Potter book is in production but for a much shorter period when a new Business Studies textbook is nearing publication.

Unit costs will be lower because the equipment can be used over and over again but time will be lost when the switch is made from one batch to the next.

Flow production involves producing long runs of the same item. In this system the product moves directly from one stage to the next. It often uses a conveyor belt that passes through a variety of stages. Many cars are produced on an assembly line so they move continuously from the initial stages of putting the chassis together through to the paint shop.

Such systems are very expensive to set up, so they are used by big businesses. They need careful planning and a great deal of investment. They are a combination of specially designed equipment and computers needing sophisticated programming. Once in place, they are expensive to change. A new car design means restructuring the line – or even starting from scratch. They tend to be used for products that have a consistently high level of demand. Many food products and sweets are made in this way.

It is critically important to keep the line flowing. Stoppages mean loss of production and, because no one can do anything, the losses will be heavy. Another problem that occurs is that staff become bored and motivation drops because they are doing the same thing all the time.

Although the initial costs are very high, the volume that can be produced means that these fixed costs are spread over millions of items, so unit costs can fall quickly.

Personalised flow

Developments in technology have meant that businesses can use flow production but make products to the requirements of the customer. Triumph motorbikes are made in this way. A purchaser orders a bike of a particular specification and the information is fed into the computer system. This ensures that the right parts are in the right place and employees receive instructions at each stage. Many car firms have moved to this flexible approach because cars come with many alternative specifications of colours, doors and extras. The process means that a business can have the benefits of both flow and job production.

Is this a threat to the small firm which specialises in job production? Probably not, because people buy handmade products because of the status attached and the hand finishing associated with it. A machine is unlikely to be able to make a wedding dress with a perfect fit and millions of individual beads.

The ins and outs of stock

Specification Content
Stock control: buffer stocks, re-order levels, lead times, maximum stock levels, diagram of stock levels; stock rotation, stock wastage, opportunity cost

starSTUDY
At a halt

1 What effect do all these problems have on the business?

2 Why does the business not keep masses of stock?

3 Which of them are the result of internal problems and which are external?

4 Can you think of a solution to each of these problems?

5 Having lots of stock of finished products means that orders can be met but why should it not be the usual situation?

Why keep stock?

If a business hasn't enough stock, production will grind to a halt. If a shop runs out of stock, customers will go elsewhere. Keeping **stock control** is therefore important. It takes careful planning within the business to manage stock levels, ensure they are of the right quality and are in the right place at the right time.

Choosing a supplier

Some clues to help the purchasing department to make the decision are:

- Has the supplier got ISO 9000? If so, it has quality systems in place.

- Has the supplier provided samples to judge quality?

- Will the supplier give discounts for bulk purchases?

- Is the supplier happy to discuss adapting its products to meet your needs?

- Will the supplier provide contacts with existing customers to check for satisfaction?

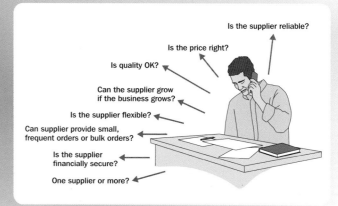

Managing stock

A business may have three different types of stock to manage:

- raw materials and components from suppliers

- work in progress that is produced within the business

- finished stocks that are awaiting orders coming in and dispatch to customers.

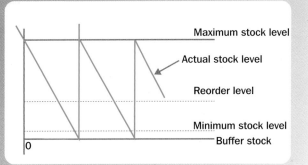

If any stocks build up or run out, it is clear that stock management isn't working. Stocks are expensive to hold so any business wants to keep them to a minimum. It is equally expensive to run out because it can bring the whole business to a halt. A hairdresser without shampoo would soon lose customers! A car plant with no wheels would have trouble rolling new vehicles off the production line! Whatever happens, keeping stocks for too long has an **opportunity cost** because the money lost could be used for something else.

Stocks are expensive because:

- they need storage space, so the factory or office has to be bigger

- if money is borrowed to acquire them, interest payments need to be made

- if cash flow is a problem, the business might be at risk of being insolvent

- they may deteriorate, become obsolete or be stolen if held for a long time.

On the other hand, not being able to meet orders threatens a loss of reputation. It can be hard to repair the damage when this happens.

Most businesses try to use old stock first and keep newly arrived stock until later. This is essential in the food industry for obvious reasons, but is good practice in any business because if stocks are left for a long time, they might deteriorate or become obsolete. This is known as **stock rotation**.

There are times when a business wants to build up stock. Easter eggs are made for a long time before Easter but do not hit the shops until the spring.

STOCK CONTROL CHARTS

In order to check that stocks are adequate – and under control – a business will keep charts to show what is happening. These are usually computer based.

When stocks are delivered, they reach the maximum level. As they are used up, the quantity falls. It reaches a point when another order is triggered. Businesses often hold a **buffer stock** to allow for delays.

The chart should not be a rigid guide. It needs to be used with other information. When a shop expects hot weather it will want to increase stocks of ice cream and charcoal. If the weather forecast proves wrong, the chart will show that stocks have remained high and the reorder level will not be hit for a while.

Critical thinking

1 Draw up a chart showing the costs and benefits of keeping stocks.

2 Give some examples of businesses that are likely to build up stocks of finished goods.

3 Draw up a stock control chart for a product of your choice in a supermarket. Label it showing factors that would influence the speed of use of stocks.

KEY TERMS

Stock control involves systems that ensure that adequate supplies of stocks are in the right place at the right time.

Stock rotation ensures that older stocks are used first.

Opportunity cost is the cost of the next best alternative that is missed because of a decision that has been made.

Buffer stocks are kept to protect a business against delays in the arrival of stocks.

Why quality?

Perfect pizzas

Canadian Pizza (UK) makes pizzas for Tesco, Asda and Morrisons and supplies pizza bases to other manufacturers. There had been 128 customer complaints at one of the manufacturing plants before a new senior management team arrived. They decided something had to be done to improve quality.

The British Standards Institute (BSI) came to the rescue. It provides quality standards and helps businesses to achieve them. Canadian Pizza had to produce a document setting out its business procedures, write a quality manual for internal use and assess its

quality management systems. Once this was all in place, a BSI assessor visited to check that everything was up to scratch. Once it had achieved the award – known as ISO 9000 – the inspectors continued to visit to ensure that the standard was being maintained.

The effort paid off. Complaints fell to 19 at one plant and there were no complaints at all about the 6 million pizzas produced at another plant. Wastage fell from 5% to 2–3% and training is now an integral part of the process.

Source: www.bsi.org.uk

Specification Content

Quality control, improvement and assurance; self-checking versus inspection

1 Why did Canadian Pizza's new management team decide to improve quality?
2 What might have happened to the business if nothing had been done?
3 How does the BSI process help a business to be more efficient?
4 What gains do you think can be made once the standards are in place?
5 How does it help in the long run?
6 Why does having achieved the standard help marketing?

What is quality?

Everyone knows that quality is important but it is surprisingly hard to define. Customers want quality but it will be related to the price they are prepared to pay and the degree of competition in the market.

In a perfect world customers want a product that looks good, does the job, is reliable, lasts as long as it is wanted, comes with good after-sales service and is value for money.

From the business point of view, the quality of design is the starting point. Whether producing a pair of designer sunglasses or the motor for a lawn mower, if the design is good, the end product can be produced efficiently and as cheaply as possible. The production process itself must be quality driven in order to meet the specifications, avoid wastage, not break down and be workable for staff.

This design specification can be driven by a powerful customer. When Nissan buys in components for its cars, they are made to its specifications. When supermarkets give contracts for ready meals, they set the specifications.

The law also influences specifications. There are laws about health and safety. These are monitored by trading standards officers. Industries also have their standards with Kitemarks of approval.

go to → page 159 to find out more about Health and Safety legislation

The important thing to remember is that quality is always changing. Just think how the quality of music equipment has changed in the last ten years.

Achieving quality

Businesses want to achieve quality in their field. Canadian Pizza became much more effective once it had established quality standards and embedded them in the business.

Once a product is recognised as being of good quality:

- customers return

- brand builds a good reputation

- marketing costs may be reduced

- retailers want the product on their shelves

- the product is perceived as value for money, so its price can be higher than the competition.

Once a product has developed a good reputation, a business has to work hard to maintain it. Measures must be in place to ensure that things only get better, so there must always be a search for ways to improve.

Prevention

Improvement

Detection

Correction

Controlling quality

Quality control

Most businesses have systems for checking that their products are up to quality. If you phone a helpline, you often hear a message saying that calls may be recorded to check on quality. This keeps employees alert because they never know when they might be recorded. It also gives customers a 'feel good factor' because they feel they are important to the business.

A system might involve

- checking the raw materials as they come in

- checking at each stage of production

- checking the finished products.

Each of these stages often involves sampling because it would be too expensive to check every one. There are different ways of checking.

- Inspectors may be employed specifically for the job. They may not be popular with other employees and often find the job repetitive and boring – which leads to mistakes.

- Everyone may be responsible. This leads to a greater sense of ownership of the product and, as Herzberg suggested, can be more motivating than just sitting on a production line.

- Many mass production systems have built-in alerts which warn staff when something has gone wrong.

BUT SOMETIMES IT ALL GOES WRONG ...

If products are not up to scratch when they reach the customer, insuperable damage may be done because reputations are hard to rebuild. If customers start complaining, it is important that the message gets to those who need to know. A business needs a system to feed customer views to people who have the power to change things.

A business which carries out market research might be alerted to problems by people's responses. If customers try things and don't come back, it can be hard to find out why. Building quality questions into research on a regular basis can help to prevent issues building up.

Critical thinking

1 What aspects of quality are important to Levi's jeans, Pizza Hut, BT, Volkswagen and Hilton Hotels?

2 Explain why. What would happen in each case if quality slipped?

KEY TERMS

Quality control involves ensuring that products meet their specification.

Improving quality

Specification Content

Total quality management; BS 5750 (ISO 9000); benchmarking

star**STUDY**

Something wrong?

A small business had been receiving a significant number of complaints that its bars of soap were not up to standard.

A call centre's customers were complaining that the staff were unable to give the support expected.

A games machine business became aware that its competitors' products were more sophisticated.

A hairdresser noticed that some regular customers were not returning.

A supplier to a major car manufacturer had a whole delivery returned because it was not up to standard.

Everything seemed OK but the managing director felt that the business might get left behind if nothing changed.

1 What effect will these problems have on the businesses?

2 Look at the strategies on these two pages to decide how each business might solve its problem. Explain your choices.

3 What are the implications for the business?

Who's involved?

Inspection is often necessary but unpopular so systems of self-checking have been developed. Many try to involve everyone so that quality control is not just the responsibility of the few. As motivation theory suggests, giving people responsibility enriches their jobs, and they become more effective employees.

If all employees are to participate in quality assurance and the search for improvement, they need greater levels of expertise, therefore training is an important part of the process. This, in turn, enhances motivation. By building quality into all stages of production costs should fall because there should be less wastage and fewer inspectors.

Quality strategies

TOTAL QUALITY MANAGEMENT (TQM) is built into the system and involves all employees being responsible. At each stage, employees aim to pass the best quality output to the next part of the process. Products will be checked to ensure they meet safety standards but all other quality checks will be carried out by departments.

It is important that senior management are seen to be part of the process because others will lose faith in the system if they aren't.

Benchmarking involves measuring the business against best practice elsewhere. It has become established as a strategy for businesses both large and small. It is usually carried out on separate aspects of the business. If there is a problem with customer service, it is useful to have a look at firms that do it well. This is done through forming an alliance with them so that they will share the information that needs to be analysed and applied to the business to enable targets to be set. The process should be carried out in consultation with everyone involved. People often feel threatened by such processes, therefore careful preparation and training is required.

The type of information to be compared depends on the business. The table shows the sort of information that a pizza delivery business might try to gather.

Benchmarking at Speedy Pizzas

	Speedy Pizzas	Faster Pizzas	Zippy Pizzas
Delivery cost per pizza	45p	42p	48p
Speed of answering phone	46 seconds	52 seconds	46 seconds
Average delivery time	22 minutes	15 minutes	27 minutes
Average price per pizza	£4.99	£4.99	£5.50
Refunds from delay	2%	1%	3%
Complaints	1%	1%	2%

In practice

Quality

Training   Motivation

Some larger businesses set up quality assurance departments to organise the process and take responsibility for ensuring that quality targets are met. In a smaller organisation, one person may be responsible.

People in the department will work with others to set targets and oversee strategies that are in place. Benchmarking, for example, takes planning, development and implementation. It therefore needs managing.

The quality assurance department will also manage quality accreditation. This enhances the role of quality because it provides a very public measure of the way the business works. Accreditation, such as ISO 9000, is often part of a business's marketing as well as its quality strategy.

Continuous improvements to quality can only be achieved by well-trained employees. It is unrealistic to expect staff to contribute in this way if they lack the expertise to deal with problems and come up with new ideas. Training generally increases motivation and quality improves, so the whole process is interlinked.

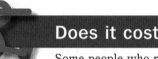

Does it cost too much?

Some people who run businesses argue that strategies to improve quality are too expensive to implement and run:

- Training is expensive

- People need time to meet and discuss the work of a cell

- Change means more cost

- Quality strategies need managing

- Accreditation involves costs.

Shareholders are often looking for a quick return so investing in the long term may be unpopular. In a market with little competition, it can be tempting to ignore quality issues. There are, however, few businesses today that are unchallenged. Applications for registration for ISO 9000 now come from all round the world.

Inevitably, the decisions made about setting up a quality system will depend on the power of customers, shareholders and employees. In some companies these will all be in favour but in others it may lead to conflict.

Benchmarking can be applied to any part of the business that is measurable – from the use of raw materials to wastage. In an office, the everyday processes can be measured and checked against others. It has to be remembered that the equipment that people use must be comparable if such comparisons are to be made.

The Upside	The Downside
Learn from others rather than starting from square one.	Processes may become more important than company objectives.
A comparison with others challenges a business.	Costs of benchmarking can be high and may not be recouped.
Introduce new ideas from finding out how others do things.	Can lead to complacency if used as a benchmark.
Improve competitiveness when companies see discrepancies.	Reduces innovation if companies just copy others.

Critical thinking

1 Explain why ISO 9000 helps the marketing strategy.

2 Why is motivation likely to be stronger in a business that takes improving quality seriously?

3 How can benchmarking help Speedy Pizzas improve quality in the business?

4 Benchmark information has to be treated carefully. Zippy Pizzas doesn't seem to measure up. What more information might you want before you criticised its activities?

KEY TERM

Benchmarking results from comparisons with other businesses or industries.

Next steps

Find out whether any businesses in your local area have ISO 9000. Check their websites or annual reports. Does it explain why they have done it and how it has helped?

Raising efficiency

starSTUDY

Reforming production to create real value

Canon has shifted from mass production using conveyor belts to a cell production method, in which small groups of employees undertake the entire production process. The shift is in line with the worldwide production system reformation aimed at eliminating labour and space inefficiencies. The beauty of cell production is that it puts the art of creation back where it belongs – in the hands of real people, rather than machines and systems.

Spearheading cell production are teams of multi-skilled individuals, who are overseen by Experts, who excel in all facets of the production process. Experts also provide sound guidance in such areas as parts procurement, machine tool refinements, product inspection and final installation. Initiatives such as these, which encourage employees to improve their skills, are being broadened to cover all companies in the Canon Group.

Source: www.canon.com

1 Why has Canon moved to cell production?

2 How does it work?

3 Why are people important in cell production?

4 Why do you think it works better than mass production using conveyor belts?

5 What extra responsibilities do Experts have? How does this help the cell, the individual and Canon?

Specification Content

Cell production: purpose and method; link with teamwork methods; self-checking and just in time (JIT)

People, process and prices

Businesses are always looking for ways of increasing efficiency. **Cell production** has removed the problems associated with flow production because staff are working in small groups on one particular item that they see through the production process.

Cell production is one way of developing a system that is 'fat free'. **Lean production** describes a group of techniques that aim to cut wastage and speed up the process at every stage.

The advantage of lean production is that it keeps costs down and therefore gives a business a price advantage. If a business can speed up the time it takes to get a product to market, it will also have competitive advantage from being innovative.

KEY TERMS

Lean production is a strategy that involves cutting out waste but ensuring quality.

Cell production uses teams of multi-skilled employees who work together to make a whole product or a particular stage.

Just-in-time production keeps stocks to a minimum to avoid wastage. They arrive when they are needed.

Kaizen is Japanese for continuous improvement. Employees constantly provide ideas to improve the process and therefore improve competitiveness.

Simultaneous development is when the processes of developing a new product take place at the same time.

Lean production

LEAN PRODUCTION aims to cut costs and ensure the efficient running of a business. It can be applied to every aspect of production from design to distribution.

LEAN DESIGN means **simultaneous development** which helps to get the product to the shop floor very quickly. This has been helped by the development of computer-aided design which allows drawings to be turned into products quickly and easily. It can cut the time taken to develop a new car by nearly half. When staff feel that their decisions are going to become reality quickly, it focuses the mind on getting it right.

JUST-IN-TIME PRODUCTION means that stock levels are kept to a minimum. They arrive when required – no sooner, no later. A factory doesn't need large stock rooms and saves money because stocks do not have to be paid for until they are needed for final production. When stocks arrive, they go straight to the place where they will be used.

There is pressure not to make mistakes because there are no stocks to rework the product. As orders for components and raw materials are put in when production is about to begin, there is less chance of over-production. When a business makes its products on the basis of an expected market for them, things can go wrong if demand is lower than expected.

LEAN PEOPLE do not have boring repetitive jobs. Instead of working on a production line which leads to boredom and reduced motivation, staff with different skills work together in cells on a complete product or a complete stage of a product. They are in competition with other teams and rewards are often associated with meeting targets. They are all responsible for solving problems and can maintain the equipment they use. If a machine goes wrong, everything doesn't stop until the engineer turns up. This means teamwork, so they have to meet to discuss what is happening and how to achieve the targets.

In many cases where cell production has been introduced:

- productivity has risen
- output has increased
- costs have been cut
- absenteeism has fallen.

LEAN QUALITY means everyone is responsible, not just the checker at the end of the production line. The aim is that nothing goes out faulty because rectifying the situation adds to costs. Mass production is cheap, so some argue that a few faults are worth the price. The lean producer would disagree because there is less reworking and waste of materials. Total Quality Management – or TQM – is one approach to achieving quality.

 go to → (Find out more about TQM on page 116)

KAIZEN, as in the Canon story, involves the staff in ensuring quality and looking out for opportunities to improve the process. This way, waste is eliminated and groups are responsible for ensuring that their team performs well. It requires well-trained, highly qualified employees.

In practice

Lean production should not be regarded as a cheap way of making things because it cuts down on staff and other resources. People have to be empowered through training and job enrichment to work this way. Some employers use it as an excuse to cut the workforce and reduce the time available for things to be done. When treated this way, it doesn't work. Employees get disillusioned and are unable to perform at the level required. Mistakes will be made and costs will rise.

Critical thinking

Lean or mass production?

Draw up a chart showing the costs and benefits of each form of production. What sort of products do you think are best suited to each production strategy?

Next steps

Why do you think quality is important for a business?

Time matters

starSTUDY

Keeping the shelves full

Specification Content

Just in Time: purpose and implications; link with flexible working and people-centred management; role in minimising waste of resources. Time-based management JIT; shorter product development times; simultaneous engineering

Customer: 'You're out of my favourite red wine again. What's gone wrong?'

Manager: 'I'm sorry. I'll have to find out what's happened.'

Customer: 'The manager of the wine department ought to get his orders in on time.'

Manager: 'Oh, it doesn't work like that. When people buy things, the information is sent straight from the till and stock is reordered as levels fall.'

Customer: 'Why don't you order more at one go – then you won't run out so often?'

Manager: 'We haven't anywhere to put it here. There's no warehouse. Everything comes off the truck and goes straight to the shelves. Anyway, the system usually adjusts the amounts ordered when we know demand will be high.'

Customer: 'So why does it go wrong?'

Manager: 'Humans aren't infallible! Some of the people on the checkout confuse the fruit. I'm always running out of pink grapefruit – checkout staff keep putting them through as white. Sometimes the warehouse is out of stock. Sometimes it's beyond their control. Where does that wine come from – Chile was it? If the boat gets held up, there isn't much we can do about it.'

Customer: 'Well thanks for explaining. I do hope it arrives soon.'

1 Explain how the stock control system works in the supermarket.

2 How has IT helped the process?

3 Does the store hold any buffer stocks?

4 Why does the supermarket use just-in-time stock control?

5 Why is any system going to go wrong sometimes?

6 How can the business work to minimise such difficulties?

7 Where do you think the customer will buy the red wine?

8 What effect will this have on the supermarket's profits?

Keeping the stock moving

Receiving stock when expected is critical for any business. The supermarket may lose a customer because, in going elsewhere for the red wine, she might discover that another supermarket provides a better service – and never return.

Businesses work hard to make stock control as effective as possible and information technology plays a major role. It has enabled businesses to use just-in-time stock control practices much more effectively.

Next steps

Ask your local shop how it controls its stock. Are the shelves usually well stocked? How does this compare with your local supermarket?

KEY TERMS

Kanban is a system of stock control involving barcoded cards that are used to reorder when stocks run low.

Time-based management uses systems which aim to cut time to reduce costs.

Speeding up the stock

JUST-IN-TIME (JIT) stock control aims at zero buffer stocks. A manufacturing plant without a warehouse has stock delivered straight to the point on the factory floor where it will be used. As the last items are used up, the next arrive. As many firms now make products to order instead of just hoping they will sell, there is no need to hold stocks of finished products either. An order comes in and stock is immediately ordered on a just-in-time basis.

A JIT system cannot be installed overnight. Any business has to be convinced that its supplier can manage to deliver the right product at the right time on a regular basis. Normally it would take effect gradually. Stocks are cut as close as possible to zero as trust is built up.

Using a JIT system means developing a close, trusting relationship with suppliers because you are dependent on them. Production will halt if stocks don't arrive on time.

JUST-IN-TIME HAS ITS UPSIDES AND DOWNSIDES ...

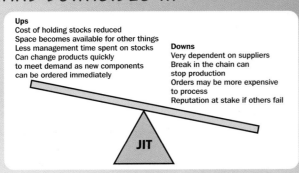

Ups
Cost of holding stocks reduced
Space becomes available for other things
Less management time spent on stocks
Can change products quickly
to meet demand as new components
can be ordered immediately

Downs
Very dependent on suppliers
Break in the chain can
stop production
Orders may be more expensive
to process
Reputation at stake if others fail

KANBAN is a system which helps just-in-time to happen. It involves having cards – or kanbans in Japanese – on individual components or batches of components. As they are used, the cards, which contain a barcoded number, are fed into the computer-based stock control system. More items are ordered and brought to place on the factory floor where they will be used. It empowers employees because they have the responsibility for ensuring that the order goes in – or they will be unable to meet their targets and hold everyone else up.

THE ROLE OF IT is clearly central to the development of JIT systems. Businesses set up systems to meet their needs. A supermarket's system will not just link to the warehouse but to the suppliers who supply the products. If the shelves empty quickly, the supplier is asked to increase deliveries.

However, the quality of the system often depends on people inputting data accurately. A failure of the system can lead to chaos as stocks fail to arrive.

BUT ...

- Just-in-time has been referred to as just-in-trucks. Guaranteeing deliveries when the route includes the M25 round London or the M6 round Birmingham can be difficult and makes production extremely erratic.

- Someone in the supply chain needs to hold stocks. Imported or seasonal resources are unlikely to arrive at 6-hourly intervals, as a producer might want. Apples grown in the UK are stored throughout the year – until the supermarkets want them.

- Stock control systems have mainly been aimed at big business but are increasingly being used in medium-sized businesses, but the small operator may still need to use a traditional approach. It may be too time-consuming to tailor a standard package to the particular needs of a small business.

- JIT may be inappropriate for a business which suffers erratic demand. It may be necessary for someone to work out expected demand and plan accordingly. It may also be necessary to hold stocks – just in case.

Critical thinking

1 Why is time an important factor for businesses? Give some examples.

2 Identify some businesses that can use just-in-time effectively and others that can't. Explain why.

3 Explain, using motivation theory, why Kanban can empower people.

4 Why is simultaneous development important for new electronic products?

Time-based management

JIT is one form of time-based management. In business, time costs money so cutting the time that processes take cuts costs. Time-based management covers a group of lean production methods which aim to reduce time. By cutting costs, the business becomes more competitive, although it may need to work constantly to achieve increasing levels of cost cutting as other businesses do the same.

Time-based management

SIMULTANEOUS DEVELOPMENT means that different aspects of new products are developed at the same time instead of consecutively.

FLEXIBLE MANUFACTURING means using production techniques which can be changed quickly from one product to another.

JIT cuts the amount of stocks held by a business.

Managing operations

starSTUDY

Built-in problem solving at Toyota

Making work flow smoothly depends on preventing big problems. To do that, Toyota designs its production system to detect and solve small problems immediately – before they become big problems.

Empowerment

Pulling on the line-stop cord lights a numbered lamp above the work place. The employee's team leader sees the lamp and comes to help. Meanwhile, the cars on the production line's conveyor belt will continue moving until they reach the next 'fixed position'. That is the position where each process on the production line has completed one work cycle.

Continuous improvement

This automatic welding machine welds a ring onto an assembly. Sometimes, an assembly comes along that is missing a ring. Toyota equips the welding machine with a

Specification Content

Continuous improvement Kaizen groups; desire for gradual change instead of major rethinks; involvement of well-qualified staff in suggesting product and process improvements

simple mechanism to detect missing rings. If an assembly is missing a ring, the welding arm comes down further than usual. It comes down far enough to depress the stop button. That lights a warning lamp and sounds a buzzer to call attention to the problem, as well as stopping the machine.

Source: www.toyota.co.jp

1 How does having control over the progress of the production line empower employees?

2 How might attitudes change if people could not stop the line if they can see that things have gone wrong?

3 How does stopping the line help the business?

4 How do continuous improvements to equipment improve quality?

5 Why do employees feel empowered when they can see their ideas being put to work?

6 What difference does it make to the business as a whole when staff feel involved? Which motivation theories support the argument? How and why?

In search of efficiency

Toyota has been practising Kaizen throughout the business so everyone involved is completely at home with the way of thinking and working. It is completely embedded in every process.

Although many businesses do not use Kaizen in this way, many individual ideas have been picked up and used to improve the way businesses work.

KEY TERMS

Business process re-engineering involves making a large-scale change in the way a business is organised.

People-centred management recognises that people work more effectively when they are well trained and valued.

Suggestion schemes provide an opportunity for employees to make suggestions for improvements in the business.

Kaizen at work

KAIZEN, or continuous improvement, is a philosophy that underpins the way a business works. Everyone is responsible for quality and looking out for ways of improving all aspects of the business. It is a strategy that was originally developed in Japan but the practice has spread round the world.

If is it to work effectively, every employee needs to be empowered so that they feel they can make decisions. This means being well trained and being happy to work in a team – or cell. If it works, development doesn't happen in fits and starts but is a constant process over time.

go to → *Find out more about cells on page 118*

Members develop expertise so they can identify and solve problems and work out how to improve the process. They will meet frequently to discuss their activities and make suggestions for improvement. This will only work, of course, if sensible ideas are accepted.

Targets are important because they help to identify problems and show whether the system is working.

QUALITY CIRCLES are often part of a Kaizen strategy. Groups of employees meet to discuss issues related to their work. A meeting might focus on a particular problem or look generally for ways to improve output.

But introducing Kaizen is not always easy ...

Persuading management and other employees to work within the system means the business must develop a democratic structure in which everyone feels free to contribute their ideas. This means trust between different levels of staff because some people may see extra responsibility as a burden rather than an opportunity. The culture of the business plays a great part in its success or failure.

Training to change attitudes can take a long time and is therefore expensive. Kaizen has to be embedded if it is to be successful.

Although the eventual gains from Kaizen will be financial, it is hard to show the effect in the short run so it may be difficult to persuade people that the shorter-term qualitative gains are worthwhile and will be effective in the longer term.

The right strategy?

Many businesses search for ways to achieve efficiency. In a search to ensure that the right products, of the right quality, reach their customers at the right price, at the right time, they might turn to TQM, benchmarking, Kaizen or time-based management strategies.

Businesses have learnt over the years that not all strategies suit all situations and workforces. Many are now looking carefully at how they can integrate aspects of the main strategies into their processes. Many businesses, for example, have **suggestion schemes**.

Kaizen is most effective when thoroughly embedded in a business, but it can be hard to introduce. Another approach is **business process re-engineering** (BPR), a term used to describe one-off changes. Instead of the Kaizen approach of continuous improvement, it advises a search for the big breakthrough. However, it is not always successful because it is:

- expensive
- disruptive
- slow to take effect
- business is playing catch up.

It also often involves job losses, therefore employees can be suspicious of the motives for change. The overall gains have been shown to be less than in businesses that go for continuous improvement.

Many businesses have appreciated that **people-centred production** methods work effectively. Motivation theorists have demonstrated how people respond much better when they are well trained, respected and their contribution is valued. Whatever strategy a business decides upon, the incorporation of a people-centred approach is invaluable.

Critical thinking

TQM, flexible manufacturing, simultaneous engineering, time-based management, benchmarking, cell production, Kaizen, lean design, quality circles, Kanban, zero defects, suggestion schemes and just-in-time are all types of lean production.

1 What is lean production?
2 Explain each one and its advantages and disadvantages.
3 Group them under the headings of time-based management and Kaizen. You may want to put items under both headings.
4 How do businesses use the ideas that have been generated by Kaizen?
5 Why is a people-centred approach important for success?

Hankins

Hankins Joinery is a small family owned business. Some 50% of its sales revenue comes from wooden components supplied to Millers plc, a large office furniture manufacturer. About 30% of Hankins' sales are components supplied to a total of five other businesses. Most of this is made in batches. The remaining 20% of sales is for bespoke furniture that it makes using job production methods especially for individual customers who make orders through the Internet or visit the show room attached to the factory.

Hankins		Millers	
Sales revenue	£4 million	Sales revenue	£80 million
Full-time equivalent employees	50	Full-time equivalent employees	400
Assets	£2 million	Assets	£20 million
Organisation by function. Finance manager and general manager, sales manager, purchasing manager, production manager, administration manager who is also the human resources manager		Introducing JIT	
25% factory space given over to stocks			

Hankins has reduced the price it pays for wood supplies by becoming a member of a buying consortium. The consortium has managed to lower the price it pays per cubic metre of wood by guaranteeing to buy in bulk from the timber mills in Sweden on a regular basis. The consortium makes weekly deliveries to Hankins. Hankins is pleased with the prices, but sometimes the quality of the wood is poor and needs to be sent back. It is concerned that its customers send back 5% of the final products as being poor workmanship or using poor quality wood. This compares with the regional average of 2.6%, according to a recent industry survey of customers.

Hankins has 25% of the factory area given over to stocks. The bespoke orders have a shorter lead-time if Hankins doesn't need to order stock and await delivery. The same is true for the orders it gets from its furniture manufacturers. Hankins' management knows that it often gets orders precisely because of its quicker delivery. That is the prime reason why the buffer stock represents about 50% of maximum stock levels. Certain types of wood can be difficult to store and the stores department operates a stock rotation system.

Millers have decided to invest in the JIT stock control system and have approached the management of Hankins with a proposal for a big increase in its orders so long as Hankins can deliver every day rather than the current fortnightly arrangement. Hankins would become a preferred supplier. Millers would buy four types of wooden component. Hankins would also be required to improve its quality control. It is a big decision, because it would mean Hankins moving towards its own JIT approach and cutting out job production and bespoke orders.

The management decided to meet with representatives from the production team, purchasing department and members from stores. The employees would have to be brought on board if business was to change. They would need to be motivated to accept change and seek continuous improvements. If not, Hankins would lose a major part of its market.

The initial meeting discussed the proposal and decided that before Hankins could go ahead it would need to think of ways of improving delivery and quality and becoming more productive.

Representatives from experienced and qualified staff were sent to other businesses and on training courses to find out more about the ways the business could set up as cell production, operate its own quality control system and become a JIT operation. The production team would see a shift in culture. The proposal would be to set up four different production cells, but would need a greater production area. The purchasing department had to explore finding new suppliers who could deliver quality wood on a daily basis. It might cost more in purchases, but there would be savings elsewhere and overall profit levels would be expected to rise.

Decision time was approaching and a final meeting was called.

1 What is meant by the terms JIT stock control system and cell production? **(4 marks)**

 Straightforward definitions required.

2 Explain how Hankins organises its production. What are the advantages and disadvantages for Hankins of operating in this way? **(6 marks)**

 The first part of the question is applying production methods to the case study. The second part invites you to make a simple analysis.

3 Why does Hankins keep a large buffer stock? What problems might Hankins face in keeping such a high level of stocks? **(8 marks)**

 You will need to know what buffer stock is and then provide a reason why Hankins feels it is important to keep large stocks. The last part asks you to come up with a couple of problems about holding large stocks. Try to relate this to working capital.

4 What comparisons can you make about the size and productivity of Hankins and its main customer, Millers (see table)? **(6 marks)**

 The first part asks you to select appropriate data from the case study. If you are making comparisons try to use ratios, e.g. 'A is 50% of or half of B'. The last part hints that if more data were available you could make better comparisons. You should know one or two further ways of comparing size.

5 Explain the advantages Millers has by being bigger. How has Hankins managed to survive despite it being small? **(8 marks)**

 Always try to recognise the key concept that can be used to support your answer. Start briefly with explaining economies of scale and then explore the different types of economies by applying it to the case study. Most businesses are small so they can survive just like Hankins.

6 Why should Hankins be concerned about its quality control system and what would you recommend it does about it? **(6 marks)**

Comment on the costs to the business of wastage and the image this has with customers. Look at internal and external solutions that provide improvement and assurance about quality control.

7 Evaluate the proposal to have closer ties with Millers and accept their offer of increased orders, but daily deliveries and improved quality. **(14 marks)**

There is so much you can write about here, but you don't have to include everything. You could look at a couple of options: 1. Do nothing and lose the contract. 2. Make the changes as required.

What are the good points about making the changes and what are the obstacles and problems? Can these be overcome? Are the disadvantages greater than the advantages? It doesn't matter which view you take as long as you can back up your arguments with evidence based on sound analysis.

End of Module 2 assessment

What to do first when opening your exam paper?

There isn't one right way of reading a case study, but it does help to highlight key terms and make sure you understand these. You should look at each sentence to see if you can relate it to a concept or issue. The examiners' instructions ask you to research the business concepts and ideas raised within this case study. It's a good idea to try to annotate your case study. For example in the second paragraph in the case study below you might think about the idea of

Another idea is to highlight any numerical data that lies within the text.

> a market segment linked to a product as part of the marketing plan.

You may not have to use what you have highlighted, annotated and thought about because the questions simply may not require it. However, going through this process will help your thinking and sharpen your mind so that you are more likely to be able to draw in the relevant concepts and ideas behind each question.

You should highlight the key terms in the questions and use a different colour to mark the command words or instructions. Look at the marks available for each question to help you judge how much detail you need to provide.

AQA Business Studies Unit 2 and Unit 3

Summer 2003

Pre-released case study

A: The idea

It all started on a Saturday morning in Electric Avenue, Brixton. Lily and her boyfriend Seyi were enjoying dipping in and out of shops with Lily's only real objective being to get some new lipstick. They went into Comfort's – an all-purpose clothing and cosmetics shop – to look at the range of lipsticks 'For women of colour'. After ten minutes Lily grabbed Seyi's hand and stormed out, frustrated by the poor range and poor quality cosmetics and the lack of interest shown by the staff.

> potential gap in the market

Seyi was interested. He had already made a successful investment into a new independent cinema nearby, and could see the germs of a fresh idea. Lily and Seyi spent most of the rest of the day talking about it. It would be a shop offering a complete range of cosmetics, toiletries and accessories for black women. Lily even thought she knew what to call it: Black Looks. The atmosphere would be quite young, with music and a young staff, but the range of products would cater fully for older women. It would have themed areas, 'For Work', 'For Pleasure' and 'Party Time'.

> market segment, part of the product mix, unique selling point

Lily spent the next few days talking to all her friends about the idea, about suitable brands to stock and about the accessories – yes to hair products, yes to underwear and yes to scarves, but no to clothing or footwear. She also visited the Halifax to talk about business banking and an accountant to discuss the right type of business organisation. Meanwhile, Seyi was talking to his friends about investing. He pointed out the potential for perhaps fifteen outlets in Britain and then perhaps in France. Sam, the cinema owner, was especially keen to invest up to £60,000.

> sole trader, partnership, Ltd

B: Preparing for start-up

> preparing and researching a business plan

As Lily researched the idea further, she was fortunate enough to get the name and number of a small-scale cosmetics manufacturer in Littlehampton. A phone call revealed that it used to supply Body Shop, but now had a great deal of spare capacity.

> able to meet demand, could get a good deal

126

Lily was sure that long-term success required a registered brand name that became synonymous with black cosmetics. So she wanted own label Black Looks lipsticks and hair care products from the start, as well as manufacturers' branded products.

A visit to the Littlehampton factory showed the possibility of low volume batch production using quite labour intensive methods. Lily was shown the factory's cell production methods, the quality inspection system, its ISO 9000 certificate and its approach to stock management and rotation. There were large stocks of raw and semi-processed materials that could quickly be turned into any grade and shade of lipstick. She discussed with the Works Manager the range of lipsticks that might be possible, then talked to the owner about prices, delivery and credit terms. He was helpful about the first two, but unyielding about credit. Experience had taught him to insist that new firms pay up front for the first month, on delivery for the next six months, and only then could credit be discussed.

Within three weeks Lily and Seyi had gathered all the data they felt they needed for a full feasibility study. They even identified a vacant site on Electric Avenue. The cash flow forecast (see Figure 1) looked difficult in the short term, but Seyi was optimistic that 'once we've opened several outlets, we can move away from the old boy in Littlehampton and use bulk buying benefits to get our unit costs right down'. Seyi was planning for the second outlet to be opened just six months after the first.

check that factory can deliver on quality, on prices, on time and in required amounts

she would want 28 days he says no

poor credit rating for new business

purchasing economies of scale, but there will be others

the cumulative cash flow forecast only becomes positive after 13 months assuming everything goes to plan

Black Looks: Forecast First Year Cumulative Cash Flow

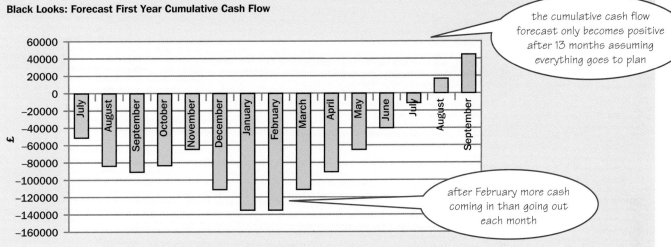

after February more cash coming in than going out each month

Figure 1: Cash flow forecast made prior to start-up

The time was coming for decisive action. It looked as if there would be only three investors, Lily, Seyi and Sam, the cinema owner. Fortunately Corinne, an old friend of Lily's, turned up having just returned from several years' working in West Africa. She had quite sizeable savings and was thrilled to be given the chance to invest. After much discussion, the capital structure of the business was agreed (see Appendix A).

C: The launch

comment on why lease and not mortgage

specialisation and responsibilities

As soon as everyone's cheques arrived, the real work began. Sam negotiated a four-year lease on the shop premises, Seyi dealt with the builders and shop fitters while Lily's responsibilities were purchasing and – later – staff recruitment and training. Sam found he had to pay £5000 more per year than had been budgeted for, but Seyi successfully bullied the builders into cutting their spending by the same sum. Lily was finding things a little harder, though. She knew she had to have key black American product ranges such as Palmer's, Luster and Sleek, but the UK distributors were playing hard to get. Credit was not an option and – to her surprise – she found that all three demanded a deposit to pay for the branded display stands. Eventually, she paid £8000 more in August than had been expected.

the saving on builders' fees would show up early on in the forecast by reducing the deficit, but the net cash flow each month would rise thereafter because the lease was more expensive. Using a spreadsheet would make it easy to adjust the forecast

the cash flow shortfall would rise in August meaning that it would take longer to come into a cumulative surplus. More money would need to be found or savings elsewhere. Think about options

With just two weeks until opening day, Lily reached a very difficult time when the need to recruit and train staff overlapped with her tough negotiations with suppliers. She coped partly, thanks to her old friend Helen, Head of School at a nearby college. Helen recommended some wonderful young students, who proved keen and responsible. All the weekend and evening part-timers were recruited in this way. For the two full-time sales staff, Lily advertised in the local paper and then had to sift through an astonishing 87 applicants. Pressure of time meant that all she did was choose eight, then spend a day interviewing them. She chose one experienced saleswoman and one bubbly school-leaver. The main form of training was a delirious day spent trying out virtually every cosmetic in the shop, plus further days with the experienced shop worker explaining to Lily and the teenager about the till, dealing with difficult customers, refunds, pilfering and much else. By the end of August they felt a team.

too small to have enough specialised roles

sounds like a poor system of shortlisting

On 1 September 2001, Black Looks opened in a wave of publicity thanks to a (free!) guest appearance by So Solid Crew. Seyi had been at school with two of the band members and they were happy to turn out for him.

The first week was incredible, as the publicity brought customers from throughout London. Lily even found herself chatting to three girls who had come down especially from Birmingham! Happily, the customers did more than look, and sales were an amazing £22,000 in the week, netting an operating profit of almost £10,000. The following weeks were also well above budget, even though they were not quite as frantic as week one.

this would be beneficial for the cash flow

D: Managing the operation

Very quickly there were serious operational difficulties. The main problem was stock. For some reason Sleek was the US brand everyone wanted and there were quickly serious gaps on the shelves. The UK distributor had some stock, but was soon sending urgent extra orders to the US factories. The own label ranges were also very popular. Fortunately, the Littlehampton factory did brilliantly, running extra evening shifts to keep up with the unexpectedly high demand from Electric Avenue. For the business, the success of the own label range was a marvellous sign for the future. Not only would it spread the name Black Looks, but the products also made a significantly higher profit per item than the imported American brands.

stock control problems

able to react quickly to orders

Meanwhile, Seyi was already looking ahead to the second store. He wanted it to be on Tottenham High Street - a shopping area as busy as Brixton. By early November he had identified a perfect site; it was almost the same size as the Electric Avenue store and was holding a closing down sale. He quickly found that the lease ran out at the end of the month, making it impossible to get the shop ready for Christmas. This was a pity, but things went quite smoothly, allowing Black Looks Tottenham to open on 10 January.

place as part of product mix

The start was not as buoyant as at Brixton, but given the time of year, sales were pretty good. Seyi had appointed Karen, the experienced saleswoman from Brixton, as the Tottenham store manager. This proved a problem, as she was better at selling than organising. One of her full-time appointments turned out to be a disaster (asked to leave after two weeks) and right from the start pilferage proved much greater than at Brixton. The first Lily heard of the difficulties was when she heard Seyi shouting down the phone: 'What on earth am I paying you for if you can't manage two staff. Buck your ideas up!' Lily was shocked to hear Seyi's bullying and unhelpful tone, but he was sure that Karen needed a severe telling off. Indeed, in the following weeks everything seemed to be going much better.

lacking some skills, so why did not recruit externally

communication, motivation and management styles

As Karen grew in confidence she started introducing some new ideas. She set sales targets for each of her two full-time and six part-time staff, and incentivised them by offering a 1% commission on their personal sales. This made them reluctant to do anything in the shop other than selling (such as stock-taking or window displays) but Karen just worked harder at filling in all the gaps they left unfilled. Within three months sales at the Tottenham branch were starting to move ahead of Brixton.

delegation

is 1% enough and would it be better as a team bonus?

With both Seyi and Lily based at Brixton, Karen loved the freedom to manage. Her only bad days tended to be when Seyi popped by. He made a huge fuss when he heard about 'giving away 1% of my takings!' but as sales moved ahead he came to trust Karen rather more.

extra costs more than matched by extra sales

E: Black Looks International

On 14 June 2002, Seyi and Lily were meeting in the office at Brixton when one of the part-time staff asked for authorisation of a customer cheque for £1723.50. Astonished, both went out to see how anyone had spent so much. They saw a young, suited man with six carrier bags full of produce. They invited him for a coffee and found out that he was from Frankfurt, Germany, and had flown over especially to investigate the business prospects of the shop. Quite quickly the conversation shifted towards the possibility of setting up Black Looks in Berlin, Paris, Marseilles and Amsterdam. Financing and ownership would be on a 50:50 basis and the German entrepreneur would take care of finding suitable locations and store managers.

expansion, but a reduction in ownership and was it too quick, and why expand abroad with associated risks when there's plenty of room for expansion in the UK?

That night, Seyi and Lily had a fierce row. Lily wanted to say no; she thought they should focus on building Black Looks in Britain before taking risks overseas. Seyi couldn't wait, though. Although he gave lots of plausible business reasons, Lily suspected that he let slip the driving force when he said 'and just think of the carrier bags: Black Looks: Brixton, Paris and Amsterdam'. At the height of the row, Seyi even threatened to get his friend Sam to outvote Lily, to force the proposal through. So Lily agreed to talk it through at the bank – to see if they had the financial backing to proceed.

Their bank manager had already become very impressed by the successes to date, and therefore was positive about the next step. Lily was surprised that there was not a greater sense of caution from the bank, especially as the newspapers had been warning of an increasing risk of recession. However, after careful cash flow forecasting, agreement was reached that the overseas expansion could proceed. The first store to open was in Paris, in September 2002. It was a fantastic success. The same happened two months later in Berlin. By now, Black Looks was buying such large quantities that the American cosmetics companies pressed to deal directly with Lily, cutting out the UK distributor. They gave her 60 days' credit and a very good deal for making bulk purchases. From now on she would be buying two months' stock at a time, but would receive a 12% discount. She was happy with this, but more concerned about Littlehampton. The factory owner had moved to a mass production system, but was still struggling to get production volume up, and prices down. When a bigger manufacturer phoned offering to produce all the Black Looks own label products at prices 20% lower than Littlehampton, Seyi said yes straight away. Lily was upset by the harsh treatment of 'a supplier who helped us to get going in the early days', but, with only two weeks' notice, all production was switched from Littlehampton to a producer in Cardiff.

economies of scale

change in stock management

a reduction in material costs would increase gross profit, but what about quality?

stakeholder and supplier relationships

F: The going gets tough

Quite soon after the change of suppliers, the Berlin store manager phoned Brixton to tell Lily that the own label face creams were bringing customers out in a rash. Lily was shocked, but found Seyi reluctant to accept that there was a problem. Complaining customers were given their money back, but the products went on being sold. Then the Paris manager phoned in a panic to say that a customer had severe ulceration on her face, and was going to sue. This brought the seriousness of the situation home to Seyi, who apologised to Lily and agreed both to offer to pay all the woman's medical costs, and also to withdraw the face cream from all the stores. Unfortunately, it proved rather more costly than that, as a Parisian newspaper took up the case of 'the scarred woman', and local sales slumped.

customer care, quality and reputation

This experience made Lily determined to stop letting Seyi have his own way. It also brought home to her the desperate need for more management input. Business had boomed, yet there were still only the two of them running the overall strategy and management of a business generating a £1 million turnover and growing at 50% a year.

Lily insisted that they should hire a Purchasing Director, whose job would be to make all the purchases and arrange all the deliveries. He or she would be answerable to both Lily and Seyi and could have an assistant. It took six weeks to find someone suitable, but Lily was delighted by the choice of a brilliant young graduate with two years' experience at Safeway Stores. He was given a £30,000 salary plus a car plus a 4% profit share. He started in April 2003.

organisation chart, people adding value, job role and responsibility

fringe benefits, motivation

By now the financial and personnel position was as summarised in Figure 2.

Figure 2: Actual and forecast financial and personnel position

Category	Actual	Actual	Actual	Budget	Budget	Budget
Date	Sept 01–Feb 02	March 02–Aug 02	Sept 02–Feb 03	March 03–Aug 03	Sept 03–Feb 04	March 04–Aug 04
No. of stores	1	2	4	7	12	18
Sales turnover	£285,000	£450,000	£1,130,000	£1,620,000	£2,850,000	£3,880,000
Profit	£40,100	£61,800	£132,000	£211,000	£450,200	£525,000
Staff (full-time equivalent)	7	12	22	40	69	106

convert data into graph, ratios and percentages

The actual profit levels seem to increase in proportion to the turnover. The forecasts show a bigger percentage growth in both these. Could these be too optimistic?

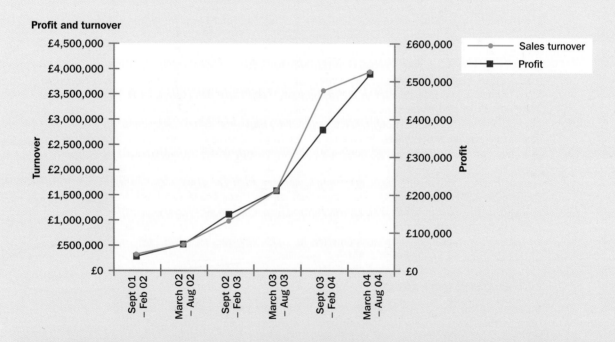

Profit and turnover

	Sept 01 –Feb 02	March 02 –Aug 02	Sept 02 –Feb 03	March 03 –Aug 03	Sept 03 –Feb 04	March 04 –Aug 04
Sales turnover	£285,000	£450,000	£1,130,000	£1,620,000	£2,850,000	£3,880,000
Profit	£40,100	£61,800	£132,000	£211,000	£450,200	£525,000
Turnover per store	£285,000	£225,000	£282,500	£231,429	£237,500	£215,556
Profit per store	£40,100	£30,900	£33,000	£30,143	£37,517	£29,167
Turnover per employee	£40,714	£37,500	£51,364	£40,500	£41,304	£36,604
Profit per employee	£5,729	£5,150	£6,000	£5,275	£6,525	£4,953

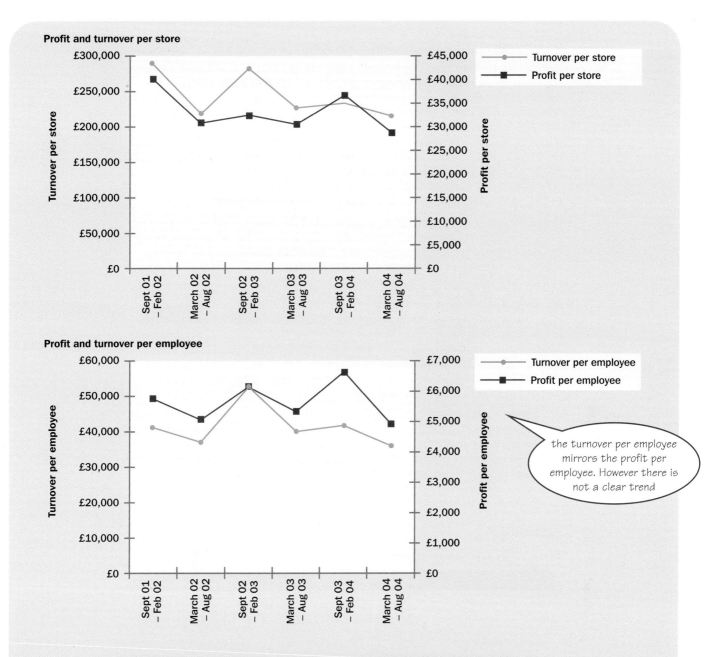

Profit and turnover per store

the turnover per employee mirrors the profit per employee. However there is not a clear trend

staff add value and the assistant has tasks to help with the new stores

The new Purchasing Director quickly hired an assistant while trying to cope with three new store openings within his first three months. At the same time he had to sort out the mess caused by the hasty switch to the supplier in Cardiff. There was still no own label face cream being produced. A trip to the Cardiff factory proved a shock. The factory was very modern, with a high degree of automation, both in the production system and in the packaging section. Yet the atmosphere between management and staff was unpleasant. The shopfloor supervisor who showed the Black Looks Purchasing Director round could not hide her contempt for 'management'. She was equally open about the mistakes that led to the wrong ingredients being mixed into the face creams. It emerged that relations in the factory had deteriorated after a new manager imposed new flexible working practices, with fewer breaks and annualised hours. A rush of orders had led to very long working days and bitterness from staff whose family lives were being disrupted.

poor motivation in supplier is a cause of concern for Black Looks

authoritarian

G: Getting the business back on track

Despite this, the Purchasing Director decided to leave production in Cardiff and to re-start face cream supplies. In the meantime he would investigate an alternative supplier in Northern France. Within four weeks he had found a remarkable plant near Boulogne, where the equipment was not as modern, but the attitudes were very impressive. There was a clear determination to please the customer, to produce high quality goods and a fanatical devotion to the environment. It seemed that recycling was fundamental to every aspect of production, and there was great concern to avoid pollution locally. This passion to do things in the right way was totally persuasive so, after producing a range of excellent samples, the Boulogne factory was commissioned to gear up production for Paris, Berlin and the new Amsterdam shop.

well-motivated staff

externalities accounted for

May 2003 saw store openings in Birmingham and Lewisham as well as Amsterdam. Despite handing over the purchasing function, Lily was still feeling hard pressed by the extraordinarily rapid expansion of the business. She was learning to be much more trusting and friendly in dealing with the store managers, but still found it hard to strike the right balance between consultation and delegation.

risk of losing competitive advantage

A more immediate problem emerged in mid-May 2003. A national chain of chemists (C.C. plc) suddenly announced the launch of a wide range of cosmetics and toiletries focused upon black women. They would be stocked only in the Birmingham, Lewisham, Tottenham and Brixton branches and sold at heavily discounted prices. The whole Luster range was on offer at 45% below the prices charged at Black Looks. As Seyi exclaimed: 'If we match those prices we'll be losing 40p on every unit we sell – and that's before allowing for overheads.'

price policy could be a price war

C.C.'s public announcement of this launch emphasised the need to 'respond to consumer pressure for lower prices at times of economic difficulty'. Seyi noted bitterly that it wasn't only the black community that was suffering from hard times. Seyi called Sam and asked him to pop by to discuss the situation with Lily and the Purchasing Director. Sam spent a bit of time on the Internet digging up the economic forecasts published by 20 City economists (see Appendix B). The four of them would have some big decisions to make, and Sam wanted to make sure they had the best available information to help them.

Limited liability for shares. Each share worth £200. Sam with 38% ownership and most of loan.

Internal finance £20,000 to loan capital of £75,000

Appendix A

Black Looks Ltd: Capital structure

	Shares	Loans	Total investment
Lily	26	–	£5,200.00
Seyi	26	£15,000.00	£20,200.00
Sam (cinema owner)	38	£45,000.00	£52,600.00
Corinne	10	£15,000.00	£17,000.00
Total	100	£75,000.00	£95,000.00

Appendix B

UK Macro-Economic Forecasts: Table 1

	Dollars per Pound			Euros per Pound			Changes in consumer spending compared with 12 months ago			UK interest rates		
	Max ($)	Ave ($)	Min ($)	Max (€)	Ave (€)	Min (€)	Max (%)	Ave (%)	Min (%)	Max (%)	Ave (%)	Min (%)
Dec-03	1.72	1.60	1.46	1.53	1.41	1.21	5.0	3.2	1.4	5.0	3.5	2.75
Jun-04	1.78	1.61	1.43	1.59	1.35	1.12	6.1	3.5	1.6	5.5	3.25	2.25
Dec-04	1.82	1.63	1.43	1.60	1.30	1.08	6.2	3.7	1.9	5.5	3.25	2.25

Max = Highest forecast made by any of the economists
Ave = Average of the forecasts made by any of the economists
Min = Lowest forecast made by any of the economists

UK Macro-Economic Forecasts: Table 2

	Inflation (% R.P.I.)			Unemployment (% of those available for work)			% Change in Company Investment (compared with 12 months ago)		
	Max	Ave	Min	Max	Ave	Min	Max	Ave	Min
Dec-03	2.1	1.4	0.6	5.1	3.9	3.1	4.5	1.2	–3.5
Jun-04	2.3	1.2	0.4	5.9	4.1	3.3	5.8	1.9	–3.8
Dec-04	2.2	1.1	0.4	6.3	4.2	3.3	6.9	2.4	–4.0

Max = Highest forecast made by any of the economists
Ave = Average of the forecasts made by any of the economists
Min = Lowest forecast made by any of the economists

- You can use a calculator, but you cannot take in your annotated case study. You will, instead, be given a fresh copy.

- You should highlight the key terms in the questions and also any command words. The command words are those that tell you what to do, like outline or assess or evaluate. Assess and evaluate type questions can earn you more marks because they demand higher order skills from candidates.

- Time allowed 1 hour.

- Answer all questions.

- Where appropriate, use examples from the case study to support your answers.

1 Seyi used internal recruitment to appoint the manager of the second store. Explain how Black Looks Ltd might have benefited from external recruitment for this appointment (see Section D). **(6 marks)**

2 Outline two possible disadvantages to the Littlehampton cosmetics supplier of holding large stocks of 'raw and semi-processed materials' (see Section B). **(6 marks)**

3 Discuss the possible problems that Black Looks Ltd might have experienced as a result of making a quick decision to switch from the small-scale producer in Littlehampton to the larger supplier in Cardiff. **(15 marks)**

4 Analyse how the Purchasing Director's performance might be improved by the introduction of management by objectives (see Section F and G). **(8 marks)**

5 To what extent would Black Looks Ltd benefit from more effective human resource management? **(15 marks)**

External influences

Module 3

External influences and objectives & strategy

The changing market

starSTUDY

We rented a house in the south of France for our holidays this year. Travelling with Ryanair and hiring a car worked out about the same price as the ferry, stop over hotels, petrol and motorway tolls. We were there in a few hours – not days.

We booked our weekend break in Prague over the Internet. The fares are so low these days.

easyJet, a low-cost airline, carried 39% more passengers in March 2002 than it did a year previously.

The combined market for easyJet and Ryanair for short haul flights in March 2002 reached £2.28 million. It surpassed British Airways' £2.17 million.

BA has reacted by lowering prices and has started to eliminate unprofitable routes.

1 Which of the three businesses, Ryanair, easyJet and BA, has the biggest share of the short haul market?

2 Why do you think demand for tickets with Ryanair and easyJet is increasing?

3 Why is BA trying to cut costs?

4 Why might people increase or decrease the number of flights they take?

5 What do you think would happen if people cut back on the number of flights they wanted to take?

What's going on?

Markets don't stay still. People want different things and businesses produce different things. Prices and costs change so markets are dynamic.

- High prices encourage existing businesses to supply more and new businesses to enter the market, but high prices discourage customers from buying.

- Customers will want to buy more if the price is lower, but there is not so much profit to be made for the business supplying the goods or services. It seems that low prices discourage businesses from providing goods and services.

Critical thinking

1 If BA could not reduce prices significantly for its European market what would happen to the business? How would this affect its stakeholders?

2 Choose a business you know and work out what is happening to prices. Are they staying the same, going up or going down? Explain why. A phone shop would be a good example.

Specification Content

The interaction of demand and supply, market equilibrium and the effect of excesses

KEY TERMS

Supply curve shows the relationship between the price and the quantity supplied.

Demand curve shows the relationship between the price and the quantity demanded.

Market clearing means that supply exactly matches demand. In reality this is difficult to achieve.

Equilibrium is the point that the market clears. It is said to be in equilibrium because there is no need for prices or output to change.

Excess demand means that the demand for a good or service outstrips the supply.

Excess supply means that too much is being supplied in the market.

Dynamic demand: dynamic supply

The **supply curve** shows how much businesses are prepared to put on the market at different prices. It slopes upwards from left to right because low prices discourage businesses from supplying the goods and services, while high prices make them want to supply more.

The **demand curve** shows how much people want to buy at different prices. It slopes down from left to right because at low prices customers want to buy more but at high prices customers buy less.

JUST RIGHT

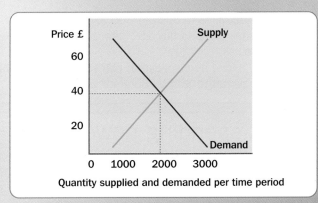

Quantity supplied and demanded per time period

Where the two curves cross, businesses want to sell 2000 items at £40 each. Customers are willing to buy 2000 items at £40 each. This is known as the **equilibrium** – the market is in balance.

But how does it work? How do businesses know what to charge and how much to supply? The answer is that they don't always get it right.

PRICE TOO HIGH

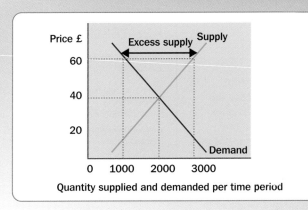

Quantity supplied and demanded per time period

At a price of £60 people only want to buy 1000 items but businesses want to supply 3000. The symptoms for a business would be a build-up in stocks or underused capacity. An airline, for example, would have empty seats.

A business may react in two different ways.

- Producing less. The airline might cut out some flights.
- Cutting prices. If prices are reduced, people usually buy more. If the price is cut to £40, the **market clears** because producers are happy to sell 2000 items and customers want to buy 2000 items.

PRICE TOO LOW

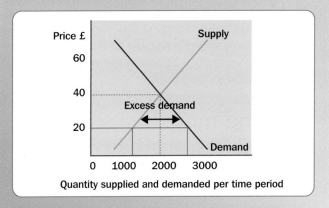

Quantity supplied and demanded per time period

If the price is £20 customers want to buy 3000 items but businesses only want to sell 1000. Demand outpaces supply. Stocks quickly run out and many customers are left disappointed.

For airlines this would show up as not enough seats in the aircraft. The suppliers have again misjudged the market. They have two alternatives:

- Supply more. This is not always easy in the short run. For example, the number of extra flights an airline business can put on is dependent on having spare planes and staff.
- Raise prices. At £40 demand matches the supply and the market once again clears.

1 Low cost airlines can pass on savings they make in lower fares to customers. Explain how this leads to a bigger market for this type of air travel.

2 Theory suggests that **excess demand** will not exist for long. Why is this?

3 BA decided to cut back on flights. Why?

4 What would happen if BA could not significantly lower costs?

Next steps

Look at the shops in your area.
When and why do they have sales?

Where's the market going?

Specification Content

How do changes in demand and changes in supply affect the allocation of resources?

starSTUDY

Flying less

Passenger numbers on North Atlantic routes were down only 7.7% last month on the previous year, compared with a 31.3% plunge in October. Air travel was already suffering because of the global downturn but the September 11 attacks delivered a devastating blow to the airline industry.

Flying more

In 2002, 5.6 million short break holidays were taken. In 1997, 11.7% of all holidays were short breaks compared with 15% in 2002 and growth will continue. Eastern European destinations have seen a surge in demand. Prague, for instance, saw a 121% increase in popularity before the floods in August 2002.

Source: ABTA.

The web accounts for 94% of Ryanair's bookings.

Plans

- easyJet aims to operate 300 aircraft.
- Ryanair plans to buy 150 new aircraft in the next 8 years.
- BA, a long haul specialist, plans to cut its fleet by 49 aircraft to 305 by Summer 2003.

UK spending power

There has been a rise in our disposable incomes. Between 1995 and 2002 they rose by over 20%.

1 Use the data to explain which parts of the air travel markets were
   a growing?
   b declining?
2 What happens to the number of people and planes in each business as things change?
3 How do you think airlines plan ahead?

Critical thinking

1 Why were customers more prepared to book online?

2 Why would Internet booking reduce costs?

3 Identify the factors which have led to an increase in supply and an increase in demand. Draw demand and supply diagrams to show what has happened.

4 What options are available to a business that faces a decline in demand for its products or services in the short run and the long run? How could you show this using supply and demand curves?

5 How do you think the growth of short haul flights has affected the demand for travel by the Channel Tunnel and the ferries? Use the Internet to research the changes in these markets.

6 Why would it be useful for businesses to keep track of changes in demand and changes in people's income?

7 What has influenced the investment decisions of mobile phone companies, cigarette companies and sports equipment companies?

KEY TERMS

Short run is the time period when businesses cannot easily react to market changes.

Shift in supply refers to the movement of the supply curve.

Shift in demand refers to the movement of the demand curve.

Business entrepreneurship means having an eye for business opportunities and taking a risk in order to achieve them.

Markets on the move

Markets can be very dynamic. Demand can change and supply can change. However change comes about, the price will change as a result. There will be **shifts in demand** and **shifts in supply**.

WHEN COSTS CHANGE

When costs are cut businesses are prepared to supply more and people want to buy more as the price falls. In this case the price falls to £20. Businesses want to supply 3000 items and demand rises to 3000 items so the market is in equilibrium again.

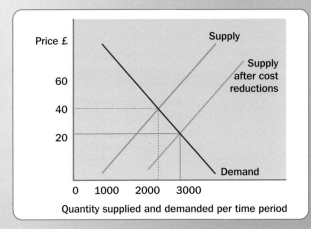

When costs rise businesses will supply less and people will want to buy less at the higher price. If the price rises to £60 businesses only want to sell 1000 items and demand falls to 1000 so the market is in equilibrium again.

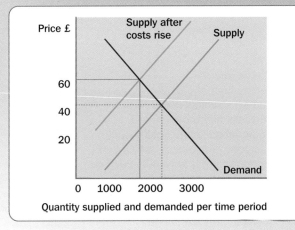

WHEN DEMAND CHANGES

People change their buying habits for all sorts of reasons:

- they earn more or less
- fashions change
- population changes
- advertising
- changes in the law
- the price or supply of other products changes.

When people want to buy more, the demand curve shifts to the right. As business costs will rise if more is to be produced in the **short run**, the end result is an increase in price. The price rises to £60 and 3000 items are sold.

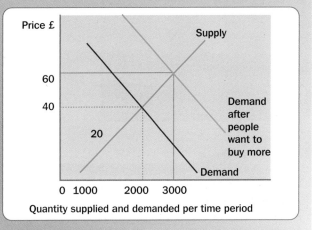

When people want to buy less, the demand curve shifts to the left and prices fall because business costs are reduced. The price falls to £20 and 1000 items are sold.

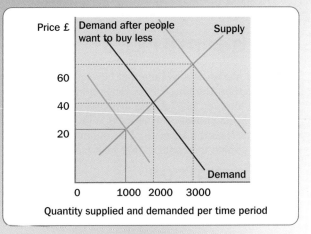

Next steps

1 The air travel industry is a rapidly changing market where consumer trends and **business entrepreneurship** help shape the direction of the market. Some markets are relatively stable but others are constantly changing. Choose six businesses and rank them according to how stable or volatile they are.

2 Changes in your local shopping centre reflect changing markets. What changes have taken place in your shopping centre lately and why do you think these changes have taken place? Look up mobile phone shops and cafés in your local Yellow Pages from a current edition and compare this with one from a few years back.

How much competition?

starSTUDY
Who wins?

Carlton and Granada worked for years on becoming one very large TV company. ITV's share of TV viewers had fallen from a half to a quarter in 20 years. As Carlton and Granada own 11 of the 15 ITV companies, this was not good news for them. They needed to cut costs and a merger would reduce outgoings by £55 million a year.

There would be winners and losers from a merger.

• The shareholders were keen on the idea.

• Advertisers hated the idea.

• Viewers might be both winners and losers.

• Employees were anxious.

1 Why would a merger cut overheads?
2 Why were shareholders keen on the idea?
3 What did advertisers fear from the merger?
4 How would viewers win and lose?
5 Why were employees anxious?
6 Explain how and why reducing competition affects customers.

Competition and the customer

Customers like competition because it means that businesses work hard for their custom. Businesses don't like too much competition because they have to work very hard to sell their products. Competition can keep prices low because businesses try hard to cut costs in order to sell their products. It can also mean that the product is kept at the forefront of the market so that it stands out from its competitors. By making their products special, they are a bit different from the others and the price can be higher.

The market

The market is anywhere that buyers and sellers come together. The possibilities range from market stalls to the Internet. Markets are dynamic so prices and products change. This process is known as **market forces**, as the strength of buyers and sellers will determine the changes that take place.

COMPETITION

Perfect competition	Monopoly
Homogeneous products	No substitutes
Free entry	Barriers to entry
Many sellers	Single seller
Price takers	Price makers

THE SPECTRUM OF COMPETITION

Differentiated products	Differentiated products
Free entry	Barriers to entry
Many sellers	Few sellers
Price takers	Price makers
	Interdependence
Monopolistic competition	Oligopoly

The degree of competition affects the relative strength of the business and the customer. Some products are sold in very competitive markets – which in the extreme form is known as **perfect competition**. Others are sold in very uncompetitive markets – which in the extreme form is known as **monopoly**. These two extremes are not often found in practice and are therefore yardsticks for comparing the degree of competition in other markets. The diagram shows four points on the spectrum.

PERFECT COMPETITION occurs when
products are all identical or homogeneous. The market is known as perfect because there is no gain in buying from one competitor rather than another so the businesses are price takers. As you can imagine, this is not a situation that businesses enjoy as it is very hard to make more than a basic level of profit.

What businesses want

Any business wants to reduce the amount of competition because it generally leads to higher profits. Price makers can set prices at levels that give higher profit margins than price takers so businesses really want to move along the spectrum towards monopoly – but so do their competitors. This can lead to unfair competition because businesses will find ways to fix either the price or the amount that is sold. Creating a shortage is a good way of keeping prices up.

Unfair competition

IN THE KNOW

If a group of businesses get together to fix the price or carve up the market between them, they are breaking the law.

go to → *Find out more about controlling business behaviour on page 164*

Their objective is to keep prices up in order to keep profits high. A tacit agreement can be hard to prove because there may be nothing written down, but it can be obvious when all competitors in a market with only a few, are selling at the same price.

If businesses are in a cartel, they are agreeing to fix some part of the market. They might, for example, divide up the country between them so they do not have to compete against each other.

Competition can also be unfair if one business looks after the environment and another doesn't. It is usually more expensive to install filters on a factory, so costs of production will be higher. Governments generally have rules on pollution but businesses have been known to set up factories in countries where the rules are less stringent in order to keep costs down.

When businesses don't look after the environment, they are passing the costs onto the consumer either directly or through taxation because the government or the individual has to meet the costs of clearing up the mess. This is known as market failure.

KEY TERMS

Perfect competition occurs when there are many buyers and sellers selling identical products.

Monopolistic competition occurs when there are many buyers and sellers selling differentiated products.

Oligopoly occurs when there are many buyers and a few sellers selling differentiated products using non-price competition.

Monopoly occurs when there are many buyers and only one seller selling a product with no substitutes.

Market forces reflect the influence of buyers and sellers in the price and output of products.

MONOPOLY occurs when there is only one seller who has control of the market so it can fix either the price or the quantity that it wants to sell. If there is only one business selling a product, it usually produces on a large scale, which creates barriers to entry. This means that it is hard for other businesses to break in to the market because it will take a lot of investment.

As markets are dynamic, a product may move along the spectrum if competition gets fiercer – or is reduced. The market for computers, for example, has become much more competitive and businesses now strive to find ways to make their products different from others. This is **monopolistic competition**.

Some products are only produced by a few businesses. Again, there are often barriers to entry. Each business will try to make its product a little different in order to attract customers. They can still compete fiercely but often try to avoid price competition because it cuts the profit margin. This is in known as **oligopoly**.

Critical thinking

1 How do the following businesses compete? Explain why.
   • DIY stores
   • Car manufacturers
   • Manufacturers of games machines
   • Shoe shops
   • Computer manufacturers.

2 Are there any companies in each industry that behave differently from the majority? Explain why.

Next steps

1 What shops are there in your local high street?

2 Make a list of them and work out what sort of competition they face.

3 How do you think this affects the prices they charge?

141

AQA BUSINESS STUDIES AS: THE COMPLETE COMPANION

What is the business cycle?

Specification Content
The business cycle: causes (durables, stock levels and investment decisions), phases and implications

starSTUDY
Booms and slumps

Businesses continue to expand but unemployment is low and land is not vacant. Businesses must pay higher wages to attract staff from other businesses. Rents for properties go up.

The increase in costs is passed onto the consumer in higher prices. The products and services are less competitive because it is cheaper to buy from abroad.

Businesses invest in new equipment and buildings to meet high demand. They employ more people. Consumers spend more even if it means borrowing more.

People become worried about their future. They may be concerned about the risk of losing their jobs so they cut back on some of their spending, borrow less and save more.

The boom gets going when consumers and businesses have confidence in the future.

The demand for UK goods and services drops. Businesses cut production and employ fewer people. As unemployment rises, consumer spending and confidence falls further.

Many businesses become more cautious and suspend their plans to buy new equipment and the recession deepens to a slump.

1 What effect does 'having confidence in the future' have on consumers and businesses?

2 Why do businesses invest in new equipment and buildings?

3 Why does this investment help the economy to grow?

4 Why do prices go up?

5 Why does it become hard to sell the products?

6 Why do people spend less? What effect does this have on business?

7 If businesses reduce investment, how does this affect consumers?

8 What will happen to prices?

KEY TERMS

Business cycle shows the patterns of growth and decline in the economy. It creates fluctuations in demand for many products.

Boom occurs when output is growing very fast.

Recession happens when output is growing more slowly after a period of rapid growth.

Slump occurs when output actually falls over a six-month period.

Critical thinking

1 What evidence of the business cycle can you see in your local area? Evaluate the effects of these changes on people and businesses. How do the changes contribute to the growth or recession in the economy of the country as a whole?

2 The reactions of businesses when the economy starts to see slower economic growth can contribute to a recession. Why might this happen? In what ways can business confidence be a self-fulfilling prophecy? Can governments talk up the economy in a recession?

3 The project to build Terminal 5 at Heathrow airport will create a shortage of building workers in the south-east for other projects. How will the new terminal contribute to economic growth? What problems and benefits will the new terminal cause for businesses in the south-east?

Next steps

Economic indicators vary from country to country and from region to region.

1 Find out the current inflation rates in the UK, some EU countries and in the USA. What has been happening over the last five years? Also find out their rates of economic growth and the interest rates.

The business cycle

Economies generally grow but not on a steady path. Sometimes they grow fast, other times they grow more slowly or even shrink. This path is known as the business cycle.

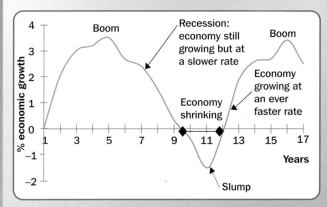

The period of rapid growth is called a **boom** and the part of the cycle when businesses reduce their output is called a **recession**. If total output actually falls, a **slump** has set in. The government tries to even out the peaks and troughs of the business cycle to make the economy more stable. They try to stop inflation and unemployment rising because of the negative effects on people, businesses and the economy in an international context.

WHAT ARE THE SIGNS?

A growing economy will make a country and its citizens better off. Governments need to know how well the economy is performing and the trends for the future. Some indicators are clearly visible. Is there a lot of construction going on or are more buildings left empty when businesses close down? Other information can come from surveys. Are people spending more or less than they used to? Are they more or less worried about losing their job? Data is collected all the time as the government and other organisations try to predict the future. The formal economy is measured by working out what has been produced in one year. This is known as Gross Domestic Product (GDP).

Businesses can often spot a change in the direction of the business cycle by looking at what is happening within the organisation. Their actions also influence the change.

Stocks start to build up when demand falls and businesses cut back on their orders. When demand increases, business have to order more so that they can increase output. Stocks are thereforc an early indicator of a change in the business cycle.

Consumer durables are products that last a long time. When consumers start to feel the pinch, they usually cut back on purchases of durables because a car or TV will usually last a little longer.

Investment decisions by businesses can influence the cycle. When there is a glimmer of light on the demand front, they start to invest. This employs more people and gives them more to spend – so demand continues to increase. If things are looking gloomy, investment will fall and demand will fall so the downturn continues.

WHY FEAR INFLATION?

Inflation is caused by:

Costs rising. If oil prices rise, costs rise for all businesses that use oil and petrol.

People having too much to spend. House prices, for example, rise fast when there are more buyers than sellers.

Businesses don't like inflation because it increases costs. They may be able to pass this on by increasing prices but they may have to cut their profit margins and absorb the increase if customers are not prepared to pay more.

Costs may rise for all sorts of reasons. Wages or materials may rise. Administration costs will also rise if there is constant change because shops will have to change prices and forms. Computer systems will have to be updated.

Businesses in one country can also lose out if inflation in other countries is at a lower rate. The price rises make our products and services more expensive to buy. Rising prices in the UK will make holidays here cost more and these will become less attractive. More of us will go abroad for our holidays and fewer foreigners will want to come here for their holidays.

WHAT'S WRONG WITH UNEMPLOYMENT?

When economies are in recession or slump, unemployment generally rises. If businesses cut production, they often make people redundant. Unemployment causes many social problems and costs the economy money because taxes are used to pay benefits to those who can't find work.

Businesses do not like periods of high unemployment because if people don't have jobs, their spending power is cut and demand falls. This makes selling products more difficult and businesses may find it hard to make a profit. Wages in some parts of the country may fall, making production cheaper but the fall in demand may offset this.

2   The rate of unemployment can differ widely between countries too. Check what is happening in your selection of countries.

3   House price changes can be used to indicate inflationary pressure in regions. Visit www.nationwide.co.uk/hpi/quarterly/prices.htm to find which areas of the UK are experiencing the highest house price rises and which the lowest. Explain your findings.

4   Find out how unemployment and wage levels vary across the country using www.nationalstatistics.gov.uk

Keeping ahead of the game

starSTUDY

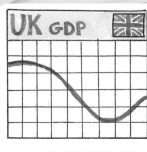

UK GDP

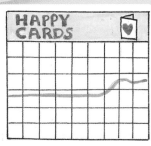

HAPPY CARDS

SHINY CARS

DOWNMARKET PRODUCTS

1 Explain the relationship between each business's sales and the business cycle.

2 What sort of businesses are likely to notice a downturn in the economy first? Why?

3 What sort of businesses are most recession proof? Why?

4 What sort of business opportunities crop up in (a) a boom, (b) a recession? Explain why.

Bucking the trend?

Some businesses are much more vulnerable than others when the business cycle turns down. Some have to work hard to survive while others sell products or services which people want whatever the economic climate.

There is a close link between the business cycle and business failure as the graph shows. As the rate of economic growth slows, more businesses fail. More British companies went under in 2002, for example, than in any year since the recession of the early 1990s.

1 Describe and explain the relationship between business failures and the business cycle.

2 Why can businesses fail even when the economy is growing?

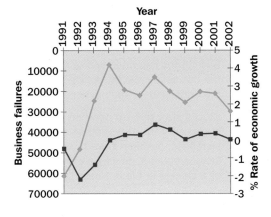

Business Cycle and Business Failures

KEY TERMS

Business failure data measures the number of businesses that go into liquidation every quarter. These can be added to give annual figures.

Discretionary spending is the spending we make after all our contracted outgoings have been met and after all purchases for basic needs.

www

http://www.cbi.org.uk/home.html

http://www.insolvency.gov.uk/

Who survives?

Not all businesses are affected in the same way from the ups and downs of a trade cycle. Some can ride out the storm easily. The demand for their products and services is hardly affected but for others a downturn in economic growth rates makes life very difficult. Some of these businesses are on the margins of survival. A small change in demand may just tip the balance and hard won profits turn into losses. A build up of stocks combined with lower sales revenue also causes cash flow problems. Banks are reluctant to lend and the receivers can be called in.

Businesses that continue to perform well in a recession would include those providing for contracted outgoings such as mortgage and insurance companies and those providing basic or necessary products and services such as food and petrol. These are things we continue to need and must buy. In fact some businesses, such as white goods and repairs, actually benefit from a recession.

Discretionary spending takes place when all necessities have been paid for. In an economic downturn the amount of discretionary spending falls because more people are out of work, or have lower incomes from less overtime. They are also more worried about their jobs, so may save more. Businesses that produce goods and services, which are paid for from discretionary spending, will suffer in an economic downturn but thrive when there is increasing growth.

The pattern can be uneven both geographically and according to the type of business. Some areas of the country are affected more than others. Variations also occur between countries. Some will grow more quickly in a period of growth and others will be more affected by a recession than others. There can also be a difference within towns.

Surviving the cycle

The data on business failures suggests that many businesses find it difficult to cope with downturns in the business cycle. These are often small businesses supplying large companies which either reduce their orders and force down prices or use their power to delay vital payments. This puts pressure on profits and also more businesses find it difficult to raise cash to pay creditors.

Many businesses are geared up to ride the ups and downs of the business cycle. They may have a flexible workforce so are able to employ a greater number of temporary workers in growth and then release them in decline. Another tactic is to employ people for a specific project so they are on short-term contracts.

In a recession

- Diversify and spread risks
- Look for greater cost cutting measures. For example they might cut training and replace equipment less frequently
- Reduce risk-taking investment
- Reduce prices and profit margins
- Release workers and cut production
- Cut overtime

In growth

- Put up prices and increase profit margins
- Increase research and development
- Increase investment
- Increase overtime
- Introduce another shift

Businesses which try to buck the trend have to watch the market carefully and control their inputs and outputs to meet demand. They also need to look for opportunities to adapt to the market. A business which sells furniture might, for example, start selling covers to people who cannot afford a new sofa or chairs. In a boom, it might switch people onto their more expensive lines as orders start coming in. Being flexible is an important part of bucking the trend.

Critical thinking

The booming Trowbridge-based company, Apetito, is recruiting more staff. Apetito is the largest supplier of frozen ready meals to vulnerable groups in the country, supplying 55% of the meals-on-wheels market. The number of vulnerable people increases year on year since we are an ageing population. These people have to eat and it becomes the local authority responsibility to make sure they get this basic need.

1 Explain why Apetito is safe in recession.

2 Identify four businesses that are recession-proof and explain why.

3 Identify four businesses that are vulnerable to recession and explain why. What might they do to become more recession proof?

Next steps

1 Find out how a business you know reacts to the business cycle.

2 Use the Internet to search for up-to-date information about our economy and business performance.

What are interest rates?

Specification Content

Interest rates: variations and their effects on demand

starSTUDY
Headlines

Local business builds new factory

The cost of borrowing money is at a 39-year low

Rise in interest rates hits small businesses

New lending falls as interest rates rise

Credit card borrowing reached £10 billion

If we all worked for 1 year and saved everything we would just about pay off our debts

1 Why do people and businesses borrow money?

2 What happens to borrowing when interest rates rise and fall?

3 How can low interest rates help business?

4 Why can businesses and people find themselves in difficulties when interest rates rise?

Why borrow?

If families or businesses haven't enough income to match their expenditure they may consider borrowing. It can be sensible to borrow money if you know you can pay it back. Individuals may expect to be paid more as their career improves. Borrowing allows individuals to buy expensive items such as cars before they have saved up enough money. Many families borrow to buy a house and pay this back over 25 years. A business may need to buy computer equipment and software in order to set up e-commerce and in turn gain more customers.

What are interest rates?

Interest rates are the cost of borrowing. A 4% interest rate means you have to pay £40 a year to borrow £1000. This is the charge a lender makes to people and businesses that borrow money.

- **If interest rates fall** then so does the cost of borrowing. This makes borrowers happy because repayments are lower. Lenders suffer because their money earns less.

- **If interest rates rise** so does the cost of borrowing. This makes lenders happy because their money earns more. Borrowers suffer because their repayments increase.

LENDER OR BORROWER?

Businesses that provide financial services, such as banks, insurance and pension companies, link lenders and borrowers.

- People and businesses that save money with these institutions are paid interest.

- People and businesses that borrow money pay interest at a higher rate.

The financial institutions hope to cover their costs and return a profit. The interest offered is also dependent on the amount of money involved as well as the risk of default.

Setting the rate

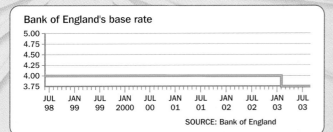

Bank of England's base rate

SOURCE: Bank of England

Each month the Bank of England's Monetary Policy Committee (MPC) has the task of deciding whether to increase, decrease or keep the **base rate** the same. It looks very carefully at what is going on in the economy now and what is expected to happen in future before it sets the interest rate for the following month.

It looks at various indicators to see how the economy is performing. These include changes in industry, trade and consumer confidence, which is measured by working out how much we spend in the high street. If this is falling, the MPC may decide to reduce the interest rate, as it believes the economy is slowing down. A fall in interest encourages borrowing and makes it cheaper for businesses to raise finance to invest. An increase in consumer spending helps the economy grow and if it is growing we feel confident about our jobs and our futures, so we borrow more to buy things we want now.

If consumer spending is growing fast, the Bank might raise interest rates. This raises the cost of borrowing and helps reduce consumer spending. Too much consumer spending is risky as people may find it hard to repay. The MPC aims to keep things on an even keel.

If we adopted the euro as our currency then the European Bank would set the interest rate for all the countries of the eurozone.

1 What might persuade the MPC to cut or increase base rates?
2 If the MPC
   a raises base rate
   b cuts base rate,
   what effect might this have on people and businesses?
3 Find out what has happened in recent months to the base rate which is set by the MPC. Why do you think these changes have taken place?

The Monetary Policy Committee and inflation

IN THE KNOW

The MPC has to keep **inflation** under control – as well as keeping an eye on the general well-being of the economy. It does this by changing base rates.

Inflation means that there is a sustained rise in prices. It is caused by:

- people and businesses wanting to buy more than is available
- a shortage of products that people and businesses want to buy.

Whether there is too much demand or not enough supply, the effect is the same – prices go up.

The MPC is given inflation targets by the government. Some inflation is considered inevitable but if it appears to be rising above the target, the MPC will increase interest rates. If it is falling below the target, the MPC will cut interest rates.

When the MPC has set the interest rate each month, banks and other institutions where people save and borrow money look carefully at the interest rates they set for customers. They all make a profit from the difference between their rate to savers and borrowers. The market is competitive as people want good interest rates for their savings but low rates when they borrow. Borrowers will also be charged different rates according to the degree of risk and the length of the loan.

KEY TERMS

Interest rates are the cost or charge for borrowing money or the reward for lending money.

Base rate is the interest rate charged by the Bank of England when lending money to banks when they are short of cash. It is used as a guide for other lenders.

Inflation is the sustained rise in average prices.

Critical thinking

Come up with ideas about how changes in interest rates affect business. Why do you think businesses like stability?

Next steps

1 Find out about banks' interest rates for borrowing money and saving money.
2 How does the length of time and the amount of money affect the rates?
3 Why do you think this is?

How do interest rates affect businesses?

Specification Content

Interest rates: their effects on overheads, the pound (£) and investment decisions

starSTUDY

Interest rates at all time low

Businesses throughout the UK welcomed the continuing low level of interest rates. Keeping business costs low is critical if businesses are to stay competitive. Anxiety is still high for businesses which trade in international markets because rates are lower still in Europe and the US.

KEY TERMS

A budget is a financial plan about income and expenditure.

Imports are products bought from other countries.

Exports are products sold to other countries.

1 Why do businesses welcome low interest rates?

2 Why are businesses anxious because interest rates in other countries are lower?

3 How does the MPC come to a decision about the interest rate to set each month?

4 How does a rise in interest rates affect customers?

5 Why is it hard to justify new investment when interest rates are relatively high?

6 What sort of businesses are most likely to be hit by high interest rates?

Not another rise!

The Monetary Policy Committee (MPC) raised interest rates by another half per cent yesterday. Many business leaders squealed with pain as they saw their costs rising yet again. They fear that customers will disappear as the cost of running a home increases. New investment becomes increasingly difficult to justify as potential costs rise.

Outside and inside the business

Businesses can be very sensitive to interest rate changes because they affect their financial situation. Careful planning will have created a budget, which a business aims to stick to. Changes in interest rates can upset plans in a variety of ways.

Customers are also affected because many borrow money, which becomes more expensive to repay. Others depend on savings so their spending power can rise or fall depending on the rate of interest.

How interest rates affect businesses

INTEREST RATES UP

Existing borrowing gets more expensive → overheads rise → profits fall or sales must rise	Customers' borrowing gets more expensive → customers have less to spend on other things
Borrowing for investment gets more expensive → new projects must make more profit to cover costs	Customers with savings earn more interest → customers have more to spend

INTEREST RATES DOWN

Existing borrowing gets cheaper → overheads fall → more profit	Customers' borrowing gets cheaper → customers have more to spend on other things
Borrowing for investment gets cheaper → more projects become viable as level of profit needed to cover costs falls	Customers' savings give lower returns → customers have less to spend

Knock-on effects

IN THE KNOW

Businesses generally don't like high interest rates because they increase costs, reduce consumers' spending power and make investment for growth more expensive.

INVESTMENT

A business will calculate the estimated return from a project and see if this exceeds the interest it receives from its savings or the interest charged if it borrows the money. It will also try to estimate likely changes in future rates. Any rise in the interest rate increases business costs and will make some projects less viable. A fall in the interest rate will increase the likelihood of businesses undertaking investment.

CHASING DEBTORS – DELAYING PAYMENTS

If costs are rising because interest rates are high a business will chase debtors more quickly to keep cash coming in more quickly. It may also try to delay payments to others in order to stop cash flowing out.

RAISING PRICES

If costs rise, businesses often want to pass the rise on to the customers by putting up the price. Their ability to do this will depend on demand and supply. If their competitors don't raise prices, it will be difficult as customers will go elsewhere. If the product is a luxury or has substitutes, customers again will be lost if the price rises. If it is something that people really can't do without and there is no alternative, people will have to pay up – whatever the price is.

COMPETITIVENESS

If interest rates in other countries are lower, it will be difficult to **export** to those countries. It may also make trading conditions difficult generally because **imports** will be cheaper than home produced purchases.

High interest rates also mean that people will buy pounds because they get a good return when they invest.

go to → *Find out more about exchange rates on page 151*

This pushes up the value of the pound in terms of other currencies and makes selling UK products abroad more expensive. Equally, it makes buying overseas products expensive in the UK.

Critical thinking

1 If we joined the euro we would have to accept an interest rate set by the European Bank. How might this affect businesses and consumers if the rate at which we joined was lower than the rate set by the Monetary Policy Committee?

2 What will be the likely effect of a reduction in interest rates on
a   short haul holidays abroad
b   house purchases
c   our purchases of vegetables?

3 Which types of businesses would be affected by this change in demand for short haul holidays abroad and houses? How might these businesses react if they believed that future interest rates were unlikely to rise?

Next steps

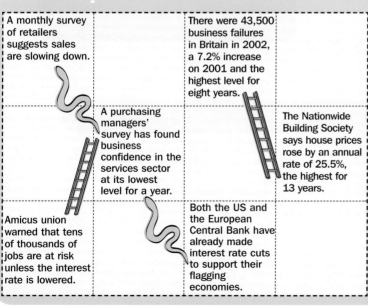

A monthly survey of retailers suggests sales are slowing down.

There were 43,500 business failures in Britain in 2002, a 7.2% increase on 2001 and the highest level for eight years.

A purchasing managers' survey has found business confidence in the services sector at its lowest level for a year.

The Nationwide Building Society says house prices rose by an annual rate of 25.5%, the highest for 13 years.

Amicus union warned that tens of thousands of jobs are at risk unless the interest rate is lowered.

Both the US and the European Central Bank have already made interest rate cuts to support their flagging economies.

1 What would business want to happen to interest rates in each of these situations? Explain why.

2 What do you think the MPC should do? Explain why.

3 Economies are forever changing and so will the pressure to change interest rates. You should track interest rate changes in the next few months by listening to Radio 4 or 5 and by searching articles on *http://money.guardian.co.uk/interestrates* and *http://news.bbc.co.uk/1/hi/business* and search the term 'interest rate'.

4 If you have contacts with a local business find out how significant interest rate changes are for that business.

What are exchange rates?

Specification Content

What are exchange rates?

starSTUDY

Web trade: Discarray

Justin Kyriakides set up a business that sells innovative, decorative CD storage. He worked hard to launch it on the market, finding the web combined with articles in magazines a successful strategy.

He soon found that he had orders from countries including Finland, the USA and Ireland, as well as the UK. He had always priced in pounds but now he had to think about selling Discarray in other currencies.

The website makes it easy as customers can choose the currency they want. He just has to work out what the price should be in each currency.

As the value of the pound changes against other currencies, he has to make sure he always has the right price. If he's behind the times, he might lose out because he would be selling at a lower price than he planned – or perhaps the price might look very expensive in another currency.

1 Selling Discarray overseas has both advantages and disadvantages. How many can you think of?

2 His sales to the USA will be in dollars. His sales to Ireland will be in euros. Find out how many dollars and euros you get for a pound. www.bbc.co.uk will help you.

3 Why does he have to be sure that he has the latest information about the value of the pound in other currencies?

4 How would the business be affected if it used resources imported from abroad?

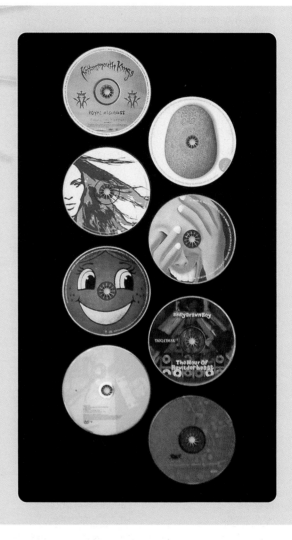

Changing currencies

Justin needs to translate the price of his products into other currencies if he is to sell abroad. He needs to know exactly what the **exchange rate** is in order to set the price for his product. The exchange rate is the price you pay if you want to buy one currency with another. The information is readily available from banks and the media.

KEY TERMS

The **exchange rate** gives the value of one currency expressed in terms of another. For example, the value of the pound (£) in euros (€).

Eurozone includes all the countries that use the euro.

What are exchange rates?

When you buy a meal in France the restaurant would want to be paid in euros (€), the currency used in France. This is the currency of **eurozone** members of the European Union, so you would also pay in euros if you bought goods and services in other European countries such as Italy and Germany.

To pay for the meal and buy other products and services in France you will need to exchange your pounds for euros. You would go to a bank or other organisation that changes money, and buy euros with your pounds. Instead of buying a product or service you are buying a currency. Paying for a currency means it has a value. Just as the euros have a value in pounds so pounds have a value in euros. If an individual or a business wants to buy pounds from a bank they need to pay in another currency such as euros, dollars or yen. The exchange rate is the price of that currency expressed in another currency.

WHY DO EXCHANGE RATES CHANGE?

When the demand or supply for a product changes, the price changes. When the supply of new houses does not keep pace with growing demand, house prices rise. On the other hand if we demand fewer houses then prices will fall. Exchange rates work in exactly the same way.

go to → Find out more on page 152–153

WHY DOES THE SUPPLY OF POUNDS INCREASE?

Going on a holiday in France is an import. We are buying a French holiday in the same way as we may buy a French car. Both are imports. Both need to be paid for in euros so we have to sell pounds to exchange for euros.

If many people want holidays and cars from France then they will want to sell pounds to buy euros. The number of pounds on the market will rise. If the number of euros stays the same, the value of the pound will fall.

In the example in Figure 1, the supply of pounds shifts from S1 to S2 and the price or value of pounds falls from €1.5 to €1.4.

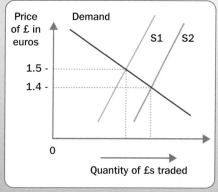

Figure 1. The effect of an increase in imports

If imports fall, people need fewer pounds to pay for them. The number being put on the market will fall so the value of the pound will rise.

WHY DOES THE DEMAND FOR POUNDS INCREASE?

Trade isn't only one way. People from France come to the UK for holidays. They also buy our music. These are both counted as exports. They will have to pay for their purchases in pounds. They will need to buy pounds with their euros. This would increase the demand for pounds on the exchange market. Figure 2 shows what happens when the demand curve shifts from D1 to D2 leading to a rise or appreciation in the value of pounds against the euro.

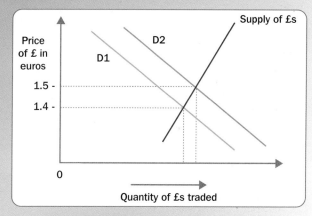

Figure 2. The effect of an increase in exports

A decline in exports would lead to fewer pounds being demanded and a fall in the exchange rate.

Critical thinking

1 Would you prefer to
a buy from
b sell to

the USA or the eurozone in the period you have been monitoring exchange rates? Explain why.

Next steps

Track the pound against the euro and the dollar for a period of two weeks by looking in newspapers or on the web.

Exchange rates and business

Specification Content
Exchange rates: degree of fluctuation; direct and indirect effects upon the economy and business opportunities

starSTUDY

Rising pound: failing pottery

Joan Beagle, the Managing Director of Archer's Pottery, announced the decision to sell its pottery in Belgium. Exports to Belgium quickly grew to 20% of sales. Plans were set to increase this and budgets calculated. However, less than two years later exports had dwindled to near nothing. The reason was a 17% rise in the value of the pound against the euro. This made the pottery too expensive for Belgian consumers. 'We cut our prices a little, but could not afford to lower them further.'

Rising euro hits economy

A rapid rise in the value of the euro against the dollar could have damaging consequences for Europe's economy, the German banking federation has warned.

The euro was trading at above $1.07 on Wednesday morning, its highest level for more than three years.

The single currency has risen almost 25% against the dollar from its low of 86 cents just over a year ago.

A strong euro dents the competitiveness of companies exporting from the eurozone, making their products comparatively more expensive.

Source: BBCi 2003.

1 Why couldn't Joan keep prices in Belgium the same?

2 What effect did this have on her business?

3 Archer's Pottery is one of many UK companies that export to the eurozone. What effect is this change going to have on them?

4 What effect would the change be likely to have on the UK economy?

5 The value of the euro had risen by 25% against the dollar. What effect would this have on the price of exports from Germany, and other members of the eurozone, to countries outside the zone?

6 What effect is this likely to have on sales of their products beyond the zone?

7 What effect is this likely to have on the economies of these countries?

8 What would an exporter have to consider before changing prices?

Changing rates

The movement of exchange rates means that businesses throughout the world must keep their eyes on the ball. They all have to watch the price of their currency in places that they trade with. Changes can have both positive and negative effects on a business's budget. Resources they buy from other countries may become cheaper, so costs fall. They may also become more expensive, so costs rise. Just the same can happen with export markets. If your products become more expensive, other countries will not want to buy them. If they become cheaper, sales will probably rise.

KEY TERMS

Transactions costs are the cost of exchanging currencies.

Hedging is minimising the risk of currency rate fluctuations by buying currency now for delivery at a future date.

Next steps

1 Investigate a business you know and find out how much it imports and how much it exports and who to.

2 Find out what effects exchange rate changes have on its business decisions.

Exchange rate costs

The effects of exchange rates on business are:

- **Transactions costs.** Every time a business changes one currency into another, the bank charges a fee. The process makes every transaction more expensive.

- Exchange rate risk. Currency values change against each other. If a business has planned its cost and pricing on the basis of the exchange rate at the beginning of the year, changing rates can affect the plans.

WHAT HAPPENS WHEN THE POUND RISES AGAINST THE EURO?

↑ Imports become cheaper because UK businesses will need to pay for the goods and services in euros. Pounds will buy more euros than before.

↓ Exports become more expensive since UK businesses need to be paid in pounds. Euros will buy fewer pounds than before.

HOW DOES IT WORK?

- A UK business exports to Ireland. Its products are priced at £20.00.

- Exchange rate: £1.00 = €1.40. €1.00 = £0.71.

- The Irish business pays €28.00.

- The value of the pound rises to €1.70, so €1.00 = £0.59.

- The Irish business now pays €34.00. It might look elsewhere for its supplies.

1 Calculate what happens to the price in pounds that a UK business would pay to import from Ireland given the same rise in the value of the pound. Assume each item is sold at €5 by the Irish business.

WHAT HAPPENS WHEN THE POUND FALLS AGAINST THE EURO?

↑ Imports become more expensive because UK businesses will have to pay for the goods and services in euros. Pounds will buy fewer euros than before.

↓ Exports become cheaper since UK businesses need to be paid in pounds. Euros will buy more pounds than before.

HOW DOES IT WORK?

- A German business supplies components to a UK business at €3.40.

- The exchange rate is €1.70 to £1.00.

- The UK business pays £2.00 for each component.

The value of the pound falls to €1.50 making each component cost £2.67 so the UK business will need to exchange £0.67 more for each component. The increase of £0.67 may force it to find suppliers in the UK.

1 Calculate what happens to the price in euros that a German business would pay the exporting UK business given the same fall in the value of the pound. Assume each item is sold at £10.00 by the UK business.

Why join the euro?

Twelve members of the EU have joined the euro – a common currency that they all use. The UK decided to stay out, but may decide to join in the future.

Is there an alternative way to protect against currency changes?

Businesses which already deal in foreign currencies often 'hedge their bets'.

They may agree to buy foreign currency at a future date but at the rate fixed today.

Why join the euro?	
Stability	Businesses know that costs and prices will not be affected by exchange rate changes within the eurozone. Fluctuations will continue beyond the zone.
No transaction costs on trade within the eurozone	Cuts costs on trade within the eurozone.
Pricing in euros makes market more competitive	More competition for business but provides larger market. Good for consumers.

Why not?	
Economic control from European Bank	Interest rates are used to control the economy. If control comes from Europe, the rate that is set may not be right for the UK. It may be hard to control inflation and unemployment.
Euro strength/weakness	If the euro is strong, trade with the rest of the world can be challenging because our products become expensive. Interest rates could not be used independently to adjust the UK economy to encourage competitiveness.

Inflation and business

Specification Content

Inflation: causes, importance of expectations, effects of inflation and deflation on firms, RPI

starSTUDY

1 How is a supermarket business affected when prices start to rise more quickly? Work your way through each part of the business in your answer.

2 How are customers affected when prices start to rise more quickly?

3 How might a supermarket chain, for example, help prevent inflation?

Going up

Prices rise most of the time. The rate of inflation is the average price rise taking place across the country. It starts to matter when the process speeds up because it imposes costs on businesses and makes customers feel poorer. If their pay is not keeping up with inflation, they will not be able to buy as much as they used to, therefore they will want pay rises to cover the difference. Inflation causes uncertainty for both businesses and customers, so it is generally considered unwelcome and bad for the country, especially if it is lower in other countries.

Measuring inflation

IN THE KNOW

The Retail Price Index (RPI) is used to measure the rate of inflation. It is worked out by watching price changes on a range of products and services that consumers buy. The change from one month to the next is worked out as an index – in other words a particular year is decided on as the starting point and the price level in that year is called 100. This is known as the base year. Any change, either up or down, is shown as a rise or fall above 100. Every now and again, the base year is updated and the index has a new start. The range of products and services used is also kept up to date.

Critical thinking

1 What is the current rate of inflation in the UK and other European countries?

2 How will the following businesses be affected by inflation? Suggest solutions if there is a problem.
   * A UK car manufacturer
   * A hairdresser
   * A greetings card manufacturer
   * A solicitor
   * A house builder.

Next steps

1 Carry out a web search for 'business' and 'inflation'.

2 What is happening at the moment?

3 How is business being affected?

Causes of inflation

IN THE KNOW

DEMAND AND SUPPLY

Inflation can occur because:

• costs rise and push prices up

• demand increases and pushes prices up.

It all comes back to demand and supply. If costs rise but people still want the products, they will be prepared to pay more. This is known as **cost-push inflation**. If people want more products but supply can increase to meet demand – the price will rise. This is known as **demand-pull inflation**.

EXPECTATIONS

People learn how to react to inflation. Over time, their **expectations** have become more sophisticated and are now a critical factor in the process. If prices are rising, they want higher wages and may use trade unions to fight for them. A **wage-price spiral** may result. It is the interaction of demand-pull inflation and cost-push inflation. If people see prices rising by 5%, they will want wages to rise by at least 5% so that they can maintain their standard of living. When wages rise, it adds to the cost of businesses – so prices may be pushed up again.

INTERNATIONAL FACTORS

• If the value of the pound falls against other countries, the cost of our imports will rise. This will contribute to cost-push inflation.

• If the cost of products we import from other countries rises, prices and business costs will rise in the UK. This again contributes to cost-push inflation.

All these factors affect the level of demand and supply for the whole economy. The terms aggregate supply and aggregate demand are used when referring to how much is produced in the country and how much the whole population buys. When aggregate demand rises and aggregate supply doesn't, we have inflation.

Because the government worries about the level of inflation the Bank of England's Monetary Policy Committee has been charged with setting interest rates in order to achieve a target level of about 2.5% inflation. If inflation rises above 2.5% the Committee has to explain itself to the Treasury.

go to → Go to page 147 to refresh your memory on the Monetary Policy Committee

The effects on business

IN THE KNOW

When costs rise, businesses face all sorts of problems.

THE EFFECT OF RISING PRICES

• The cost of inputs rises – whether wages, raw materials or overhead costs.

• Operations costs rise because computer systems have to be updated whenever there is a change. Keeping a supermarket system in shops and on websites is expensive if prices are constantly changing.

• Marketing costs rise because people have to be informed of changing prices.

• Transport costs rise for distributing products.

• The cost of borrowing often rises as interest rates tend to rise to match inflation.

• Customer behaviour changes because they feel uncertain about the future and the value of their savings is falling. People may try to save more to compensate – so they spend less.

• Overseas sales may fall because UK products have become relatively more expensive. If prices are rising at 10% in the UK but only 3% in the USA, people in the USA will look to their home market rather than buy products from the UK. UK **competitiveness** will have declined.

The behaviour of businesses will depend on whether they can pass the increases on to customers. If not, they must search for ways to cut costs generally. Once businesses start cutting back, fewer people will be employed and spending will start to fall. This may start the beginning of a recession – the downturn in the business cycle.

go to → Go to page 143 to refresh your memory on the business cycle

KEY TERMS

Competitiveness compares the attractiveness of products in different markets.

Cost-push inflation causes inflation because costs rise and businesses pass the increases on in higher prices to guarantee profit margins.

Demand-pull inflation causes inflation because people want to buy more than is available so prices rise.

Expectations change people's behaviour according to what is happening in the economy. High inflation, for example, will lead them to ask for higher wages.

Unemployment and business

Specification Content

Unemployment types (structural and cyclical) and effects

starSTUDY

1 If you ran a business and were looking for staff, which situation would you prefer? Why?

2 What sort of business is finding it hard or easy to find staff?

3 Use demand and supply curves to show how wages might be different if there are lots of jobs available or just a few.

4 What problems might a business face if there is lots of unemployment?

Employees or customers?

People often have more than one role. They are always customers and often employees; therefore businesses are affected considerably by changes in the employment market. Even if there are lots of people available for work, they might not meet your requirements. If you are looking for a website developer, it is not much help if the local biscuit factory shuts down.

Types of unemployment

Every month data is collected showing the number of people who are unemployed and looking for work. However buoyant the economy, there are always some people looking for a job. If the economy is in recession, there will be many. During an upturn in the business cycle, the numbers will fall.

 go to → page 143 to refresh your memory on the business cycle

There are a variety of reasons why people are unemployed.

Frictional unemployment occurs when people are between jobs. People often have a week or more after leaving one job and before starting the next.

Cyclical unemployment shows the pattern of the business cycle. In recession, numbers rise. In an upturn, numbers fall.

Seasonal unemployment reflects the time of year. Few Father Christmases are employed in August and jobs in seaside resorts are few and far between in January.

Structural unemployment occurs when business changes and needs fewer staff or people with different skills. This may happen because:

* new technology requires more capital and fewer people

* reorganisation to improve competitiveness often means cuts in employment

* demand for the products of an industry fall

* imports increase from countries which can produce more cheaply.

Unemployment: the effects on business

Unemployment affects both production and sales in a business.

- It needs people to make things or provide a service.

- It needs customers to buy its products.

THE EFFECT ON BUSINESS

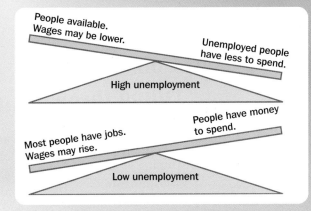

People available.
Wages may be lower.

Unemployed people have less to spend.

High unemployment

People have money to spend.

Most people have jobs.
Wages may rise.

Low unemployment

ON THE HUMAN RESOURCE DEPARTMENT

When unemployment is low, people move jobs frequently as there are many opportunities. The human resource department will be kept busy looking for ways to retain people and having to recruit and train new staff. It may be hard to find staff with the right skills, so training will be important. In a recession a business may need to make staff redundant. Both these activities add to a business's costs.

ON PRODUCTION

In times of high unemployment a business may have spare capacity because sales have fallen. Businesses then cut back on both staff and office or factory accommodation. In times of low unemployment, demand generally increases so a business might expand capacity by taking on more staff and moving to larger premises.

KNOCK-ON EFFECTS

If a big company in a local area closes down, it can have knock-on effects on many other businesses in the area. The business will have bought supplies from others in the area – which will suffer. People who are now unemployed will have spent money in shops in the area – which will also suffer. If no other businesses open up, the area will continue to decline.

Unemployment and society

When unemployment rises, more people need unemployment benefit so government spending increases. At the same time, the government collects less in taxes because fewer people are working; therefore it becomes increasingly difficult to balance the books.

Most people would prefer to be working, so unemployment creates a range of social problems. Being short of money can mean inadequate food and clothing, ill health and children's absence from school, so education suffers. It is then hard for people to find employment because they do not have the skills a business needs.

Businesses don't want to be located in depressed areas as it may limit the range of customers and increase the risk of crime.

Critical thinking

1 A medium-sized business is trying to recruit people for its IT department but is having difficulty. What effect might this difficulty have on the business?

2 Why do you think there might be a shortage of IT staff? What strategies could the business use to overcome the problem?

3 A factory in a small town is closing down. What are the knock-on effects likely to be?

Next steps

1 Research 'unemployment' and 'business' on the Internet.

2 What is the current level of unemployment?

3 How is it changing?

4 How does it affect business?

KEY TERMS

Frictional unemployment reflects the number of people between jobs.

Cyclical unemployment reflects the stage of the business cycle. There is more unemployment in recession and less in an upturn in the economy.

Seasonal unemployment reflects the time of the year. Builders are often laid off in the winter when the weather is bad.

Structural unemployment occurs when changes take place in the economy which affect the employment market. It may relate to demand or technology, for example.

Employment rights and wrongs

Specification Content
UK and EU law (outline knowledge only); awareness of the purpose and degree of impact of laws regarding health and safety and employment

starSTUDY

Man sacked after 11 years with no complaints

A man sacked unfairly after 26 years' service said his reputation has been restored after an employment tribunal awarded him maximum compensation.

Malcolm Clark was awarded £58,300 after the tribunal ruled he had been dismissed unfairly by Moores Furniture Group Limited.

The company, which sells kitchen and bathroom units to bulk buyers, claimed that Mr Clark was not up to his job, despite having been regional sales manager for 11 years without any complaints from his bosses.

Asian employee wins case

Amit Bhadhuri was overlooked for the post of anti-racial harassment co-ordinator. Despite the fact that he speaks three languages apart from English and met all the criteria for the job, it was offered to someone else. The employer claimed that he had not performed well when interviewed but the notes taken at the time did not reflect this.

The job should have been an internal appointment but was given to a white woman from outside the organisation. The tribunal ruled that this was a serious case of discrimination.

Collar and tie ruling thrown out

Matthew Thompson was celebrating last night after winning his case for sexual discrimination. He had challenged a ruling by Stockport Jobcentre that men had to wear collars and ties while women could wear T-shirts.

The tribunal ruled that he was being treated less favourably because the requirement to wear a tie was gender based.

1 What was the cause of discrimination in each of these cases?

2 Why is it important for businesses to keep records such as interview notes?

3 Why are people paid compensation if their ex-employer is found to have broken the law?

4 Why is it important to have laws about fair employment?

Who holds the power?

Employees usually hold a weaker position than their employers, so laws are in place to protect them. Laws are passed by parliament, having gone through many stages to ensure that they are well conceived and agreed by the majority. In this field, laws are civil rather than criminal so people who feel that their rights have been infringed will take a case to a court, known as a tribunal, rather than being dealt with by the police.

Employees, business and the law

The law protects people who work, or are seeking work, in a range of ways. The laws apply to everyone who works, whether it is in a business or government organisation.

- Organisations must not discriminate between people because of their sex, religion, ethnic origin or disability. From recruitment to promotion, all decisions must be seen to be even-handed. It is important to keep records so that there is evidence to show how decisions have been made.

- Organisations must not dismiss people unfairly. There have to be very clear reasons why people are dismissed and formal processes must be carried out. If things are changing, they will be entitled to training rather than dismissal. If the job has really come to an end, the person can be made redundant. An employee can take the employer to an **Employment Tribunal** if they consider the decision to be unfair. The Tribunal will come to a conclusion about whether the employer's action was fair and the process was carried out properly. If the employer is found to have broken the rules, the ex-employee will be granted compensation.

- Organisations must provide a safe and healthy working environment. There are standards laid down for many aspects of the working environment. They range from the safe use of computers to protection on machinery and fire risks. Visitors must be protected too.

go to →
Find out more about the law on page 160

Most larger organisations employ human resource managers to ensure that the systems are in place to deal with recruitment, selection and other aspects of responsibility to employees. Part of the job involves checking that the legal requirements are met and keeping records to show that everything has been carried out correctly.

go to →
Find out more about human resource management on page 93

You don't need to know the names and details of the laws. What is important is why they are there and how they affect people, businesses and other organisations.

Employees have responsibilities too

The law is there to protect people in employment because they are usually in a weaker position but, as an employee, they also have responsibilities. Their legal responsibility is based on the **contract** they sign when they start a job. This will specify their working hours, holidays and what they are expected to do.

The criminal law also applies of course. People should not steal, damage property, hurt people or break any of the other laws that affect everyday life.

go to →
Find out more about people's ethical responsibility on page 166

Next steps

Local newspapers are a good source of information about businesses and the law. Have a look at a local newspaper's website and search for Employment Tribunal to find out what's been going on locally.

Critical thinking

1 Employment law can add to the cost of a business. Explain how. Why do you think people are more likely to work effectively if they feel that they are being fairly treated?

2 Change can be challenging for a business and its staff. Draw up a spider diagram showing the issues that might arise if a business wants to put in a new, automated system of production on a new site. How might this affect the staff?

KEY TERMS

Compensation is paid to people when a business has broken employment law.

Contract – a legal agreement between people. An employment contract will lay down the rights and responsibilities of employee and employer.

Discrimination occurs when people are not given equal opportunities. Such action breaks the law if it is on grounds of sex, religion, ethnic origin or disability.

Employment Tribunals are set up to decide whether employers have acted illegally towards employees.

Redundancy occurs when the work a person does is no longer required.

The law, customers and businesses

Specification Content
UK and EU law (outline knowledge only); awareness of the purpose and degree or impact of laws regarding consumer protection and competition

starSTUDY

£20,000 pirate CDs seized in market raid

Four men were arrested after trading standards officers raided Walton Street market in Hull. Computers and copying devices plus thousands of master disks were subsequently removed from houses in the city.

The real value of the CDs, in terms of losses to the music industry, was approaching £1 million.

The trading standards department said they frequently received complaints from local retailers who were suffering because of the activities of these pirates and customers who have bought these low quality recordings.

Prison for crooked car dealer

Gordon Booth, a car dealer from Bexhill-on-Sea, was sent to prison for three months after being found guilty of five trading standards offences.

He had turned back the clock so it showed a false mileage and pretended to be a private seller rather than a business. A customer had returned a car on discovering that the clock had been turned back, but Mr Booth sold it to someone else who had no idea that it had a false mileage.

A spokesperson for Sussex County Council said, 'Our Trading Standards Officers will continue to focus on the rogue element of the motor trade and bring to book those who set out intentionally to mislead the public.'

Source: adapted from www.eastsussexcc.gov.uk

Honesty is the best policy

A complaint by a customer was accepted by the Advertising Standards Authority (ASA) when Dell made the following claim about one of its computers: 'Everything about it is bigger except the price – over £120 off – was £1,121'. There was no evidence to show that the price had really been cut.

The ASA has a voluntary code for advertisers, which is generally respected. When criticisms are made, companies take notice and change their ways.

1 How were customers hurt by each of these offences?

2 How were other businesses hurt by the offences?

3 Why is it important to challenge businesses that try to take advantage of customers?

4 Why do you think that organisations abide by the rulings of the Advertising Standards Authority?

Customers and the law

The law tries to prevent businesses and other organisations from misleading and endangering customers and other businesses.

- Cars that are inaccurately described may turn out to be death traps.

- People can be tempted to buy one company's product rather than another's because of inaccurate advertising claims.

- 'Fake' products may be poor quality and damage genuine competitors.

The law therefore expects products to be:

- as they are claimed

- safe.

A range of laws covers these aspects of consumer protection. They are enforced by Trading Standards Offices, who work for local authorities. They inspect catering premises and other outlets as well as responding to complaints from unhappy customers.

The main effect on business is to increase costs. New legislation on safety, for example, means a tighter specification and more inspection of products. Safety is obviously of paramount importance but sometimes businesses feel that the requirements are excessive.

BUSINESS POWER

Customers are very dependent on the businesses that supply their utilities such as water and power. Although there is now competition between these businesses, the government has set up bodies to oversee the industries.

Ofwat and Ofcom control the water and communications businesses. Profits are limited in the hope that customers will not be exploited. Competition itself can have this effect but these bodies offer additional protection.

Protecting the customer

Customers hope they will receive the product they think they are buying. When they see an advert, they expect it to reflect the product that is on offer. This is not always the case. Customers are usually in a weaker position than the companies they are buying from unless there is a lot of competition. Even then – if a product doesn't match the claims, it can be hard to get redress despite companies' offers of customer service. The law is there to protect people.

Business power

www

www.dti.gov.uk
www.competition-
commission.org.uk

Customers are very dependent on the businesses that supply their utilities such as water and power. Although there is now competition between these businesses, the government has set up bodies to oversee the industries.

Ofwat and Ofcom control the water and communications businesses. Profits are limited in the hope that customers will not be exploited. Competition itself can have this effect but these bodies offer additional protection.

starSTUDY

Brewing power?

Interbrew, a Belgium brewing company bought the brewing part of Bass plc. It had already acquired Whitbread's brewing business and now had a market share of up to 38% of UK beer production and distribution. The merger was referred to the Competition Commission, a government agency which investigates the effect of mergers and takeovers. It's objective is to maintain a level of competition that prevents any business becoming too powerful.

After looking carefully at the effect on customers and other businesses, Interbrew was told that it would have to sell Bass.

1 Why do you think Interbrew wanted to buy Bass?

2 What effect do you think it would have had on customers and competitors?

3 What effect do you think the existence of the Competition Commission has on businesses which are thinking of taking over or merging with another business?

IN THE KNOW

Competition rules

Should Granada merge with Carlton? Should newspapers in one area all belong to the same company? Should Safeway be taken over by one of the other major supermarkets groups? Should Blockbuster take over Apollo? Should shop keepers be allowed to put Mars ice creams in a fridge provided by Walls?

These are all issues that are dealt with by the Competition Commission, a government body which investigates mergers and takeovers. If one business controls too much of the market for a particular product, it can have an adverse effect on both competitors and customers. It may mean that the price of the product increases or competitors' products don't get a look in so choice is restricted.

The Commission takes all these things into account and comes to a conclusion which is 'in the public interest'. Sometimes, just being referred to the Commission means that a business thinks again. When Blockbuster wanted to take over Apollo, it withdrew when it realised that the plan had been challenged.

The Competition Act, the law which is the basis of the Commission's decisions, relates to European Law. In an attempt to have a 'level playing field' for businesses in Europe, laws are the same across the EU.

Critical thinking

1 The government banned all advertising of tobacco. Draw up two spider diagrams showing the winners and losers from this decision.

2 Find out about a recent decision made by the Competition Commission. Explain why the decision was made.

3 Why might one business think of the Competition Commission as a constraint while another is pleased that it exists?

KEY TERMS

Mergers occur when two businesses join together.

Takeovers occur when one business buys another. It may or may not be amicable.

Competition Commission is a government agency which aims to maintain competition between businesses in order to protect the consumer and the businesses.

Next steps

Have a look at the website of your local trading standards office. You will find it on the local council's website. How does it aim to protect consumers? Is there evidence of recent prosecutions? If so, what are they about?

Responsibility

Specification Content

Social responsibilities: responsibilties to employees, customers and other stakeholders

starSTUDY

Making magic

DJW designs and installs audio-visual experiences. The Premier League Hall of Fame and Explore@Bristol are among its customers. The business started life by providing the audio-visual expertise for the Motor Museum in Beaulieu, Hampshire, where it is based. It then found there were other people who wanted to buy the services that it offered. It now employs 13 people and has a range of experts it can call on for specialist jobs. Most of the employees live in the local area.

The business buys all sorts of things – from hi-tech equipment to jars of coffee – from a range of suppliers.

Sometimes DJW needs to borrow money from the bank. It might want to use the money to buy some new equipment. There are times when customers haven't paid their bills on time so the business needs to borrow to fill the gap.

The business, which was set up by David Willdich, is owned by its **shareholders** who are members of the family. This small group of shareholders puts money into the company and shares the **profits**.

David and his wife Lynn, who is responsible for finance, work hard to make DJW a success because they enjoy running the business and want to make a profit. This means ensuring that each installation covers its **costs** – and makes a little more.

Businesses and stakeholders

WHO ARE THE STAKEHOLDERS?

Stakeholders all have an interest in an organisation. They may:

- work within the business – employees and managers.
- have financial relationships – lenders, suppliers and customers.
- be affected by the way the business functions – people in the local community and beyond.
- own the business or hold shares in it.

Sometimes the interests of stakeholders might conflict. When a business wants to expand, it may put pressure on the local environment. Owners may put pressure on employees to increase profits.

Stakeholders may wear different hats. Employees are often members of the local community. Expansion, for example, will secure jobs but will make the roads busier and put pressure on local schools. What should they do?

MEETING STAKEHOLDER OBJECTIVES

The primary function of any business is to make a profit for the owners or shareholders. If this is not achieved over a period, the business will cease to exist and other stakeholders will lose out as jobs will be lost and suppliers will find that their order books get thinner.

Businesses have different priorities in dealing with stakeholders. Carphone Warehouse, for example, puts customers and employees at the top of the list because they think that this is critical for success in the phone business.

Often the most powerful stakeholder wins attention. A vociferous campaign in the local community, for example, can prevent a business from making an unpopular decision. The business may want to protect its reputation because negative stories in the media can drive customers away.

Working with stakeholders

Companies, large and small, are aware that stakeholders need to be looked after. They know that a good reputation is important and once it is lost, it is hard to regain.

Stakeholder	How to look after them	Effect
Customers	Sell a good product at a fair price	They will keep coming back
Employees	Good working conditions	Produce better results
Suppliers	Pay them on time	Supply what the business needs, when it needs it
Creditors	Pay back loans regularly	Lend willingly – the next time
Shareholders	Make a good profit	Keep their money in the business
Community	Look after people and the environment	Support if you want to expand or make other changes

BP is the UK's largest company and has activities all over the world. Its stakeholders are many and varied because of the nature of the business. Chemicals and oil production affect people in many ways so the company must work with its stakeholders to try to avoid conflict. Like all big companies, it has policies on working with stakeholders and is aware that objectives might conflict. Instead of fighting with organisations like Greenpeace, it tries to work with them to achieve ends that satisfy everyone. Despite much care, it doesn't always get it right.

Suppliers to any company feel under pressure to sell their products at the lowest possible price because if others do it more cheaply, they might lose the business. Some companies have started working more closely with suppliers in order to give security and develop a relationship which makes both businesses work better.

1 Make a list of the people and organisations that have an interest in DJW.
2 Explain why each one is interested in this business.
3 Can you think of anyone else who might be interested in what the business does? Explain why.

KEY TERMS

Stakeholders are people who have an interest in a business. They include employees, managers, customers, creditors, suppliers, owners/shareholders and the community.

Critical thinking

BP's Cleaner Fuels strategy includes:

- Making cleaner fuels available in 90 cities throughout the world.
- Working to reduce emissions of the greenhouse gases produced by its manufacturing operations by 10% from a 1990 baseline by 2010.

1 Work out how these activities:
a benefit BP
b benefit the stakeholders.

Evaluate these benefits.

2 Identify a business which you know and work out whether its approach to stakeholders helps it to achieve its objectives.

Next steps

Choose a business that you know about. It could be one you work for, a large business such as McDonalds or a small local company.

1 Who are the stakeholders?
2 Work out the objectives of each stakeholder group.
3 How do you think these objectives affect the way a business works?
4 In what ways might the objectives conflict?
5 What might happen if a business makes a 'wrong' decision?

Good behaviour

star**STUDY**
The new store

Worcester has its fair share of supermarkets but there was a gap in the St John's area on the west side of town. Tesco planned to build a new store on the site of a school, which was badly in need of updating. It proposed to put up £12.6 million to build a new school on another site – a tempting offer for the county council since it knew the school needed a lot of money spent on it.

Children go to school along St John's busy High Street

Sainsbury's also put forward a proposal. This involved keeping the school but providing a sports centre, youth club and an all-weather pitch.

Local people were keen on the idea of a new supermarket at this end of town but weren't sure that it should be Tesco because there were already two in the city. They were also anxious about the extra traffic that would come through the area – Sainsbury's plan might bring in more traffic because it was keeping everything on the same site.

It would be great to have a new school but, with Tesco's plan, students would have to travel out of St John's to the new site. There was some concern about the effect that it would have on the local community.

The traders in St John's High Street campaigned ferociously against any supermarket, because they knew it would take their customers away.

1 Which stakeholders live in the local community?

2 How would the new store affect the local community? Draw up a table showing the pros and cons of each scheme.

3 How do you think the following stakeholders would respond to the proposed developments:
   a suppliers
   b creditors
   c shareholders?

4 Which plan would you go for? Why?

Keeping everyone happy

A business's prime objective has to be to keep its **shareholders** happy. They own the company because they have bought shares in it, so they expect to be paid a share of the profit. This is known as a **dividend** and it is a reward to the shareholders for buying into the business. If they do not receive the reward they expect, they will probably sell the shares and buy into another company instead.

There are other stakeholders who need to be kept happy if the business is going to be successful.

A new store means:
• new jobs
• easy shopping for customers

• more orders for suppliers
• more borrowing from creditors and interest payments
• more traffic in the local area.

It may also mean that the local area benefits. The business wants to persuade people that the new store is a good thing – in Worcester, Sainsbury's and Tesco were in competition, so each company was keen to make a tempting offer to the community.

Both businesses are **accountable** to their stakeholders. Upsetting any of them can lead to problems but often a business has to decide which stakeholders are most important when changes are made.

Accountability in practice

IN THE KNOW

SHAREHOLDERS have bought shares in a business and hope to be paid a dividend each year if the business is making a profit. They must be kept informed of events so they know how the business is going and be given the opportunity to have their say.

SUPPLIERS expect to be paid on time. Most suppliers give a period of credit but some companies delay payment to help their own financial position. Suppliers can add interest if bills are not paid on time but many don't do this because they don't want to upset the customer.

CUSTOMERS can expect to buy products that live up to the claims of the business. If they don't, the law protects them. Customers can turn to the local Trading Standards Officer or the Citizens' Advice Bureau for help if they feel that they have been unfairly treated.

CREDITORS have lent money to the business and expect it to be repaid with the right amount of interest. A bank that has not been paid may call in the loan and the business might fail as a result. It is always sensible for a business to discuss problems, however small, with the bank before the problems get too serious.

go to → Find out more on page 160

THE LOCAL COMMUNITY around a business can be critical to its success. By working with them, a business can develop a 'licence to operate'. If a business wants to expand, having a good relationship with the community may make the process much easier. Big businesses like BP have found that working with Greenpeace, for example, helps when environmental issues are at stake.

EMPLOYEES expect to be treated fairly by employers and are protected by the law if things go wrong. The law covers unfair dismissal, discrimination, disability, and health and safety among other areas. Someone who feels that an employer's decision has been unfair can take their case to an Employment Tribunal where a judgement will be made.

go to → Find out more on page 158

Critical thinking

Vodafone's mobile phone network broke down for a whole day. Customers were not happy!

- **Work out who Vodafone's stakeholders are.**
- **How was each of them affected by the network failure?**
- **If you were responsible for communicating with Vodafone's stakeholders, what would you have done?**

KEY TERMS

Shareholders own part of a company because they have bought shares.

Dividends are the share of profits paid to shareholders as a return for investing in a company.

Accountability describes the relationship between a business and its stakeholders.

Next steps

1 Draw up a spider diagram for a business you know. Show its stakeholders and its accountability to each one.

2 How do you think this accountability affects the way the business works?

What are business ethics?

starSTUDY

Yeo Valley stands by its values

'Our aim remains to produce high quality, value for money organic products and we promise that as the range and availability of organic raw materials improves, we'll keep on innovating and producing new products to give our customers more and more choice.'

Yeo Valley combines its organic and environmental ethos with a strong business objective. It didn't find it easy to move into organic products because there is still an inadequate supply of the milk and fruit it needs for large-scale production. Tesco and Sainsbury's will not stock your products if you cannot guarantee a reliable supply. To overcome the problem, Yeo Valley devised a way of encouraging farmers to convert to organic production.

Not only did it set a price for the milk that guaranteed a profit for the farmers, it also bought the milk that wasn't organic to sell to other people. This strategy ensured that

it had enough organic milk and demonstrated its commitment to an ethical relationship with its suppliers.

Its ethical agenda is to be found in other aspects of the business too. Packaging aims to be as recyclable as possible, lorries go out with full loads to avoid wasting fuel, water is conserved wherever possible and employees are encouraged to cycle to work.

1 What ethical principles does Yeo Valley demonstrate?

2 How do these values help the business?

3 How do you think a strong ethical ethos affects the attitude of the staff?

4 What do you think would happen to the business if it were discovered to have been breaking its own rules?

5 Write an ethical statement for Yeo Valley which comments on the relationship with each of its stakeholders.

Specification Content

Moral and ethical: recognition of possible conflict in addressing different perspectives

There's a place where the grass really is greener.

YEO VALLEY

It's what goes into it that makes it taste so good.

At Yeo Valley Organic we know that to get the best out of cows you have to put the best in. That's why they only graze on the finest, juiciest, organic grass and clover (no pesticides or artificial fertilisers for us). And it shows in the creamy milk they generously provide for us to turn into thick, smooth yogurt at our Somerset dairy. Why not grab a spoon and try some. You'll find that Yeo Valley doesn't just have the best earth, but the best yogurt on earth.

www.yeo-organic.co.uk

Ethics and business

Many big businesses now have **ethical statements** that set out the relationship of the business with stakeholders. Some people suggest that they are just a cynical way of making the business look good, but once a business has made a statement of this sort, the media and pressure groups tend to be quick to identify and publicise any contraventions.

Businesses started to develop such codes in the 1990s after a series of corporate disasters that led to environmental damage and financial disaster. To begin with, having an ethical code or statement was something special. It gave a business a unique selling point, which made it stand out from the crowd.

An ethical approach needs to be embedded in the business. If it is just a superficial statement that is never put into practice, the company will soon be caught out by the media or pressure groups. The Institute of **Business Ethics** helps organisations of all sorts to develop a code that involves everyone.

Making ethics work

THE INSTITUTE OF BUSINESS ETHICS' FORMULA FOR AN ETHICAL STATEMENT

It should include:

THE PURPOSE AND VALUES OF THE BUSINESS. The products which are being provided – financial objectives and the business's role in society as the company sees it.

EMPLOYEES. How the business values employees: working conditions, recruitment, development and training, rewards, health, safety and security, equal opportunities, retirement, redundancy, discrimination and harassment. Use of company assets by employees.

CUSTOMER RELATIONS. The importance of customer satisfaction and good faith in all agreements, quality, fair pricing and after-sales service.

SHAREHOLDERS OR OTHER PROVIDERS OF MONEY. The protection of investment made in the company and proper 'return' on money lent. A commitment to accurate reporting of achievements and prospects.

SUPPLIERS. Prompt settling of bills. Co-operation to achieve quality and efficiency. No bribery or excess hospitality accepted or given.

SOCIETY OR THE WIDER COMMUNITY. Compliance with the spirit of the law as well as the letter. The company's obligations to protect and preserve the environment. The involvement of the company and its employees in local affairs. The corporate policy on giving to education and charities.

IMPLEMENTATION. How the code is issued, used and reviewed. Ways of obtaining advice. Training programme for staff.

More than just the law

The law of most countries lays down how many of these relationships should be handled. Business ethics takes things a step further. Businesses can often make decisions that are within the law but don't treat stakeholders ethically. There is nothing to prevent a business having short-term contracts with suppliers but an ethical approach might mean taking a longer-term view, as Yeo Valley does.

The number of businesses that have developed ethical statements has increased rapidly through the last decade. The change gives a clue to the perception of such statements within business because they cost money to develop.

Critical thinking

Draw up a spider diagram showing why a business might develop an ethical code. How might it affect the relationship with its stakeholders?

Next steps

1 Have a look at some big companies' websites to find out about their ethical codes.

2 What similarities can you find?

KEY TERMS

Business ethics are a code of behaviour that is morally correct.

An **ethical statement** or code is a business's view of the way it behaves. It explains how ethical decisions are made throughout the organisation.

WWW

Institute of Business Ethics:
www.ibe.org.uk

Ethics and/or profit?

Specification Content

Business ethics: morality in decision-making; potential conflict of ethics and making profit

starSTUDY

A tough decision

Core values of the Corus Group

Corus Group's 'Core Values' detail company beliefs, which both current and future policies are built upon, enabling all employees to work towards the common goal of maintaining our position as a global leading metals provider.

Objectives

Corus aims to be recognised as a leading global metals provider with a strong technological base and an outstanding level of service. To achieve this requires the combined efforts and professionalism of all our employees.

Corus seeks to be an excellent employer:

- Through a commitment to creating a stimulating work environment and enhancing employability.

- By seeking to provide competitive remuneration.

- By creating opportunities for employees to develop their skills.

- By providing an open and fair working environment.

The Group places the highest value on:

- The health, safety and welfare of all employees.

- Teamwork, based on mutual trust and respect.

- Personal commitment and individual involvement.

- Integrity and reliability in all circumstances.

In Corus, respect for all stakeholders and open communication are leading business principles.

Corus and the individual

Management will encourage employees to buy into Corus Group's common purpose and responsible business practices.

All employees must be assured of clear and open access to management to discuss matters of personal concern as well as those of wider interest to the Group.

Source: part of Corus Group's 'Core Values'

Steelworkers face uncertain future as Corus admits job losses are inevitable

THOUSANDS of Welsh steelworkers face an uncertain future, as up to 3,000 jobs at British plants are threatened in the wake of Corus's failed rescue bid.

The knock-on impact has plunged the company, which is £1bn in debt, into heightened uncertainty after it admitted earlier this week that redundancies and plant closures were inevitable.

Last night speculation was rife that the cash crisis would trigger the end of steel production at the Redcar works in Teesside, which employs 3,000 – sparing Corus's major plants at Port Talbot and Scunthorpe, with 4,000 workers each.

But sources revealed there was also disquiet that Llanwern could close completely with the loss of 1,400 jobs.

Source: adapted from The Western Mail, 14 March 2003.

1 What message is Corus's 'Core Values' giving about working for the company?

2 Why is Corus in difficulties?

3 How is this affecting its commitment to its core values?

4 Which stakeholders appear to be most important?

5 If Corus did not take tough decisions, how might the future of the business be affected?

6 What effect would this have on remaining stakeholders?

Who comes first?

When a business sets out its ethical agenda, it shows how it aims to work with its stakeholders. When everything is rosy, this works well. When the environment becomes more challenging, it becomes harder to treat everyone as equally and openly as the code suggests.

A business that is in difficulties may want to keep its plans to close a plant under cover until the last moment, despite consultation with employees being part of its ethical statement. Its commitment to its shareholders, and employees who will be retained, might come before the employees who will lose their jobs in order to protect its future.

IN THE KNOW

Testing the code

Businesses make their codes available to the public, so they must think that they help. There is, however, a cynical view that they are simply an attempt to show the business in a good light and are therefore really part of the marketing strategy.

It can also be difficult to embed a code if employees are wedded to a traditional shareholder perspective. Persuading people that an ethical code can actually make a business more effective can take a long time.

Some parts of a code are easier to comply with and demonstrate to be working than others. If a business is making environmental claims, it is reasonably easy to

show that they are being upheld. It may be more difficult to demonstrate that bribes are not being paid to officials, a common practice in many less developed economies, as it is in the interest of both parties to keep quiet.

The real test of an ethical code occurs when a business has to make tough decisions. When weighing up the long-run impact on the business, it can be difficult to give all stakeholders equivalent status, especially when a business's survival is at stake.

Win–win?

A business's prime responsibility has to be to its shareholders. If potential investors were in any doubt about this, they would be unlikely to buy shares in the company.

There is, however, a body of evidence suggesting that businesses that have an ethical code are more successful than those that don't. The research, carried out by the Institute of Business Ethics, looked at a range of businesses with and without explicit codes of ethics and compared financial indicators. It found that ones with a code tended to be more successful. This suggests that there is a positive but not definitive relationship. It might mean that a business with a code is well run.

It may also mean that:

- good employees are attracted to an ethical business and stay with it

- suppliers will make more effort for a business that treats them well

- banks will lend more cheaply to a well-run profitable business

- customers prefer to buy products from a business that behaves ethically.

There is obviously a close relationship between behaving ethically and having a stakeholder culture.

Critical thinking

1 What is the difference between obeying the law and behaving ethically?

2 Why is it sometimes difficult for a business to keep to its code?

3 Why is there a close relationship between behaving ethically and a stakeholder culture?

4 Can a business be expected to keep its ethical code when its future is under threat? Explain your answer.

Next steps

1 Search for stories about businesses that are in difficulties.

2 Does the business have an ethical code?

3 Is it keeping it?

4 If not, which aspects are being broken?

5 Why do you think this is happening?

Technology: threat or opportunity?

Specification Content

Technological change: business opportunities (new products or process); fear and cost of change; effect on staff

starSTUDY

A virtual business

Virgin Mobile is a technology business. It sells technology and it runs on technology. It doesn't make phones and it doesn't run a network. It sells phones that run on the T-Mobile network.

The business runs from a call centre in Trowbridge, Wiltshire which employs 1200 people. It has 2.6 million customers who are sold products and looked after from Trowbridge. Virgin Mobile's objective is to grow. Customer care is Virgin Mobile's key strategy for adding value so the systems have to guarantee that every customer is contented. The Customer Service Agents (CSA) have to be well trained, motivated and monitored and technology can help.

The company has a huge management information system which monitors the

• quality of the call

• CSA performance

• reaction time in dealing with a call.

The Real Time Management system juggles the workload. When things get hectic, multi-skilled employees are brought into the front line. When all is quiet, CSAs are taken off duty for training.

Monitoring is carried out by another system that enables calls to be selected randomly. The aim is to improve staff retention and motivation by financial rewards for good performance. This in turn serves to improve the quality of the service as well as identifying training needs. This all saves team leaders' time.

Vision is Virgin Mobile's intranet. It provides staff with information about orders and payments. It also has e-learning material for staff to use at quiet times.

The Knowledge is an expert diagnostic system that helps CSAs to meet customer needs to best effect by picking out key words and giving alternative solutions. The agent can then choose the one that fits the bill.

Despite all the technology, Virgin Mobile tries not to forget the people. It is hard to recruit in Trowbridge, so trained people are valuable. The rate of turnover was very high but is now coming down as the company develops strategies for keeping people involved and happy.

1 How does Virgin Mobile use technology to achieve its objectives?
2 How does it use technology to save money?
3 How can it use technology to motivate its staff?
4 What would happen to Virgin Mobile if it got left behind in the technology stakes?

Keeping ahead of the game

Businesses have always had to watch how technology changes. It just seems to change more quickly today than it did a hundred years ago. There is often a fear that technological change leads to unemployment – and in specific industries this is often the case. Introducing a laser operated cutting machine in a clothing factory will probably put people out of work but it may also mean that the clothes are cheaper, therefore people can buy a greater variety of products – so demand and employment increase in other areas.

Technology has resulted in falling prices for many products. Electrical goods of all sorts are relatively much cheaper than a generation ago so we all have more of them. Technology has therefore helped businesses grow and has improved our standard of living. Things we now take for granted, such as washing machines and battery operated radios, were luxuries fifty years ago. Microwave ovens had not even been invented.

Some businesses thrive on doing things in the traditional way but most need to watch developments if they are to keep their place in the market.

Opportunities and threats

OPPORTUNITIES

• To make business more efficient

Technology is often used to cut costs or raise quality. Both developments can make a business more competitive. Cutting costs may lead to falling prices and higher sales so both the business and customers win.

Technology can raise quality because a computer which is well programmed does not make mistakes. It is very difficult for a human being to be perfect every time. Quality has become a critical factor for most businesses because customers expect high standards. Cars now break down less frequently because they are built with much more sophisticated systems.

• To create exciting, new products for customers

Businesses that develop new products can achieve an advantage over others. It may not last long because others are always trying to catch up. Many work hard to stay ahead of the game. It is important to

be able to recognise potential success. The Sony Walkman nearly never made it to the marketplace because the company's directors could not imagine that people would want to take music wherever they went!

THREATS

The main threat is that other businesses will get there first. Another is that your business will simply cease to exist because people don't want your products anymore. The final typewriter factory shut down because even the most stuck-in-the-mud typist had finally started to use a computer!

A threat to one stakeholder can be an opportunity for others. Cheap, easy communications, which led to the introduction of the call centre for businesses to access its customers, has changed dimension as call centres are now shifting to India and other places with a cheaper, skilled workforce. This means cost and prices stay low but there is less employment in the UK.

Critical thinking

Broadband comes to Marlborough

The Chamber of Commerce in Marlborough is organising a public meeting to discuss the advantages of broadband. The objective is to discuss ways in which businesses can turn the fast, cheap internet connection to advantage. It is also hoped that the availability of broadband will help to attract businesses to the town.

1 What sorts of businesses might be attracted to Marlborough by the arrival of broadband?

2 How might existing businesses turn it to advantage?

3 What effects might the development of such businesses have on the town?

4 How might it affect places nearby which do not have broadband?

Next steps

What sorts of businesses are there in your area which use technology to good effect? Use Yellow Pages to see what's there.

testing–testing

External influences – assessment

Specification Content

The interaction of supply and demand, how changes in supply and demand affect the allocation of resources, the degree of competition.

Part A: The market and competition

Cinema proves pundits wrong

The resurgence of the cinema business during the past decade or so has been astounding. For years doom and gloom pundits had written off cinema as a mass entertainment industry. Television and later home videos were the nails, which would finally close the coffin of this once all-powerful media. The dark days of the 1970s and early 1980s witnessed countless once much-loved local cinemas across the country converted into bingo halls or just simply left to rot. UK cinema audiences hit their lowest point in 1984 when 54 million visits were made. How things have moved on. Events have changed and the 1990s saw a resurgence in the film industry. Improved marketing combined with better films shown in new comfortable multiplex cinemas began to attract back customers.

Today sees work start on Bath's first multiplex cinema complex as the city – rather belatedly – jumps on the back of an entertainment revolution.

Many fear that Bath's existing cinemas will not survive for long when the Odeon multiplex opens in around 18 months' time. One small independent cinema will focus even more on specialist films in an effort to survive.

Source: Bath Chronicle, Cinema admissions

Cinema admissions and screens

	Admissions	Screens
1980	101 million	1562
1984	54 million	1450
1990	91 million	1715
2000	142.5 million	2700
2001	155.91 million	3164
2002	176.91 million	3258

Source: British Film Council

Disposable income

Between 1995 and 2001 disposable income rose by 20%.

easyCinema

easyCinema has chosen Milton Keynes for its first cinema. Booking early means you pay less. Booking off peak also means lower ticket prices. You must buy online as there is no box office at the cinema. It's a no frills service.

Source: easyCinema

assessment questions

1 What evidence is there that demand to see films has changed? **(2 marks)**

 help! Look for data in the evidence in the form of numbers, graphs or text. Remember: demand can fall as well as rise. Think about whether the market is a volatile one.

2 a How has demand changed? **(2 marks)**

b Suggest possible causes for this change. **(6 marks)**

help! Part (a) wants you to point out if the change has been in one direction or has it switched? You should use some of the data to illustrate the change either by quoting directly or preferably by providing a percentage change. Part (b) wants you to link the evidence to some of the standard reasons for people changing their buying habits.

3 Demonstrate the change in **demand** between 1980 and 2000 using a diagram. **(8 marks)**

 You will need to be able to construct a simple diagram showing the shifts in demand curve. It is easier if you keep the price the same and then you can use actual admission figures on the x axis. Your diagram must have a written explanation.

4 How might the cinema industry react to the trends in the short run and in the long run? **(8 marks)**

 You must consider both the decline in demand and the increase in demand to see films. Remember that businesses react differently in the short run from in the long run.

5 Demonstrate the change in supply using a diagram. **(6 marks)**

 A change in supply is referring to the long-run position. You will need to plot three different supply curves to show the shifts in them. As with question 3 it will be easier if you keep the price the same and then you can use the actual number of cinema screens on the x axis. Your diagram must have an explanation.

6 To what extent is there a danger of over supply in the market? **(6 marks)**

 You should consider reasons why there might be an over supply. There could be a short-term explanation, but also consider the long-term factors. Risk takers can get it wrong for a number of reasons. The introduction of a new player in the market with a different strategy might also be significant.

7 a How is easyCinema attempting to gain a competitive advantage? **(4 marks)**

  b What effect will easyCinema have on the competition should it be successful and open cinemas throughout the UK? **(8 marks)**

 Part (a) wants an explanation of what competitive advantage might be and for you to apply this to the strategy adopted by easyCinema. Part (b) will want you to consider the negative effects on the other cinemas, but also how they may react.

Part B: Macroeconomic issues in relation to businesses

Conversions

Terry manages and owns shares in W.H. Bence Ltd. The business converts vans and lorries into mobile libraries, exhibition units and any other vehicle the customer wants. Terry's business is sensitive to the business cycle and other external influences, because the firm depends on other companies and local authorities' spending plans. When money is tight these organisations cut back on their orders to W.H. Bence. The opposite happens during times of economic growth.

A couple of years ago the order book was full for the next three months. Orders were coming in thick and fast and Terry was turning away customers. He even introduced additional shift work, as deadlines could not be met with overtime alone. To recruit workers Terry needed to attract them from other businesses by offering higher wages. He was able to pass the increased costs onto his customers. After all, he had a full order book.

How times have changed. The economy is slowing down and some forecasters believe we will soon be entering a recession. The government increased National Insurance rates to both employees and employers. These higher costs have affected all businesses. Many of Terry's customers have to find savings in order to manage their budgets. Some have cancelled their orders and others are asking for the bare minimum to be done on conversions. It is bad news for Terry, his business and his workforce. Orders have nearly dried up and he has already made several of his employees redundant. Less cash is coming in and he still has the same overheads. At least the cost of borrowing has fallen with lower interest rates, but the bank won't support him forever.

With all these pressures Terry still has to devote more time to finding new orders. This means looking into European markets to export his products. He has been on several trips to France and Germany, both countries that are part

of the Eurozone. The value of the pound has been falling against the euro, which means the exchange rate gives him a price advantage over his foreign competitors especially since he buys most of his materials from UK-based businesses and so has few imported components. However, buyers would have transaction costs to consider in exchanging euros for pounds. He doesn't like all the paperwork involved in trading with the EU but he feels that he has to look for new markets.

Skills shortage may be causing an increase in wage costs.

Interest rates to rise for the first time in a few years

The Monetary Policy Committee has decided to raise interest rates after fears about the house price rises fuelling inflation…

Should interest rates have been changed?

Fears from some economists that the latest rise in interest rates will lead to an increase in unemployment.

Specification Content

Interest rates: their use and purpose; impact of an interest rate change on the firm and its market; exchange rates; impact of changes in exchange rates on the firm and the market; taxation; the business cycle and its impact on the firm and the market; unemployment

assessment questions

1 What is meant by the terms 'business cycle', 'recession' and 'boom'? **(3 marks)**

 Straightforward questions asking for definitions, but do try to relate the three terms together.

2 What decisions did Terry make during a period of economic growth? How might such decisions affect the inflation rate if adopted by most businesses? **(6 marks)**

 Use the evidence to state the decisions he made and then you must comment on the connection between these decisions and changes in inflation levels.

3 a Why might a skills shortage lead to a rise in wage costs? **(2 marks)**

  b What effect will such rises have on businesses? **(4 marks)**

 This is a straightforward question.

4 a How will a rise in interest rates affect businesses? **(4 marks)**

  b If rising interest rates affect businesses why might the MPC bother to increase them? **(6 marks)**

 You should look at how interest rate rises increase business costs and discourage investment. The second part suggests that the MPC is prioritising keeping inflation under control. You should also mention how inflation may be seen to be a bad thing for businesses.

5 Evaluate Terry's strategy of looking for new markets in Europe. **(8 marks)**

 Evaluations ask you to look at arguments for and against as well as short and long term. Explain the need to look in the Eurozone and then comment on the advantages of the declining value of the pound in the short run. Suggest some difficulties Terry may face and then make a comment about exchange rates moving in both directions.

6 How might an increase in the UK exchange rate affect UK businesses? **(8 marks)**

 Comment on the rising value of the pound on both importing and exporting businesses. Think about the worry of currency fluctuations and how this can be resolved. Does this present opportunities in the domestic market?

7 What effect will changes in interest rates have on Terry's business and on the economy in general? **(8 marks)**

 You need to consider both rises and falls in interest rates and whether this has a positive or negative impact on Terry. Can Terry's business easily cope with interest rate changes? Are others subject to the same difficulties?

Part C: UK and EU law, social responsibilities, business ethics and technological change

Case study A: Technology and consumer laws

Making e-commerce work

The E-Commerce Directive sets strict rules for UK businesses which advertise or sell goods either via a website, mobile phone or through e-mail. These firms will now have to offer key features on their sites such as contact information, a swift acknowledgement of orders, and the chance for customers to amend an order. The laws are good news for consumers, but they will add to the costs of businesses as they prepare for the change.

Goodnessdirect.co.uk is an online shop selling over 2000 health products from foods to health supplements. There's lots of product information on the website and you can even e-mail an expert. The site meets the European Directive. You can cancel goods after receiving them and there are clear contact addresses. The business operates out of Daventry and uses broadband in order to speed up its service.

The UK has seen a staggering growth in broadband, due largely to falling prices, fierce marketing campaigns and new ways to install the technology. The government is encouraging all of the UK to use the new technology, but we have a long way to go.

The Wentworth Wooden Jigsaw Company sends its products all over the world, and increasingly needs to download pictures and artwork to use in creating puzzles. It operates in a rural part of Wiltshire that does not have access to broadband. Without the fast computer facility, the company's future in its rural location is threatened, together with the jobs of its 18 staff. It has unsuccessfully campaigned to have broadband installed locally over the last two years.

The companies providing fast computer access say it costs a lot of money to convert telephone exchanges and there must be enough demand to make this viable. BT expects 90% of the country to have access to broadband by mid 2005.

Source: BBCi

assessment questions

1 The E-Commerce Directive is one of many laws that support the consumer. Why might some businesses welcome laws like these while others see them as yet another burden? **(8 marks)**

 This question is about encouraging good practice, making an even playing field for businesses and understanding why we need laws to protect the consumer.

2 Why might small rural businesses that do not have access to broadband be concerned at it not being available? **(4 marks)**

 Go to page 170

3 How has the growth of information technology led to new opportunities for businesses like Goodnessdirect.co.uk? **(4 marks)**

 This question asks you to comment on cost savings available and how the technology allows these types of business to reach a larger audience. These provide them with a competitive advantage.

Case study B: Employment laws

Women now benefit from better maternity leave rights. Women are now entitled to 26 weeks off, regardless of how long they have worked for their employer. Under the new system the first 6 weeks maternity leave is paid at 90% of average earnings, and for the remaining 20 weeks it is £100 a week, or 90% of average weekly earnings if this is less. It has got better for fathers as well. They can now take 2 weeks' paid paternity leave. There is even more good news for working parents. Mothers and fathers of children aged under 6 will be legally allowed to request flexible working.

A senior examiner, who claimed he was sacked for complaining about the grading of exam papers, has failed in his bid to take the case to an industrial tribunal. The tribunal, in Norwich, agreed with Edexcel that Mr Mead was a contract worker, not a salaried employee, so had no legal right to claim unfair dismissal.

When Fineline Cymru, a swimwear factory, went bust the 35 workers, mainly women, claimed they were left without redundancy pay and back wages. Just two weeks after closing the factory, owner John Potter reopened the swimwear factory and began trading under the name Cherub UK.

Lawyers for the GMB union, which represents the former workers, are going to an employment tribunal to claim compensation against the former owner. 'When Fineline closed and Mr Potter opened Cherub UK, all of the contracts of employment should have been transferred over to the new firm,' a spokesperson from the GMB argued.

Source: BBCi

assessment questions

1 Why did the government want to improve working parents' rights? **(2 marks)**

 Go to page 158

2 Evaluate the effects of the new working parents rights to a small business and a large company. **(8 marks)**

 A small business employing a small workforce may not be able to spread these costs as well as a larger business.

3 What is an employment tribunal? **(2 marks)**

 Go to page 159

4 What is meant by a contract? What arguments are there for and against the swimwear workers' case against their former employer? **(8 marks)**

 Go to page 159

Case study C: The environment and Shell...

Specification Content

Environmental, moral and ethical influences

Shell is a very large global petrochemical company. The company's website provides an insight to its views on a range of sensitive issues such as:

- Human rights
- Globalisation
- Politically sensitive areas
- Climate change
- New energy
- Water use
- Biodiversity
- Product stewardship.

'We have a responsibility to stick by business principles based on honesty, integrity and respect for people. We must make a constant effort to live by them. For example Shell operates in countries where bribery and corruption is endemic. Shell will not tolerate this and employees will be sacked if they are found to be involved in it.'

'Must work with sensitive stakeholders, e.g. inform interest groups before going into new areas.'

Shell believes that being sustainable:

- Encourages innovation, e.g. cleaner fuel.
- Attracts and motivates best staff.
- Reduces project risk.
- Opens new markets.

'It's a matter of enlightened self-interest,' claims Shell's CEO Malcolm Brinded. 'Being transparent within annual reports and published environmental audits helps us gain and maintain trust.'

Shell has promised to reveal which 210 of its 1100 petrol stations have mobile phone masts hidden inside the forecourt price signs. The oil company, which has a deal with T-mobile, said the transmitters were safe but campaigners have expressed concerns.

...and T-mobile

T-mobile spokeswoman Gill Kerr told BBC News Online the antennae ensured 'that about 46 million people with a mobile in the UK get the best possible service'.

But Mast Sanity, a pressure group, said operators were 'making a mockery' of the planning process. 'They promised faithfully they would consult with residents before they put these masts up.'

Source: BBC October 2002

.... And Unilever

'Supplier relationships –– practices of suppliers must be in line with our own, say Unilever, makers of detergents, soaps, perfumes and the like.

assessment questions

1 What is meant by a stakeholder? List three stakeholders for Shell and say what they might want from Shell. **(6 marks)**

 Go to page 162

2 a What motives does a company like Shell have for trying to be ethical in the way it behaves? **(4 marks)**

b Is there any potential conflict between having an ethical approach and satisfying shareholders? **(4 marks)**

 You should comment on the need for big businesses to be aware of environmental and ethical issues that affect them and the law. Consider undertaking a PEST-G analysis to provide a framework for your answer. You should also consider whether this approach would reduce profitability.

3 What would happen if the government increased the restrictions on erecting
mobile phone masts? **(4 marks)**

 Consider why the government would take this action and then explore the effect on
the businesses involved. You need to recognise there will be a trade off. How might the
businesses react to the restriction?

4 What does Unilever mean by 'the practices of suppliers must be in line with our own'? **(6 marks)**

 This implies that suppliers as stakeholders must be in on the act too. Think why this
might be important for Unilever.

Spotting an opportunity

Specification Content

Identifying an opportunity: small budget research and marketing; identifying a profitable product or service; protecting it (patents and copyright)

starSTUDY

Harriet Kessie started a hair salon targeted at a particular segment of the market

go to → Find out more on page 56

David Hanson set up his own market research company having worked in the business for some time

go to → Find out more on page 12

Justin Kyriakides had a bright idea and set up Discarray

go to → Find out more on page 150

David and Lynn Wildich developed a business creating interactive hi-tech displays based on the work they were doing at the Beaulieu Motor Museum

go to → Find out more on page 162

1   What opportunity did each of these businesses take?

2   Where do you think the idea came from?

3   What preparation do you think they had for starting a business?

4   Which do you think are most likely to be successful? Why?

5   What might make things difficult for each business?

Bright sparks

Businesses start for all sorts of reasons:

- Some people turn hobbies into businesses.

- People with a specific training set up a business.

- Some people set up a business as a sideline to their existing work.

- Some people use resources that they have available.

A potter, a carpenter, a tutor and running a bed and breakfast are the types of businesses that might begin in this way. The examples in the Star Study all had experience in their business before they began, apart from Justin who just came up with a good idea.

However a business begins, they all have one thing in common. The people who run them have to be prepared to take a risk. Working for someone else carries the risk of being made redundant but you don't have to worry about balancing the books. An **entrepreneur** usually has to put money into the business and risks losing the investment if things go wrong.

Research on a small budget

IN THE KNOW

Most small businesses don't have enough resources to invest in research but it does help to reduce the risk. If people have been working in a particular industry, they will have a good picture of what customers expect. A brand new idea is harder to test. They can, however, work out what the market is like and how it works by carrying out market mapping.

go to →

Go to page 11 for a reminder on market mapping

Buying in market research is probably too expensive, but looking carefully at other businesses in the same field will help to show what works and what doesn't. A new estate agent would look at the location of others and the type of properties that they deal with. They could easily find out how the competition markets properties – and think about more customer friendly or more efficient strategies. In businesses of this sort, primary research is quite easy to carry out personally. Secondary research would tell a potential estate agent how the house buying market is going and the pattern of properties in the area.

MARKETING ON A SMALL BUDGET

As the first part of this book shows, marketing can be an expensive activity. There are lots of possibilities and some have high costs attached. There are, however, some strategies that can be cheap and effective.

A new restaurant might
- Ask the local newspaper to come and write a review
- Pay for an entry in Yellow Pages
- Leaflet the local area
- Offer introductory discounts
- Advertise in the local paper or local websites
- Visit or telephone local businesses that might bring clients for lunch
- Set up a website

Success or failure?

No new business can guarantee success but research and marketing can help to reduce the risk. The problem with having a good idea is that other people copy it. It can be hard to prevent. A new bar in a part of town that is becoming trendy often leads to others opening quickly.

It can be beneficial because it brings more customers into the area but in other circumstances, businesses don't want to be copied. It is hard to stop people opening a new bar but innovative ideas can be protected.

Protecting the product

IN THE KNOW

A new invention can be **patented**. This means that the inventor owns the idea and noone else can copy it. A patent can be taken out for the UK, the USA or worldwide. This is an expensive process and may be beyond the reach of many small businesses. To overcome this, an inventor might license a large company to make the product. This has the advantage that the idea is protected, the product is made and the inventor receives a financial reward. After 20 years, the patent comes to an end and anyone can make the product.

Music and books are protected by **copyright**. It is illegal to copy them without paying a fee to the writer, composer or performer. Every now and again a songwriter is taken to court because a new song sounds very like something that already exists.

Critical thinking

1. If you wanted to set up a sandwich shop, what research would you carry out? How would it help you to make decisions?
2. How could you market the new business cheaply but effectively?

KEY TERMS

Copyright gives protection to authors and composers because books and music cannot be copied without permission and payment.

Entrepreneurs run their own businesses and bear the risk of doing so.

Patents protect inventions because others are prevented from copying them

Making it legal

starSTUDY

First cut

Harriet Kessie's hairdressing salon Harriet Kessie Hairdressing in Edmonton, London, is owned by Harriet and Joseph Cudjoe. Being a small business it has its upsides and downsides. Despite all the hard work it has taken to start her business, Harriet never looks back. 'Every time a door opens you forget the obstacles that have stood in your way.'

Her dreams haven't stopped there. She now plans to develop a high street chain – the first black hair salon with a national profile and training scheme. Harriet enjoys making things happen.

1 Why do you think Harriet and Joseph enjoy running their own business?

2 Why do you think it can be difficult to run a business on your own?

3 Use the information on these two pages to work out

  a what sort of legal structure Harriet and Joseph used when they first set up the business

  b what will change as the business grows

  c why she decided to change the legal structure?

Getting going

Harriet and Joseph run the business as a **partnership**. Many small businesses start as **sole traders** or partnerships because they are easy to set up. They are the most common form of business organisation, but the businesses are usually small and turnover is low. As Harriet's business grows, she will want to think about changing to another type of organisation that suits a bigger business.

Sole traders and partnerships

Sole traders are businesses that are run by one person. The main drawback is that they have **unlimited liability** so, if the business fails, the owner risks losing everything he or she owns to pay off the debts. It does, however, give the owner a lot of freedom because he or she doesn't have to consult anyone.

THE UPSIDE

• The owner is in control

• Freedom to organise work

• Personal relationship with customers

• Fewer legal restrictions

THE DOWNSIDE

• Unlimited liability

• No one to share decisions

• Only one set of skills

Most plumbers and electricians are sole traders. New businesses – from IT advisors to beauty therapists – also function in this way.

Partnerships are very similar to sole traders but involve more people. A group of people who trust each other make a legal agreement to work together. Trust is very important because all the partners are liable for the actions of the others. As a partnership has unlimited liability, each partner's possessions are at risk if one does something wrong.

A partnership can increase the range of skills in a business but it still remains difficult to raise finance for expansion.

Solicitors, doctors and other professional groups tend to work in partnerships. John Lewis is also a partnership, which is unusual for a large retailer.

Bigger business

As the business grows, Harriet will probably set up a **private limited company**, which means that a small group of shareholders can contribute to the finances and own their share of the company. Setting up a company will reduce Harriet's risk because if it were to go under, she would only lose the money that she has put into the business as she would have **limited liability**.

If her dreams come true and she has a shop on every high street, she may well decide to 'go public'. This means setting up a **public limited company** and selling shares which can then be traded on the Stock Exchange. They can then be bought by anyone and provide more capital for the business.

Private and public limited companies

IN THE KNOW

A company has a legal identity of its own. This brings both rights and responsibilities. It can enter into agreements in its own right. It can be sued if it does wrong. To set up a company you have to register with Companies House and submit the Memorandum and Articles of Association and an annual return. These documents give all the details of what the business does, who is involved and how it will be organised.

The main drawback of becoming a public company is loss of control. If people are putting money into your business, they will expect to have a say

in what happens. As the shareholders – or owners – of a big company cannot run the business, they appoint a board of directors who take responsibility. In turn they employ managers who take day-to-day control. Although the shareholders own the business, they only have control through their contribution to the Annual General Meeting. This is an annual event where the directors report on the state of the company. If shareholders are anxious about activities, they can call a special meeting but this does not often happen.

A public company must send detailed accounts to Companies House and their shareholders. The reporting requirements for a private company are less demanding.

	Private company – Ltd	Public company – Plc
Limited liability	Yes	Yes
Buying and selling shares	Must have permission of existing shareholders	Open to the public
Raising capital	Easier than sole trader	Easier than private company
Control	Tight – in hands of small group of shareholders	In hands of shareholders; may be takeover battles
Legal constraints	Yes	Yes
Value of shares	Stable	Fluctuates according to public view of value

Critical thinking

1 If a business is responsible for using other people's money, it has to be accountable. Explain how each type of legal structure is accountable to people who put their money into a business.

2 Why is accountability important?

Next steps

Find out about the legal structures of the following businesses. Explain what each business does and its structure.

1 The Virgin Group

2 Richer Sounds

3 Unilever

4 Dixons

5 Your local shop

6 A local builder

KEY TERMS

Sole traders run their own businesses. They have complete control but bear all the risk as they have unlimited liability.

Partnerships are groups of people who decide to run businesses together. They take joint control but have unlimited liability.

A **private limited company** belongs to a small group of shareholders who all have limited liability.

A **public limited company**'s shares are traded on the Stock Exchange. All shareholders have limited liability.

Limited liability provides protection for people who own shares in a company. It means they can only lose the money they have put in. Sole traders and partners have unlimited liability.

Solving the problems

Specification Content

Practical problems of start-ups: finance, location, building a customer base, cash flow, business plan

starSTUDY

Indulge

Roger and Kathy are the owners of Indulge. They started out in a small way buying and selling high quality soaps for cash sales in local markets in and around Wiltshire. Their initial budget was £2000, which they spent on buying stock and marketing. They decided to take no wage or salary to keep costs down. To begin with they lived off Roger's income from his teaching and lecturing.

The first 6 months of trading:

- Sales revenue £1900

- Purchased stocks of soap to the value of £1250

- Remaining stocks of £250

- £200 for hiring pitches at 5 events and paying the petrol.

Putting the second phase into operation meant a loan from the bank. They had decided that there was a market for their products and set about manufacturing their own

products. Kathy ran the business. A shop was rented and they managed to buy soap-making equipment for £450. They made a range of soaps in quantities reflecting the demand in the first 6 months.

The second 6 months of trading:

- Sales revenue rose to £25,000

- Purchase of £5000 of stock to add to the £250 left over from the previous 6 months' trading. All new stock was ingredients needed to make the soap and package it.

Costs went up considerably to £18,550. They rented a shop that cost £5000 for the first 6 months. The business rates were £4500. Kathy was paid a salary of £5000 during this period. They also had to pay for promotion, telephone and power, not to mention insurance and interest on the loan, adding another £4000 to their costs.

1 How did Roger and Kathy overcome the initial problem of covering all the costs of starting up Indulge?

2 What effect did this have on the first 6 months' cash flow?

3 What sort of market research were they able to carry out in the first 6 months? How did this help them to make decisions for the future?

4 How did their initial experience help them market their products?

5 What factors do you think they took into account when they decided on the location of the shop?

6 Why do you think the bank was happy to support their venture?

Hit or miss?

A very high proportion of new businesses fail. Sometimes it is bad luck but on most occasions, the planning process has lacked the detail needed to generate success. People who start businesses are generally enthusiastic about their idea and desperately want it to work so they may be optimistic about sales and their ability to keep costs under control.

They may make silly decisions about setting up a shop. It is easy to spend too much when you really want it to look good. It is easy to compromise on location when the rent is high near the high street – because you just *know* that everyone is going to go out of their way to *your* shop.

Being realistic is therefore very important.

What are the problems?

CREATING A REALISTIC BUSINESS PLAN

Most successful businesses have started with a plan. It makes potential entrepreneurs think hard about how the business will work in the first year or so. It is still easy to run away with enthusiasm for the idea and assume higher sales than are likely. The plan should cover:

- The business activity
- How it will be carried out
- Evidence about the market for the product in the area
- The marketing plan
- Who will work in the business
- Premises to be used
- Financial planning: budget, cash flow, breakeven
- Money to be contributed by owners.

Once in place the plan will help in the monitoring process because the cashflow and variances from the budget can be checked.

RAISING FINANCE

Many new businesses need to raise finance and the business plan will help. It shows that there are clear ideas about how it will all work. The choices for new businesses are quite limited as much money comes from savings, other individuals or the bank.

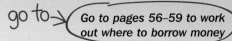

go to → Go to pages 56–59 to work out where to borrow money

CHOOSING THE RIGHT LOCATION

Any business that needs an office, shop or factory is going to have to consider which factors are important in making it successful. A shop needs customers. An office and a factory need staff with the right skills. Cost often plays an important part in the decision. There is often a trade-off between costs and convenience. The shop is often the hardest to choose because it must be visible to potential customers – and that can be expensive.

FINDING CUSTOMERS

Building up a **customer base** can be hard work. It is often easy to persuade people to buy once but you have to show them why it is worth coming back. When running a new business, you have to put yourself in the customers' shoes and work out what they want. Once they have bought your product, you need to look after them and keep in touch.

What do customers want?

- Value for money
- Quality at the price they're prepared to pay
- Good service when buying
- Good service after the purchase

KEEPING THE CASH FLOWING

go to → Go to pages 52–55 for a reminder on cash flow

Cash flow is often the downfall. Getting revenue in before having to pay the bills is often harder than people running new businesses imagine.

When starting up a business it is very easy to spend more than you planned. As few new businesses have much cash to spare, this is an easy way to get into difficulties. You might delay paying bills or ask the bank for a bigger loan. Unfortunately banks don't like lending working capital and it doesn't look promising if the owners want to borrow more so quickly.

Critical thinking

How did Indulge avoid cash flow problems? Look back to pages 180–181 and work out how cash flow might have been a problem for the businesses in the Star Study.

Next steps

Most banks have a business plan form and guidance for completion on their websites. Download one and work out how Indulge – or another business that you know about – would have completed it. What factors do you think a bank manager would be looking for before lending money?

KEY TERMS

Business plan sets out the initial planning for all aspects of a business or developments within an existing business.

Customer base is the regular customers who return to purchase the products.

Important objectives

Specification Content

Corporate aims and goals; purpose of agreeing aims from which objectives can be derived; short- versus long-term objectives; circumstances in which each may apply; implications for decision-making throughout the business

Our phones have happier lives

Helping customers at Carphone Warehouse

starSTUDY

Carphone Warehouse: Aims to Objectives

Our aims:
'We firmly believe that by remaining wholly focused on the customer, while also deepening our relationships with network operators, we will deliver superior returns to shareholders.'

Our objectives:
- To continue to expand our retail presence and gain further market share in our key markets
- To expand our Telecoms Service business through growth of our UK and French operations and the identification of similar opportunities in other countries where we have a significant retail presence
- To develop compelling residential fixed line and corporate mobile offerings for the UK market through integration with Opal Telecom

How?
- If we don't look after the customer, someone else will.
- Nothing is gained by winning an argument but losing a customer.
- Always deliver what we promise. If in doubt, under promise and over deliver.
- Always treat customers as we ourselves would like to be treated.
- The reputation of the whole company is in the hands of each individual.

Source: Carphone Warehouse website

1 What is the focus of Carphone Warehouse's aim

2 How does the company transla[t] aims into objectiv[e]

3 How is the busine[ss] aim put into prac[tice]

4 Why is its commitment to customer service likely to be the w[ay to] achieve its aims?

5 How is the busine[ss] relationship with [its] staff likely to influ[ence] its success?

Setting objectives

Businesses have one or more of several broad **objectives**.

- **PROFIT** Without profit, a business won't survive in the long run. The owners of a business need reward for taking a risk. It also provides resources for running and developing the business.

- **GROWTH** Many businesses are in search of growth. It is difficult to stand still because markets change, so most businesses aim to grow. Some small businesses are looking for a quiet life and are content to stay as they are.

- **DEVELOPING CORE CAPABILITIES** Some businesses identify their strengths, such as innovation, high quality staff or a good reputation, and build on them in order to develop new products or increase sales of existing ones.

- **DIVERSIFICATION** Developing new types of products makes a business more secure because if there is a downturn in one area, another may stay strong. Many supermarkets, for example, have started selling clothes and homewares.

- **SURVIVAL** The vast majority of businesses want to survive. It only becomes an objective when they are under threat.

The objectives are turned into a **strategy**, which sets out how the business will achieve its aims and objectives.

The diagram shows the decision-making process. As things rarely stand still, a business is constantly going through the cycle of asking questions about what it is doing in order to achieve its objectives. This may mean changing the strategy if objectives are not being achieved.

Communication plays a big part in any business. Ensuring that the staff are [aware] and understand the objectives and str[ategy] is an essential part of running a succe[ssful] business.

MAKING DECISIONS

KEY TERMS

Objectives are targets which can be measured and therefore help to drive activities.

Strategy shows how objectives will be met.

Long-term objectives are set for the next three to five years.

Strategic objectives are set to achieve the aims of the business over the next three to five years.

Short-term objectives are set for the next twelve months.

Tactical objectives are set by the departments in a business to achieve the strategic objectives.

Operational objectives are short-t[erm] practical objectives for managing d[ay to] day activities.

Core capabilities are the strength[s of a] business. They might be innovation, [or a pool] of highly skilled employees, for exa[mple.]

Aims → Objectives → Actions

A business usually has to have a clear idea of where it is going if it is to be successful. Carphone Warehouse has been at the forefront of the mobile phone business from the early days. Charles Dunstone, its founder, realised that the mobile phone had great potential for ordinary people at a time when phones were just for big business and the rich. He could, for example, help builders or plumbers stay in touch with their customers. He knew that if this market was to grow, there had to be clear, accessible information and helpful staff who wanted to ensure that each customer got the phone and contract which suited them best. This philosophy has underpinned everything since. It has led to profits and rapid growth.

Profit, in simple terms, means that revenue is greater than expenditure. In Business Studies, it is important to distinguish different sorts of profit because any confusion may mean that the wrong decisions are made.

IN THE KNOW

Short- or long-term objectives

LONG-TERM OBJECTIVES are set by a business for the next three to five years. These strategic objectives are set to meet the big targets of the business.

SHORT-TERM OBJECTIVES relate to the next six to twelve months. There are two types.

• Tactical objectives help to meet the strategic objectives. A business which wants to expand by opening new stores might set a tactical objective of opening ten new stores in the next year. Tactical objectives can be adapted to circumstances if the market for the product changes.

• Operational objectives refer to the practical running of the business. Completing the purchase of a new shop site in the next month or organising the grand opening are both operational objectives.

Setting these objectives involves the whole organisation. While strategic objectives are generally set at a very senior level, tactical and operational objectives are developed by departments within the business.

Wider objectives

Many businesses now consider a sense of responsibility to the community to be critical to success. Customers tend to expect a high standard from businesses and will reject the products of those that behave badly. Social responsibility and profit can be hard to separate so some consider this to be part of the objective of making a profit.

go to →  Find out more on page 168

www

www.carphonewarehouse.co.uk

www.tesco.co.uk

www.sainsburys.co.uk

Charities aim to make a surplus rather than a profit. The surplus is then used to further the activities of the charity. Public sector organisations are expected to break even. They can spend within the limits of the money they receive from the government and any revenue from activities.

Critical thinking

1 Some supermarkets are more successful than others. Compare two that you know and work out what their objectives are. Do you think they are achieving them? Is one more successful than the other? Why?

2 You can find out more about the companies from their websites. Their objectives are often set out in the front section of the Annual Report and Accounts. Have a look.

Next steps

1 What are the objectives of your school or college?

2 How are they put into practice?

3 Do you think they are effective?

Objectives in practice

starSTUDY

Carphone Warehouse's strategy circle

REPLACEMENT
Fashion, wear and tear and new technology all lead to phone replacement. The company anticipates that this will continue and develops its staff to support changing technology.

REPAIRS
The company repairs nearly 1 million phones each year. Almost half of these have been bought from other suppliers. Providing an excellent service attracts customers to come back for their next phone.

CONTENT
Developing technology means that customers are in search of content for their phones. The company aims to meet this demand.

ACCESSORIES
Accessories add to the customers' spending especially as new technology has increased the value of individual items. As phones become more sophisticated customers return to customise their phones.

DISTRIBUTION
More, high quality stores in prime locations. Develop web sales and telephone sales across Europe.

RANGE
Maintain wide range at good price. Size of the business gives strong buying power so customers have wide choice and latest phones.

INSURANCE
Maintain quick, efficient service for customers. 90% of claims are honoured so customers return. It adds value to customers and a steady profit stream.

SERVICES
Income stream comes from managing customers for networks and therefore protects the business from the volatile handsets market. It keeps the company in touch with the customer when contracts come to an end so gives access to the replacement market.

Strategy circle:
1. distribution
2. range
3. insurance
4. services
5. accessories
6. content
7. repairs
8. replacement

...for a better mobile life. all round

1 How does each of these elements of the strategy contribute to the company's profits?

2 How do they contribute to the company's objectives?

3 How do they help the company to grow?

4 What should departments be doing to achieve these objectives?

5 What do you think the company should do to make sure that the strategy works?

6 How will the company be able to measure whether it is being successful?

Strategy and success

Most businesses that are in search of success have worked out their strategy. Sometimes success just happens – but not often. It may be a chance event of a change of fashion but without a strategy, it is likely to be short lived. Barbour, a maker of country wear, suddenly became cool but quickly faded from the fashion scene. Burberry followed soon after.

Carphone Warehouse has developed a strategy. It wants to gain market share in the mobile phone market and expand its services both in the UK and elsewhere. Its strategy circle aims to do both.

It is based on attracting and keeping customers and therefore investment in employees is critical to its success.

Well-trained, motivated employees are much more likely to persuade customers to return. Knowing how a strategy will be turned into reality is very important.

The **culture** of the business will affect people's willingness to implement a strategy. Carphone Warehouse wants employees to have fun. It even runs to monthly sessions at the local bar or pub!

From objectives to strategy

IN THE KNOW

A business decides on its objectives and develops a strategy. To make things happen, the departments within the business must plan their contributions and make sure that they all fit together.

Meetings will be held to decide what must happen if the objectives are to be achieved. This may involve:

- research and development to update a product

- packaging design

- market research to test it in the market

- checking that the figures add up

- organising production

- an advertising campaign

- organising distribution.

The marketing department will have made set objectives for the product. They will include the target market, pricing policy and expected sales. The plan will be detailed – even setting targets for sales staff. A business that is **product oriented** rather than **market oriented** will produce the product they want to sell rather than looking at what the market wants. This can be a recipe for disaster, as the products may not sell.

STAYING ON TRACK

It is important that everyone is kept informed. People don't like being kept in the dark and it affects motivation. Communication within the business must be built into the strategy.

Monitoring at every stage must take place if deadlines are to be met and quality is to be maintained. If some products don't reach the market at the right moment, the expected profit will turn into a loss. Who wants Christmas trees in January?

Any strategy needs to be flexible. If the source of raw materials fails, another will have to be found. A plan that relies on distribution by train may have to change if the rail network is disrupted.

The process needs to be under continuous review and future plans will be amended in light of the lessons that have been learnt.

A positive culture

Developing a culture

Culture will vary from one business to another. There is not one perfect solution. The attitude of employees will be affected both by the nature of the work and the working environment, but the way people are treated can have the greatest impact.

Changing the culture of an organisation can be difficult. It often underpins everything that goes on. Without a positive culture, strategies are unlikely to succeed because employees are unlikely to persevere when things get difficult. Good leadership and careful management of people are most effective. There are many strategies for motivating people in different circumstances. Find out more on page 82.

Critical thinking

Your current objective is to get good grades in your AS studies.

1 Work out your strategy for doing this.

2 Which are tactical and which are operational?

3 Are there any factors that might mean you need to change the strategy?

4 What will the impact be?

5 What sort of culture keeps you working effectively?

Next steps

1 You often talk to people who work in businesses. It may be on a helpline or in person. Try to work out the culture of their organisation. You can often tell from their approach, friendliness, willingness and knowledge to solve your problem. Give them marks out of ten.

2 What persuades you to go back to a business?

KEY TERMS

The **culture** of a business covers the attitudes, customs and expectations of staff. It affects how they carry out their roles.

A **product-oriented** business focuses on the product rather than the customer.

A **market-oriented** business aims to make the product match what the customer wants.

Who influences strategy?

Specification Content

Conflicting and common aims of stakeholders – shareholders, employees, customers, suppliers, residents, the state; differing stakeholder and organisational objectives and priorities

starSTUDY Pizza Express

A Pizza Express restaurant

1 Who are Pizza Express's stakeholders?

2 What effect can each stakeholder have on the business?

3 What should Pizza Express do to keep its stakeholders happy?

4 How can government actions affect the business?

5 Why is it important to think ahead about changes that might be taking place in future?

Strategic influences

Pizza Express must keep a close eye on its stakeholders when it develops a strategy for the future. If it doesn't take their objectives into account, they may be dissatisfied with any changes and this may damage the business.

All businesses should be watching the objectives of stakeholders if they are to make successful progress. Government policy should also be taken into account because it will probably affect customers' spending powers either positively or negatively.

Critical thinking

1 Work out what gives each stakeholder power.

2 Think of two examples for each stakeholder – one showing a weak position and another showing a powerful position.

KEY TERMS

Pressure groups are groups of people with common interests who try to persuade business, government and others to take their views into account.

Stakeholder objectives and strategy

IN THE KNOW

OWNERS

The objectives of owners depend on the type of ownership. Sole traders, partners and people who run small private companies are looking for a return for their efforts and the risks involved. They may also be looking for growth and security. Strategy will obviously reflect the objectives of the people who run the business as they are the owners.

In larger private companies and public companies owners often do not run the business on a day-to-day basis. They risk their money through buying shares. These shareholders are mainly looking for a return on their investment. Without a good return, they will quickly sell their shares and buy ones in a different company that provides a better reward. Providing a reward for shareholders must therefore be part of the strategy.

CUSTOMERS

Customers buy things from businesses that meet their needs. Businesses want to keep existing customers and attract new ones so they have to take customers' objectives into account. A bad experience drives customers away – if there is an alternative. Many of the products we buy need aftercare and this has to be part of the strategy, although many businesses don't seem very good at it.

Customers can have considerable power, especially when they join together. The Consumers' Association is a **pressure group** that influences the activities of businesses and government. There are laws that determine how businesses behave towards customers.

go to → *page 161 for a reminder on customer protection*

A business's strategy may incorporate a range of actions which are designed to attract and keep customers in order to achieve other objectives. It might mean opening more stores, setting up an online service or making its customer service work more efficiently.

EMPLOYEES

People often have a variety of objectives when working. Everyone wants to be paid well but other factors are important too. Job satisfaction, training and opportunities are often on the list. An employee who feels well looked after is usually more effective than someone who feels that the employer doesn't really care.

go to → *page 82 for a reminder on motivation*

If a business wants to make the most of its staff, it must know how to motivate them and build this into the strategy. It must also make sure that its actions are within the law.

go to → *Find out more about employees and the law on page 159*

SUPPLIERS

Suppliers, like any other business, want to make a profit. They are dependent on the businesses, which are their customers, to pay on time. These customers are dependent on them to send supplies as requested. If there are only a few reliable suppliers, they will be in a more powerful situation. If there are many – or they are dealing with very powerful businesses – they will have less power.

Some businesses build a supplier relationship into their strategy. If a supplier feels that there is a close working relationship, he or she are more likely to work hard to send products quickly in a crisis, for example.

LENDERS AND CREDITORS

Businesses often depend on borrowing to keep going. It is therefore wise to make sure that lenders and creditors are considered in the strategy. Becoming a bad risk makes it harder and more expensive to borrow money in future. Creditors will want rapid settlement and won't give any leeway on payment time.

A lender or creditor can close down a business when no payments are received. This may not be the best way of dealing with the situation because the money may never be paid once the business ceases trading. It is often worth trying to negotiate an agreement, but in the end it may be impossible.

THE COMMUNITY

The community often has strong views when businesses want to make changes. A new factory may add to noise and traffic nuisance but on the other hand may provide more jobs. The development of an airport is almost always subject to heavy pressure from the community because of its impact on the community around it.

Many businesses work with the local community to produce schemes which reduce the impact on the neighbours. They also devise inducements to compensate. This might take the form of a new school or leisure centre incorporated into a development scheme.

go to → *page 162 for a reminder on social responsibility*

THE GOVERNMENT

The government always has objectives for the economy. These can affect businesses in all sorts of ways. Higher taxes mean people have less to spend and reduce a company's profits. Reducing unemployment may mean setting up schemes to help businesses train people. The government has organisations that aim to help businesses develop and make the most of government support.

A business needs to be aware of government objectives and strategy if it is to plan effectively. Changes in interest rates and taxes, including national insurance, can have a big effect on businesses, so they need to be alert to what might happen when they develop strategy.

go to → *Refresh your memory about government strategy to control the economy on page 142–147*

Getting the strategy right

Specification Content

SWOT analysis: purpose and method; application in a wide range of functional and integrated/corporate situations; value in gaining a full understanding of the market and the competitive forces within it

starSTUDY

The Crikey Moment

The crikey moment struck Terry Leahy, then the newly appointed marketing director of Tesco, when he was charged with finding out why the company had been hit so badly by the recession.

He commissioned masses of customer research and found that they had less money to spend because of the recession and felt that Tesco has let them down by being obsessed with copying Sainsbury's instead of meeting their needs.

From that moment, Tesco became a customer-led business. It stopped following the competition and followed the customer.

- It introduced the Value line which generated sales and goodwill.

- It set up the Clubcard, now regarded as a masterpiece of loyalty marketing.

- It developed smaller Express and Metro shops.

- It introduced petrol, clothing, music and, most important of all, financial services.

- It opened stores abroad.

Terry Leahy later became Chief Executive of Tesco.

Source: adapted from *The Sunday Times*, 16 November 2003

1 Why was Tesco in trouble?
2 What had it been trying to do?
3 Why was the customer research so important?
4 How did it affect Tesco's objectives?
5 What strategy resulted from the rethink?

A change of direction

Many businesses have had major turning points when they have rethought their objectives and developed new strategies. Such change is often associated with a crisis. By keeping a continuous eye on the company and the competitive environment in which it functions, such major changes should be unnecessary. To do this it needs to carry out an **internal audit** – by looking at the company itself – and an **external audit** which provides information about the environment beyond the business. SWOT and PEST-G are two methods a business can use to analyse itself and its position in the market.

SWOT analysis

go to → Go to page 17 for a reminder on how SWOT is used in a marketing department

SWOT stands for strengths, weaknesses, opportunities and threats. Strengths and weaknesses look at the internal aspects of the company and opportunities and threats are external. A business often uses brainstorming techniques to carry out a SWOT analysis and then uses it as the basis for developing or revising its objectives and strategy.

Strengths are successful aspects of the business which could be developed further, such as a strong brand name or a network of successful shops.	**Weaknesses** are unsuccessful aspects of the business that need to be sorted out. Customer service might be poor or a product range might be lagging behind competitors.
Opportunities are openings in the market for product development, for example. New technology might help the business to be more efficient or a new export market might be opening up.	**Threats** might come from competitors who are encroaching on the market or developing new products more quickly. Legislation to ban high-powered cars would affect some motor manufacturers, for example.

PEST-G

No business is insulated from the world, so it must be aware of external influences that will affect it. PEST-G reviews five aspects of interest to any business.

POLITICAL activity, in the form of changing legislation, affects all businesses. Each time the Chancellor sets the budget there are tax changes which alter how much consumers have to spend. Regulation affects all aspects of business. People's working conditions or pensions, consumer protection and safety can all have an impact on businesses in different ways.

ECONOMIC change affects businesses. As the economy moves through the business cycle, customers' spending patterns change and the employment market changes. As interest rates change to control the economy, borrowing becomes more or less expensive.

SOCIAL change alters the market. As the population grows older, people want to buy different things. The market for baby products shrinks. As more women are now at work, they buy more convenience foods.

TECHNOLOGICAL change can help a business produce more efficiently, make its products obsolete or increase competition because others can now enter the market cheaply.

GREEN issues can affect business behaviour. Businesses have to be seen to be environmentally friendly in order to maintain a good reputation. Pressure groups constantly monitor major companies to make sure that they are not breaking rules or carrying out damaging activities.

Making plans

A business will use the results of SWOT and PEST–G analysis to develop its strategic plan for the next 3–5 years. It may also use them on a continuous basis to review and revise existing plans.

When the strategic plans are in place, the departments within the business must make their own. These will be much more detailed because they will lay out the strategy and tactics to be used.

Reviewing plans

Once plans are up and running, reviewing the outcomes will show whether targets are being achieved. If they are working well, it is important to ask why and develop the plans to build on success. If they are not being met, some questions must be asked. The answers should then be fed into a revised plan.

What went wrong?

KEY TERMS

External audits survey the competitive environment in which the business functions.

Internal audits survey the way in which the business is working.

PEST-G is a way of evaluating the external environment. It stands for political, economic, social, technological and green issues.

Were the objectives realistic?
Could the departments achieve what senior management had in mind?

Did the plan work?
Could people achieve what was in the plan? Did they need more machinery? Did people need more training?

Can the culture cope?
Some businesses have a culture that is averse to change. It can be very hard to change so a business must decide whether to work on the culture or change the strategy.

Did objectives conflict?
Marketing wanted more products in the shops but logistics couldn't get them there.

Is anything beyond our control?
Changes take place that a business cannot control. It might be economic or technological, for example, but may mean a rethink of the strategy.

Critical thinking

1 What would Tesco have spotted if they had applied SWOT and PEST–G before the 'Crikey moment'?

2 Carry out a SWOT and PEST–G analysis for Marks and Spencer. What advice would you give them in light of your conclusions?

testing–testing

Objectives and strategy – assessment

Case study A

Daniel is a young chemist. He is fed up with the long hours for little personal reward. However, Daniel has thought up a brilliant idea that will use his chemist skills. Should he cash in his investments and use the money to set up his own small business? He desperately wanted to be more in control of his destiny.

His bright idea is to set up a business producing and selling recycled printer ink and laser cartridges. It's dead easy really. He would buy empty cartridges from customers for £1 and then clean and refill them using specialist equipment. He would then sell them for about £10–£13, which is way below the rate charged for selling the brand names in outlets like PC World. Research suggested that business clients preferred delivery. He would consider delivery to local businesses for an additional cost of £2.

Customers would gain by paying a lot less for their cartridges and feel that by recycling they are contributing to the environment.

He found an old grocery shop for rent near the main road about a mile out of the town centre with some limited on street parking.

Daniel worked out his start-up costs. They were £10,000 more than the £5000 he was able to put in. He reckoned he would be fairly accurate in estimating that monthly overheads would be around £3500 with variable costs as little as £3 an item, but would he get enough revenue to more than match this? He would certainly want to start making a profit in the second six months.

assessment questions

1 What might Daniel's business objectives be? **(2 marks)**

 Go to pages 86–89

2 What budget is required to cover Daniel's start-up costs and what might the start-up costs include? **(4 marks)**

 Use the figures given in the case study and use clues like old grocery store and specialist equipment to help form your answer.

3 What ownership would you recommend Daniel should consider? **(6 marks)**

 Remember it's a small business and Daniel wants to make his own decisions. You should also mention the drawbacks of the ownership you decide to recommend.

4 How can Daniel reduce the risk of failure? **(8 marks)**

 This is all about producing a business plan. Comment on what should go into his plan and why it is important to plan.

Case study B

Amazon delivers

There is a big new warehouse off the M1 at Junction 13 near Milton Keynes and it belongs to Amazon, a private limited company.

Amazon used to be a business, which existed entirely on the net. The original concept Jeff Bezos had was that Amazon would run the website and take the money, but book distributors would do the difficult stuff, namely hold the stock and handle the deliveries. Good thinking because you have none of the big overheads.

But the strategy has changed. Amazon has recognised that to provide a superb service to customers it is dangerous to rely on others. The warehouse is its new distribution centre.

The belief is that big rewards from e-commerce would be gained by businesses that succeeded in blending bricks-and-mortar expertise with the power of the net. Anyone can put up a website and accept credit cards, but it takes organisational skills to ensure that the goods are delivered on time. In Britain Tesco developed its online shopping business by doing it in-house via its own software and stores; John Lewis moved into cyberspace by acquiring a financially weak but technologically sound e-business called Buy.com.

If you want a simple test of whether a company knows what it is doing online, try this: can you find out what a product or service costs in three clicks or less?

Source: Adapted from The Observer, 11 May 2003

Amazon's mission

'Amazon seeks to be the world's most customer-centric company, a place where people can find and discover anything they might want to buy online. We are not a book, music, or toy company; we are a customer company.

Our mission requires us to innovate constantly while continuing to provide our customers with an unparalleled online shopping experience. We've been able to succeed in these categories by building superior technology and world-class fulfilment capabilities.

As we grow, we continue to promote small working teams and cross-functional teamwork. This team diversity encourages creativity, an open exchange of ideas across groups, and a respect for the challenges and trade-offs present across our business.

Our employees also have a stake in the success of the business. They are given the option to buy shares to promote a sense of ownership.'

The Royal Mail

The Royal Mail, a public sector organisation, has cut its annual losses to £611 million after its first improvement in trading performance for five years.

'We're largely still being pretty inefficient but this is the first time in five years the numbers have gone in the right direction,' chairman Allan Leighton told BBC Radio 4's Today programme. 'I'm pretty confident we'll be profitable this year.'

The Royal Mail is already one year into a three-year renewal programme designed to turn the company round.

Nearly 17,000 jobs have already gone and more than 30,000 will have been lost by 2005. The Royal Mail also proposes to close 3000 sub-post offices by 2005.

The number of days lost through strikes last year fell by 90%, making it the Royal Mail's best year for industrial relations in a decade. Postal workers have stopped the rot, claims the chairman.

The Royal Mail has targets to reduce the number of road journeys, experiment more with electric vans and use more gas as a fuel. When bikes are renewed the old ones are reconditioned and given to charities, which are linked with Africa. Post and passenger service buses are seen as an important lifeline to rural communities.

Source: BBC Radio 4, 22 May 2003

assessment questions

1 a Provide two pieces of evidence that suggests Amazon is a market-oriented business. **(2 marks)**

 b Is the Royal Mail market or product oriented? Explain why. **(2 marks)**

 It is useful to provide a brief definition and then say why you think some evidence in the case study supports this. For the second part, if the organisation is making a loss what does this suggest about it meeting customer needs?

2 What is an aim? Give an example using Amazon. **(2 marks)**

 Straightforward definition and application to the case study. Amazon's aim should be stated in one sentence.

3 What is an objective? What objectives did the Royal Mail set itself? **(4 marks)**

 Objectives need targets that can be measured. Look for some data that has improved. The data is usually a symptom that something is wrong, getting better or getting worse.

4 Suggest an objective that Amazon might set itself. **(2 marks)**

 Use something within the mission as an objective and then try to translate this into a target.

5 What is a strategy? How did strategy change in each organisation? **(6 marks)**

 Straightforward definition and application to the case study.

6 Construct a simple SWOT analysis for each organisation. **(8 marks)**

 The phrase 'simple SWOT' implies that you need only recognise one relevant example of each element of the SWOT to earn four marks. The last two marks are testing if you can relate your SWOT to the strategy adopted. You may decide that the strategy was either sensible or misguided given the SWOT. Both responses are acceptable so long as you back up your argument.

7 Contrast the culture differences between the two organisations. **(10 marks)**

 Go to pages 188–189

8 What is meant by social responsibility? To what extent is the Royal Mail meeting the social objectives of its customers, the community and its owners? **(8 marks)**

A clear definition is worth 2 marks so the bulk of your answer asks you to recognise some social objectives from the evidence that the Royal Mail claims to be meeting, but also look for evidence to suggest it is not always a positive picture. Try to conclude as to why the customer as a stakeholder will not always be satisfied.

End of Module 3 assessment

AQA Business Studies Unit 3

Summer 2003

- Time allowed 1 hour
- These questions are based on the pre-issued case study on pages 126–133.
- Where appropriate, use examples from the case study to support your answers.

Answer all questions

1 Outline two significant strengths in the way Lily and Seyi started up Black Looks Ltd (see Sections A and B). **(6 marks)**

2 Analyse whether C.C. plc's strategy for launching the range of cosmetics and toiletries should be regarded as fair or unfair competition (see Section G). **(8 marks)**

3 Discuss the possible effect on Black Looks Ltd of exchange rate changes proving to be in line with the minimum figures forecast by City economists. **(15 marks)**

4 Seyi's long-term hope is to turn the business into a public limited company. Explain how Black Looks Ltd might benefit from this. **(6 marks)**

5 Some experts believe that there is an inevitable conflict between the aims of shareholders and those of the other stakeholders. To what extent did this prove true in this case? **(15 marks)**

Assessment answers

Marketing: Chester Zoo

1 In what ways does the zoo's marketing objectives help support its overall objectives? (4 marks)

The zoo's marketing objectives are to increase the number of visitors and what they spend. This will increase its revenues overall and the zoo will be able to spend more on supporting and promoting conservation. If marketing succeeds in getting more to attend during slack months it will help the zoo to ease its cash flow especially since it will have high overhead costs (see Finance section).

2 In what ways is the zoo both customer and product oriented? (4 marks)

By supporting conservation of animals and plants Chester Zoo must be product oriented. However, the zoo's main source of income is through its customers and if their needs are catered for they will continue to visit the zoo and spend. Its market research activities focus on providing high standards of care and high quality visitor facilities that cater for all ages.

3 Discuss two promotional methods and strategies that might be suitable for the zoo to use to encourage new customers. What methods might be suitable to encourage repeat customers? (8 marks)

The zoo spent £670,000 on advertising and promotion and much of this was to encourage new customers or repeat customers. Encouraging new customers requires above the line direct advertising. Most visitors to the zoo have heard about it through television adverts and by promotion in regional papers. To be cost effective the adverts will start around April in time for Easter and be aimed at media watched or read by socio-economic grouping C1 and C2 who make up 70% of visitors. It is best to tempt customers to repeat a visit while they are in the zoo. This is point of sales promotion.
Below the line advertising may be the more effective method. For example, leaflets handed out may offer discount vouchers and visitors may be encouraged to enter a prize competition. The name and address included will allow direct marketing through mail shots.

4 What is market segmentation? How and why might the zoo segment its market? (4 marks)

Market segmentation is when different types of customers are identified. Chester Zoo might try matching customer groups to different products on offer thereby finding new market niches. For example, the zoo offers conference facilities especially in winter when there are fewer traditional visitors. The Halloween evening seems to be targeted at families with teenage children and the Safari is perhaps aimed at work social outings.

5 Explain two internal and two external factors that have influenced the rate of growth of customers to the zoo. (6 marks)

An internal factor would be the investment in new and better facilities to attract the public. Another might be an improvement to the quality of customer care. Both these should lead to an increase in demand. External factors might include the general rise in living standards, but a recession or an external shock such as the foot-and-mouth outbreak can have a negative effect, such as new competitors from theme parks. The marketing department needs to be aware of all this by undertaking market research and must liaise with other departments so that everybody is working towards meeting the overall objectives.

6 Assume a new marketing campaign costs £20,000 and manages to bring in an extra 3000 adults. Would it be regarded as successful? (4 marks)

The extra 3000 adults have an average spend of £12.39, which means extra revenue of around £37,000. This is £17,000 above the marketing budget. However, extra visitors will add extra costs, such as the food and beverages they buy. If these are a lot less than £17,000 then the campaign may be viewed as successful. The marketing campaign is adding value by persuading more customers to go to the zoo.

7 Why is market research important to the zoo? (4 marks)

Market research provides the zoo with essential information about how it is doing and how its competitors are performing. It also provides useful information about past and current trends on people's spending habits and these can be used to forecast future trends. The information gathered can be used to help make more informed decisions about matters such as investment, pricing and promotion.

8 How might it best carry out its research? (6 marks)

Like many other organisations, Chester Zoo targets research at likely customers. Sampling too few people will not produce accurate results. However, consulting too many can make it very expensive. The zoo employs marketing consultants to help make sure the research is sound. The primary research has a confidence level of 96%. It means the data is reliable in that it will be right 96 times out of 100. This type of research involves finding out information tailor-made to the business's needs, such as what the zoo visitors feel about the facilities, where they come from, their ages, how long they stayed and what were their likes and dislikes. Secondary research collects together information that already exists. The zoo will be interested in finding out what people spend their money on and probably collect this electronically from the tills. It will also add up the number of visitors each day to provide the number of visitors per month. Other secondary sources might lie outside the organisation. Chester Zoo will want to know what its competitors charge and what facilities they offer to the customers. It will also want to know readership socio-economic groups for newspapers so it could choose the most appropriate to advertise in. Government statistics can provide useful information on spending trends as can market intelligence reports.

9 Analyse the results of past market research. (8 marks)

The majority of visitors, some 70%, are from the C1 and C2 socio-economic grouping made up of clerical, administration and manual skilled type workers. About 40% of visitors are under 15 and these will most likely be accompanied by parents or grandparents (11%) of visitors. More detail on the breakdown of the average number in a family and the relationship between younger and older members would provide a more complete picture.

Over two-thirds believe their visit was very good value or excellent value and this may explain why over 60% of visitors return within 3 years. However, only 13% return in the same year and improvements to this figure might be a target for the marketing department.

The promotion techniques seem successful, as 54% have heard about the zoo's promotion. However, the zoo still might aim to increase this figure. Television is the most effective way of reaching potential customers but it is expensive and the reason why some other methods might be ineffective is because little effort is made. More detailed research would help provide the real reasons here. The monthly attendance figures are no surprise, largely reflecting the traditional leisure peaks starting at Easter and slowing down in September. The worst months are in winter.

10 Why has the zoo been able to regularly raise its prices over the past 12 years? (8 marks)

Chester Zoo has increased prices from £5 to £11 in 12 years. This significant increase cannot be wholly explained by inflation. Despite these increases Chester Zoo has seen an overall rise in visitor numbers. How can this be?

The zoo has added value through effective promotion. This reinforces its good reputation and boosts demand. People also have higher incomes and it is more fashionable to spend this on leisure activities. If the percentage change in demand has been higher than the percentage change in income the zoo will be highly income elastic. It is good news when incomes rise, but bad news if there is a recession. The numbers of visitors to the zoo fell between 1990 and 1992, which was a time of recession in the UK economy. However, the trend continued downward after 1992 even when there was economic growth. During this period the zoo raised prices from £5 to £7. Prices had increased by 40% when overall inflation levels were less than 13%. A rise in prices of 27% resulted in only a small percentage drop in demand of less than 2%, making it highly price inelastic.

This means that the zoo's total revenues will rise. Effective promotion is one factor that may explain this, because it makes alternatives to a visit to Chester Zoo seem inferior. The promotion, however, must be combined with a positive customer experience and the zoo has probably used the increase in revenues to invest in facilities such as the glass-sided penguin-pool, the Twilight Zone bat cave, the orang-utan breeding centre and the Tropical Realms.

Chester Zoo, however, must be careful about raising prices because as prices rise so demand becomes more price elastic. It may have reached this point, since a recent 10% discount increased revenues by £25,000 suggesting that discounting works because lowering prices is price elastic. It has sensibly decided to become more scientific about its price rises.

11 Produce and justify a marketing plan to increase customers who might be attracted to an event outside normal zoo hours. How might such a plan be monitored? (10 marks)

The product life cycle is seasonal in nature with many more spring and summer visitors than during other seasons. The trend over the years indicates that the zoo is either in the late growth stage or early maturity. Chester Zoo's marketing plans should meet its marketing objectives. Namely, to encourage customers to come back, get new visitors, spread them more evenly over the whole season, raise awareness of the zoo's work in conservation and sell more food, drink and souvenirs. For this to happen the zoo will need to develop a product portfolio and this means experimenting with different events aimed at different market segments.

Such a niche market might be to aim at various festival dates such as organising a Halloween event. Tickets are priced higher than the normal entrance fee as there is a disco and supper so they will be buying more food and drink. The price of tickets could be contribution pricing, as the fixed costs of the zoo will be accounted for in the normal entrance price. The shop will have a Halloween theme to its products. Past experience will inform the purchasing department of what to order. The creepy happenings might easily be linked to bats and a quiz may provide educational information on conservation, which then meets another objective. Halloween is held during an unseasonable period and this should help bring in extra cash. However, promotion can be a problem as it is a period when the zoo spends less on this. The promotion could be niche marketing by targeting members through mail shots. Advertising on the website and making leaflets available within the zoo during the summer period might bring in a few more customers. This may attract existing customers who are likely to be those most interested in the event. To attract new customers the zoo might advertise locally in the press and on radio. At the very least it will raise brand awareness.

Monitoring such a plan would involve setting targets for the number of tickets sold at various times. This can be checked and related to the promotional activities especially if these activities are lagged. That way the effectiveness of each type of promotion can be assessed especially as each promotion will have a budget attached. The information gathered can then be used to help inform marketing decisions for future similar events.

Finance: The Carpet Barn

Part A

1 What is the purpose of budgets? How might The Carpet Barn have reduced the budget for start-up? (4 marks)

A budget is a financial plan linked to the business objectives. It helps to make sure that money is allocated sensibly and it should support the objectives. For example, a start-up budget is like a shopping list, looking at all the expenditure required to get a business going. The Carpet Barn may believe its shopping list is too expensive and could seek to cut this down by trying to arrange to pay for the computer system in instalments. This would save £4000 initially but may cost more in the long run. The owners could consider buying a cheaper van for less than £2000, but it may prove to be unreliable. The owners could go for cheaper shop fitments, saving perhaps £1000, although this may look tacky. They may decide that cutting the start-up budget will not be worth the problems this may cause and therefore they would need to look at raising more finance.

2 Name two variable costs for this business. (2 marks)

The cost of carpets is variable because they are dependent on sales as is the cost of fitting the carpets.

3 Explain two types of fixed costs faced by The Carpet Barn. (2 marks)

The Carpet Barn pays its owners a salary and this has been fixed for the year. The business will have to pay rent and business rates irrespective of the amount of carpets it sells.

4 What is the contribution made by each sale? What is the relationship between contribution and profit? (4 marks)

The contribution is the sales price minus the variable costs or £500 − £375 = £125. This means each carpet sale contributes £125 towards covering the fixed costs of the business. Once the fixed costs have been covered then the contribution from each sale could then be regarded as profit.

5 Calculate the break-even point. (4 marks)

For The Carpet Barn the break-even point is the amount of sales per month that will neither give it a loss or a profit. It is the fixed costs divided by the contribution. That is, £6250 divided by £125 = 50. The Carpet Barn would need to make 50 sales per month to break even.

6 What was the forecast margin of safety? (2 marks)

The projected sales were 60 per month and the break-even 50 per month giving a small margin of safety of 10 sales per month.

7 What would be the average overhead if sales were 40, 50 and 60 a month? (2 marks)

Monthly overhead	Sales per month		Average overhead
£6,250	40	=	£156.25
£6,250	50	=	£125.00
£6,250	60	=	£104.17

The average overhead diminishes with increased sales. The rate of decrease gets less.

8 Use the data in the case study to explain the difference between profit and cash flow. (6 marks)

Cash flow is the movement of cash in and out of the business. For example, in the cash flow forecast for June, The Carpet Barn expected to receive £30,000 from sales and pay out £28,750. Although this would be a positive net cash flow of £1250 it would be more than swamped by the £3750 owed from May when the shop was fitted out and a van purchased. Murray would need to arrange an overdraft with the bank to cover the shortfall estimated to be £2500. Cash payments are made for materials, wages and other costs. They are often paid out before cash comes in from sales. A business like The Carpet Barn needs working capital to pay these bills. In this sense a business may have a large order book that will turn in profits but have a cash deficit. The projected profit for the first 6 months of trading is £7500, but more cash flows out in the first 3 months than comes in from sales and other sources. Clearly if cash flow is negative all the time then costs will be higher than revenues and the business will make a loss.

Part B

1 In which months did The Carpet Barn need to draw on its overdraft facility? (2 marks)

The forecast suggested a shortfall of cash in the first three months, but in reality the business was short in all six months.

2 What happened to the overall budgets on expenditure and revenue over the first 6 months of trading? What might have caused the difference between the budget forecast and the actual performance? (6 marks)

The owners' funds and bank loan remained as forecast. The turnover was a significant £30,000 or 20% down on the forecast. This may have been caused by the owners overestimating demand especially in the light of national data, indicating a fall in the number of carpets sold. The start-up costs were as predicted, as were the overheads. Since sales were down so was the purchase of new stock and the direct costs, as less carpets were fitted. Hence total payments were down by just over £24,000.

3 Evaluate various options open to Murray and Ellen when the bank refused to give them the entire loan they required. (10 marks)

They could have interpreted the bank's response as a signal to give up especially when the bank imposed personal liability conditions on the loan. However, they would stand to lose much of their investment as the stock held would not be valued much if a quick sale had to be made and the shop fittings would not command a high price. They had also invested considerable time already in getting the business going. The diversification seemed logical given the growing demand for laminate flooring. Murray would be able to fit these as well as carpets. However, having made the decision to go ahead they would need to cut back expenditure to reduce their exposure to the bank.

This might mean looking closely at cutting the cost of refitting out the shop, plus ordering less stock. Perhaps Murray could use his communication skills to arrange two months' trade credit with suppliers, but they may be reluctant to give any credit since the business is only a few months old.

They could cut overheads by taking a drop in salary, but this is demotivating.

They might demand a bigger deposit from customers or at least quicker payment. However, this could reduce demand. Finally, they could put more of their savings into the business or invite others to become owners, but it may be difficult to persuade them given that the business made a £2000 loss in the first 6 months of trading.

4 The decision Murray and Ellen needed to make after 6 months was whether or not to cease trading. Comment on their decision to carry on. (12 marks)

Murray and Ellen have put in considerable effort and some £6000 each of their personal savings into this venture. However, the business has made a loss of £2000 in the first 6 months. They are liable to pay the creditors.

The bank's loan was granted only on the basis that, as a final resort, they would have to sell their personal assets to make good the sums owed. In short, they have unlimited liability for the debts they incur.

Currently they have an overdraft with the bank of £3000 and they owe their creditors (suppliers) £11,000. On top

of this they have a long-term loan of £7000 making the total short- and long-term debt £10,000. However, their debtors owe them £22,000, which should cover their creditors' demands.

If they ceased trading they would be able to sell their assets. They might receive only a portion of the value of the fixed assets and the stock. They would stand to lose some of their original investment. If they carried on trading and things got worse they would remain liable for further debts.

With the decline in carpet sales nationally it would seem difficult other than to perhaps break even. They could earn a similar salary by working for someone else. Given these circumstances I would recommend ceasing trading. However, if they were really determined and liked being their own bosses I would give them another year, so long as they diversified their business to include laminate flooring. They would only need a few more customers per month to be successful. Murray could use his skills as a carpet fitter to lay laminate flooring. The Carpet Barn would need to change its name, perhaps to The Carpet and Flooring Barn and revised objectives and budgets would need to be made.

5 Why was it useful to divide the business into two profit centres? (2 marks)

This way Murray could monitor which sector of the business was performing the best and which the worst. It would support decision-making.

6 Complete the variance table. State what was favourable and what was adverse. Comment on the allocation of overheads. (6 marks)

It looks as though carpets have outperformed laminate flooring because they made a profit and the laminate flooring a loss. However, without the latter the overhead allocated to carpets would have been much higher. It may have been more realistic to allocate overheads as a percentage of the sales. This would roughly be an extra £5000 on overheads for carpets and a drop of £5000 on laminate flooring. Both would then be making a similar level of profit.

		Second 6 months of trading in £s			
		Budget	Actual	Variance	
Carpets	Revenue	150,000	130,000	−20,000	Adverse
	Direct cost	112,500	97,500	−15,000	Favourable
	Overhead allocation	24,000	25,000	1,000	Adverse
	Profit	13,500	7,500	−6,000	Adverse
Laminate flooring	Revenue	75,000	90,000	15,000	Favourable
	Direct cost	56,250	67,500	11,250	Adverse
	Overhead allocation	24,000	25,000	1,000	Adverse
	Profit	−5,250	−2,500	2,750	Favourable
Total	Revenue	225,000	220,000	−5,000	Adverse
	Direct cost	168,750	165,000	−3,750	Favourable
	Overhead allocation	48,000	50,000	2,000	Adverse
	Profit	8,250	5,000	−3,250	Adverse

End of Module 1 assessment

Unit 1: Summer 2003

Question 1

a What is meant by the term 'budget'? (2 marks)

> A budget is a financial plan linked to the business's objectives. Penman Ltd had anticipated gaining a certain amount of sales revenue from its new publication, but sales were lower than expected. The budget was too optimistic.

> *This answer relates well to the case study.*

b (i) How many copies of Vitality would have to be sold in the year from July 2003 for the magazine to break even? (5 marks)

> The variable costs per unit can be calculated by dividing the projected variable costs (£550,000) by the projected sales (500,000). This calculates out to £1.10 per magazine. The contribution is the price minus the variable cost per magazine. This becomes £2.50 − £1.10, which means each magazine sold contributes £1.40 towards covering fixed costs. Fixed costs of £602,000 divided by the contribution £1.40 = the break-even sales figure = 602,000/1.40 = 430,000, so Penman Ltd would need to sell 430,000 magazines to break even.

> *This is an excellent answer as it demonstrates a good understanding of break even and the calculations are correct. It also shows the methodology, so that even if there was one error in the calculation it could earn 4 marks.*

b (ii) If sales in the year from July 2003 were actually 600,000, what level of profit would Vitality earn? [Assume that fixed costs and variable costs per unit are unchanged.] (3 marks)

> Since 430,000 were needed to break even, the contribution of any sales beyond this would go towards profit. Therefore profit = 170,000 × £1.40 = £238,000.

> *The answer could also be calculated by working out sales revenue then calculating total costs. Sales revenue is 600,000 × £2.50 = £1,500,000.*
> *Costs are the total variable costs, 600,000 × £1.10 = £660,000, added to the total fixed costs of £602,000 giving a combined total of £1,262,000.*
> *Profit = £1,500,000 − £1,262,000 = £238,000.*

c Analyse one reason why Penman Ltd should draw up a cash flow forecast for Vitality for next year. (6 marks)

> By producing a cash flow forecast, Penman Ltd can calculate periods when it thinks it might have a cash surplus and periods when it is likely to have a shortfall of cash. It can then make plans to cover this, either from other budgets within the business or from arranging an overdraft with the bank.

> *This is fine, but would benefit from being related to the case study. For example, reference could be made to what type of costs it may incur, such as printing and paying staff to produce the articles. The evidence suggested there were high start-up costs.*
> *On the money coming in side, sales figures are likely to be sluggish at the start and it might be difficult to sell advertising space if sales are low. However, the annual subscription would bring in necessary working capital to help cover this period.*

d Discuss the case for and against Penman Ltd's management team deciding to publish Vitality for a second year. (9 marks)

> Penman Ltd has invested a considerable amount of time and money in this project and recent sales have been more promising. If this trend continues it is likely to break even some time within the next financial year and then go into profit with a forecast of £98,000. The product is still in the growth stage of the product life cycle.
> On the other hand, £400,000 is a significant loss and may indicate that the competition from the larger publishers is too strong. The business will yet again have to find more working capital. The project has not been a success and the last sales budget forecast was way out.

> *The argument is two sided, but it should come to a conclusion even if it was to comment that further information was required, such as data on monthly sales. What would happen if the competition releases new titles aimed at the same market segment?*

Question 2

a Distinguish between 'market share' and 'market size'. (4 marks)

> The size of the market is the total value of the sales of all the businesses in that market area whereas the market share is the percentage of that market that one business has.

> *Try to apply the terms to the case study where appropriate. In this case Mars and Nestlé have about 19% each of the market for snack purchases which is behind Cadbury's, the market leader.*

b Mars bars have been a cash cow for many years. Explain one benefit the company may have received as a result of this. (3 marks)

> A cash cow is part of a company's product portfolio. The Mars bar is a cash cow because it has low market growth, but a high market share. The company will need to milk this cash cow to provide money for investment for newer products, some of which may turn into stars like its competitor, Nestlé, with Chunky KitKats.

> *As asked, one benefit was explained and then applied to the case study. Alternatively the answer could have considered cash cows as:*
> *· A steady source of profit*
> *· Ones that require less promotion*
> *· A brand that could be used to promote related products, e.g. Mars ice cream bars.*

c Examine two problems Mars might have faced as a result of the large fall in sales of Mars bars in 2001. (8 marks)

A large fall in sales is likely to affect the profitability and the cash flow of the company especially since Mars was a cash cow. The profitability of the company would fall. There would be a drop in sales revenue because less bars were sold. In addition, if overheads remain the same it would also make less profit per bar sold.

If the drop in sales was unexpected then stocks may be too high and Mars would be less likely to have had a chance to reduce costs. As a consequence, roughly the same amount of cash is going out of the business as before, but less cash is coming in.

The first paragraph outlines the two problems and looks more closely at profitability. It might have mentioned that shareholders would not be happy with a decline in profitability as they may receive lower dividends and the share price might fall.

Another problem that might arise from the fall in sales would be a drop in market share and therefore the reputation of the company.

d Mars decided not to reduce prices as part of the new marketing strategy for Mars bars. Evaluate the case for and against this decision. (10 marks)

There are good reasons for not reducing prices. First, a few major producers dominate this market and they tend to compete on non-price factors. Experience has shown that dropping your prices would encourage competitors to follow suit making all sellers worse off. It is important for Mars to avoid a price war. Secondly, the reason for a fall in sales is not down to price, but down to the product not being attractive to the main market segment, which comprises females.

Perhaps Mars should consider reducing prices as sales have dropped. Impulse buyers who make up 66% of all purchases are more likely to be influenced by price once they get into the shop. If the bars were price elastic then a reduction in price would lead to an increase in the company's revenue as well as helping increase market share.

Price would be only one part of the strategy to tempt more females. Mars also needs to consider better promotion and providing a product more suitable to female wants that is made available at places convenient to them. Mars will also have available data on the price elasticity of its products. Given that it does not intend to reduce prices this suggests that Mars is relatively price inelastic, perhaps due to its strong brand image.

People in organisations: more nurses needed

1 What do you understand by the terms recruitment and retention? (2 marks)

Recruitment is the process of identifying the need for new employees through to attracting applicants and finally selecting the best ones for the vacancies.
Retention is keeping the employees with your business.

2 What is workforce planning and why is it important in a large organisation like the NHS? (4 marks)

Large organisations usually employ many people in a range of specialist posts, all of which are necessary to help them meet their objectives. It is essential that such organisations estimate the need for new recruits in the face of changes in demand and of changes in levels of staff turnover. For instance, there is a growing demand for increased healthcare because we are an ageing population at a time when staff turnover has increased. Workforce planning does not stop here. It will account for how organisations cater for new technologies and new objectives. People will then require training to support them in undertaking new tasks. For example, more sophisticated operations demand different styles of nursing care.

3 What might explain the high labour turnover in the past and what has been proposed to reduce it? To what extent do you believe these proposals will be sufficient? (12 marks)

High labour turnover may be the norm for nurses in the NHS as many of them are women who take a career break to raise families. However, if working conditions worsen or pay levels are uncompetitive with other jobs nurses will leave for reasons of dissatisfaction. One worry the government has is losing experienced highly skilled nurses. The pay restructuring is designed to reward these employees more than others. In this way it is targeting the key shortage areas with greater financial rewards. High pay awards for all nurses would cost the NHS too much and mean that there would be less money available for equipment and medicines. It is difficult to predict how successful this measure would be without further information, such as detailed labour turnover figures and data on the changes in those applying for training. The government may well need to take note of the RCN research on stress and poor morale. Perhaps the NHS needs to ensure it is providing Herzberg's hygiene factors, such as having better staffroom areas, and more crèche facilities. The new pay structure may provide some motivators if it encourages achievement by giving skilled staff more responsibility and a wider range of tasks through job enlargement and multi-skilling. The induction process may need to be improved to make new staff more settled in such big organisations. Perhaps each new nurse should be attached to a mentor who could provide informal support.

People in organisations: Amazon.co.uk

1 Explain the stages in the recruitment process described by Amazon in the article above. (4 marks)

Determine the need for posts and establish the qualities and skills it feels important for the jobs. Inform the public of these positions through the Internet. Invite them to apply. Undertake some form of shortlisting and invite those shortlisted for interviews.

2 What are the advantages of Amazon using this system? (4 marks)

The Internet is a quick, cheap and easy way of reaching a large audience. Phone interviews would be used as an additional way to the CV to shortlist further. They would quickly inform Amazon about some of the interpersonal skills of the applicants. This may be sufficient for more junior positions. Both actions help keep the costs of recruitment down which may be significant if the business is growing rapidly or if the labour turnover is high.

3 Recommend other methods Amazon might use to let potential applicants know about vacancies. (6 marks)

It is highly unlikely that this business will solely use the Internet to let potential applicants know, because it would not reach a wide enough audience and this in turn would narrow the field it has for selection. It may be looking to promote internally for some positions. This rewards current employees and you know you are recruiting people who are already used to working towards your culture and objectives. Hence weekly newsletters or an employment notice board would be necessary. A second measure is to advertise in the media locally either on radio or in the local newspaper. This will cost money but it is targeted at people who live within commuting distance. It is free to advertise in the local job centres and many of those attracted by this method would be unemployed and ready to work. For more specialist work commanding higher salaries the company may advertise in professional magazines or newspapers. These employees are more prepared to move in order to get the job. The methods chosen are likely to be cost effective and meet the relative urgency of the appointment.

4 How does Amazon structure the company? (6 marks)

Amazon structures its business by its product or services such as books, electrical and photo departments and also by functional departments such as customer care, finance and other administrative posts. It attempts to get staff to work in small teams and interestingly has some teams that are cross-functional allowing employees to meet others with different experiences. Amazon believes this allows for creative approaches and improves performance. It is a little like a matrix approach.
In addition all employees have to spend some time in the distribution centre, especially during busy periods, making sure they understand the key objective of the business of getting products to customers on time.

5 Evaluate the methods Amazon uses to motivate its employees. (10 marks)

Amazon's financial incentives to motivate its employees include share options and fringe benefits. By offering shares in the business Amazon is both rewarding employees and giving them a small stake and incentive in the company. If the company performs well the share price will rise. However, share prices could fall and there is nothing to stop people selling their shares. Amazon also offers a range of fringe benefits including life and medical insurance after 3 months' service. Amazon may have reached a good deal with BUPA if most of the employees

are young because they are less likely to claim. This benefit will be well received by employees as it demonstrates the company cares about the individual. Its non-financial incentives to motivate link to the human relations approach to motivation. First, its cross-functional team approach suggests parallels with motivators such as being recognised for your work and feeling a sense of achievement. It is a type of job enrichment since some of the tasks and challenges given will be beyond the employee's current experience. Such empowerment is indicated in the company's leadership style that encourages learning in an accountable environment with ideas being encouraged and rewarded. This approach may help to encourage employees to meet their self-esteem needs by recognising achievement and providing promotion and responsibility. In this sense it has used Maslow's hierarchy of needs to improve motivation. Amazon must make sure its words are put into practice, by employing the right type of managers during the recruitment process and by undertaking surveys of its workers to see if they share the views put forward by its website. It could also check to see if there are fewer customer complaints.

People in organisations: Co-operative Bank

1 State one 'person specification' and one aspect of the 'job description' associated with this job. (2 marks)

Person specification looks at the skills and qualities necessary for the post. The skills can be taught in training. Working in a team and good communication skills seem essential for this post.
The job description tells you what the job involves, including your responsibilities such as dealing with customers on a face-to-face basis.

2 Why might the bank be using the phone to shortlist rather than wait for written applications? (4 marks)

Using the phone lessens the recruitment costs, as there is less administration required. It also allows the human resources department to shortlist or filter applicants quickly. It is unlikely that anyone will get through to the next stage of recruitment if they don't have the right phone manner and don't show a good level of enthusiasm. Many large firms are using this system for more junior positions.

3 Define the terms flat organisation structure and flexible employees. (4 marks)

A flat organisation structure has few levels within the organisation structure and a wide span of control where a manager is directly responsible for a large number of employees in the level of the hierarchy below.
Flexible employees can adapt to changing circumstances. They can change tasks and times they work to meet the needs of the business.

4 Evaluate the benefits and drawbacks of a flat structure to an organisation like the Co-operative Bank. (12 marks)

The flat structure fits in with the ethos and culture of the bank. It means less emphasis is placed on supervision and more on teamwork. It requires the company to adopt a more democratic approach to management so that employees feel comfortable and empowered by working in a team. The Co-operative Bank is adopting some of Herzberg's motivators such as recognition of efforts and giving responsibility. The bank believes these motivators help the business to reach its objectives and improve the quality of work as well as encouraging a culture of change and flexible workforce.

To help further empower its employees the bank pays close attention to finding out the opinions of its employees on a regular basis for all issues. This approach links well with the human resources management ideas put forward by Mayo. Staff training on the democratic approach and delegation will need to be a priority for all managers. With this in place the flat structure will improve communications and employees will feel more equal with their contributions valued. The reduction in bureaucracy will allow more time for discussion. Decisions will be based upon the expertise of the team as a whole.

One problem with flat structures is that there is less scope for promotion as there are fewer levels in the hierarchy and a much wider span of control for the head of teams to co-ordinate. This could demotivate staff. However the bank has other motivators in place. Teams are set up to undertake specific project work. Employees become experts in their teams. They are given responsibility and power to come up with solutions that take the company forward and enrich the employees' experiences. This continuous improvement supports the Kaizen principle. It seems that the Co-operative Bank places a high value on job enrichment. There must be leaders within the team who have overall responsibility and there should be clear guidelines otherwise the approach could be laissez-faire and lead to decisions being made that did not fit comfortably in with the culture of the business. The democratic approach is not suitable for all types of worker and so it would pay the Co-operative Bank to look for the more flexible worker when recruiting new staff. The bank would be highly unlikely to recruit an autocratic manager who is paid according to meeting personal targets. Such a system would make the manager put pressure on subordinates to perform and go right against the culture of this business.

Operations management: Hankins

1 What is meant by the terms JIT stock control system and cell production? (4 marks)

JIT or Just-in-Time stock control system attempts to keep the costs of holding raw materials, work in progress and finished stock to a minimum by carefully scheduling the flow of materials through the production process. Materials and components are made available just when they are needed. It needs a reliable ordering system. Cell production uses teams of multi-skilled employees who work together to complete a self-contained unit of production. Each cell becomes a supplier for the next cell and is a customer of the previous one. In this way it can link in with JIT.

2 Explain how Hankins organises its production. What are the advantages and disadvantages for Hankins of operating in this way? (6 marks)

Hankins probably has two types of production. For bespoke or individual orders it uses job production. Although more expensive it can motivate Hankins' employees as they can use their skills to produce high quality furniture. Customers are prepared to pay higher prices for unique, quality-made products.

To supply the components to Millers and other businesses the firm will most likely use batch production as it produces a large number each of a small range of products. Once the machines have been set up this is a cheap method of production for volume runs. It may not motivate employees so much, but allows Hankins to employ people with lower skills. Due to lower prices there is a higher demand for this type of work reflected by it representing 80% of Hankins' business revenue.

3 Why does Hankins keep a large buffer stock? What problems might Hankins face in keeping such a high level of stocks? (8 marks)

Buffer stock represents the minimum level of stocks required by the business. This seems high for Hankins, but it likes to have enough stock in to start a job immediately an order comes in. It reduces the lead-time between the order being made and delivered. Hankins believes it gains a competitive advantage from this. However, holding large amounts of stock can cause a number of problems. Even with stock rotation (using oldest stock first) some of the stock of wood is likely to warp over time especially if stored under damp conditions. Also of significance are the costs of holding such a large buffer stock. It ties up working capital in having a large stock area full of stock. This can lead to cash flow problems.

4 What comparisons can you make about the size and productivity of Hankins and its main customer, Millers (see table)? (6 marks)

Hankins is a much smaller business than Millers. Its sales revenue of £4 million a year is 5% of that of Millers (£4m / £80) × 100. Each employee worker in Millers generates £200,000 of sales revenue compared with £80,000 per employee in Hankins. That is 2.5 times as much. Millers also has a higher investment in capital expenditure. Each £ of capital at Millers generates £4 of sales compared with £2 for Hankins. This might be explained by economies of scale or that Millers' stock purchases represent a greater proportion of sales than Hankins'.

5 Explain the advantages Millers has by being bigger. How does Hankins manage to survive despite it being small? (8 marks)

A bigger business can gain considerable advantage from economies of scale. This is when the unit costs fall as output increases. It means the business has become more efficient and productive. Lower unit costs means the business can charge lower prices and this boosts demand. By being bigger Millers can buy in bulk and negotiate bigger discounts. For example, the Millers order from Hankins is very important to Hankins who can't afford to lose it. Hankins will be prepared to charge less to keep the contract. Being smaller Hankins' management has to share some responsibilities, but Millers can employ more specialists. For example, it will no doubt have an expert purchasing manager and assistants who have the time and expertise to find and arrange the best deals. Millers can also employ technology more efficiently with the fixed costs of the items being spread over a much larger output. The cost of marketing Millers' office furniture in trade magazines and at displays is also spread over more sales, making the unit cost of marketing lower. It is also easier and cheaper for bigger businesses to raise finance. Millers, by making different types of office furniture and having a number of suppliers and customers, is able to spread the risk more effectively than Hankins.

Hankins has survived because it supplies components to a few businesses, therefore it doesn't require a huge amount of marketing. It also joined other small businesses in a purchasing consortium enabling the consortium to buy in bulk. The bespoke side of the business is more suitable to job production and this cannot so easily gain from economies of scale. Big businesses can lack co-ordination and have poor motivation if not managed well. This can result in diseconomies of scale. Hankins, being a small family business that attempts to empower its workers, can be more flexible to changes in the market. However, Hankins is at risk of losing a substantial part of its market. It will need to seriously consider specialising in one area or with one customer. This may make it worthwhile purchasing new equipment, but there are risks to this. In particular it would need to make sure its customer would not quickly find a cheaper supplier. It will also need to make sure it is efficiently managed to get the most out of the investment. Raising productivity will lead to lower unit costs.

6 Why should Hankins be concerned about its quality control system and what would you recommend it does about it? (6 marks)

Benchmarking indicates that Hankins' quality is about half that of the national average for regional furniture makers. Quality control seems to be weak at checking the raw materials when they come in and in checking the finished product. It may be there are no checks at each stage in the production process except perhaps in sampling. The benefits of choosing a sampling system is lower quality control costs, but there are costs to having poor quality products. Firstly, Hankins stands to lose its reputation, which could result in a loss of business. It would not wish to upset Millers. Secondly, there is a waste of materials, which have a cost to them as well as the labour costs spent to correct the mistakes.

It may pay in the long run to employ inspectors, but inspectors are often unpopular with the workers. Hankins could consider making everyone responsible for quality control. It would make sense especially if Hankins went over to cell production. This gives ownership and can be a motivator. This TQM needs to be built into the system. One way of achieving this is to go for the ISO 9000 award where the British Standards Institute would support and assess Hankins as they introduced a quality management system.

7 Evaluate the proposal to have closer ties with Millers and accept their offer of increased orders, but daily deliveries and improved quality. (14 marks)

If Hankins decides to reject Millers' proposals it will lose half its sales revenue. Finding new markets will be difficult and the business may have to make workers redundant. On the face of it accepting the proposal has significant benefits. For example, the orders would significantly increase and Hankins would become a preferred supplier. Concentrating on just four components would mean the investment in new equipment would be more cost effective. However, Hankins would require more finance and have a good business plan available for the bank. Millers may offer to buy some shares in Hankins, but this would change the emphasis of ownership. Hankins would need to be sure that Millers' own markets are strong. If Millers' market declines so will Hankins'. If Hankins dropped the bespoke side it may demotivate its more skilled employees. However, empowering the workers to come up with solutions means that hard decisions are more likely to be accepted and change more likely to succeed.

By moving to a JIT operation the level of stocks and the need for a large stock area will be reduced. The extra space released may allow the bespoke production to continue or enable the factory to meet the higher production targets, which is important because Hankins is operating at full capacity or 100% capacity utilisation. By moving to JIT the capacity utilisation could be maintained but the maximum possible output would increase, so helping spread out the fixed costs and lowering unit costs. However, if Hankins had orders beyond its capacity it would have to think about increased overtime or shift work or alternatively subcontracting (out source) work. This has its own problems in that Hankins would need to be sure its supplier can deliver quality and on time.

There is an opportunity cost to holding stocks. Lower stocks means there will be less working capital required to run the business so releasing capital for equipment and training to enable JIT to go ahead.

The JIT operations would mean the stock room staff changing their role to include more deliveries. It would also require leaving the consortium and finding a supplier who can also deliver daily.

Working in four cells leads to more teamwork and a commitment to meet targets such as increased output, less waste and higher quality. Each team will take on more responsibility including its own quality control. Roles are less repetitive, there is a sense of teamwork and team rewards can be gained when targets are met. Techniques such as this would promote efficiency and speed up production at Hankins and is called lean production. It shouldn't stop here, because employees develop expertise and become empowered to provide ideas to improve production and make for continuous improvement. The Japanese have coined the term 'Kaizen' to describe this process. However, if Hankins used the system to rationalise and lay off workers and the teams started blaming members for poor quality the system will not work. It means managers need to be supportive and workers need to be empowered. The approach Hankins is taking to get employees on board is a promising start. For example, by encouraging employees to attend training courses and visit firms operating in this way Hankins has a strong chance of making this work.

Overall I would recommend they go down this route at it has a more secure future and will make the business more efficient. Millers will have built up a strong relationship with Hankins. The main drawback is that Hankins will be dependent on one customer. If Millers fail at least Hankins' greater efficiency will give it a chance to capture new markets. In the short run Hankins will need to raise more finance. It is a risk, but one worth taking.

End of Module 2 assessment

Unit 2: Summer 2003

This is not a model answer and will have typical good and bad points.

1 Seyi used internal recruitment to appoint the manager of the second store. Explain how Black Looks Ltd might have benefited from external recruitment for this appointment (see Section D). (6 marks)

External recruitment means employing personnel from other organisations rather than promoting from within Black Looks Ltd. Karen was internally recruited and lacked some of the managerial skills at first. By recruiting from outside these skills could have been made essential requirements for candidates to be shortlisted. Recruiting from a wider source should increase the quality of the applicants and bring in people with creative ideas and experience who have worked in similar retail outlets. This would fit in with the ethos of the business.

There is a clear understanding of the difference between internal and external recruitment and some idea of the benefits of recruiting from outside. It is well applied to the case study especially the reference to Karen.

2 Outline two possible disadvantages to the Littlehampton cosmetics supplier of holding large stocks of 'raw and semi-processed materials' (see Section B). (6 marks)

The Littlehampton supplier would have to tie up large amounts of cash by holding large stocks of raw and semi-processed materials. The working capital is not working so efficiently. Further, there will be an increase in costs because of the extra storage required and the increased wastage especially if stock rotation methods are poor.

This answer needs extending in order to gain full marks. For example, the business faces an opportunity cost in that the money tied up in extra stocks would have an alternative use. This might have been investment in better machinery. The answer could be further applied to the case study by suggesting that there is a risk in holding semi-finished stock for a large customer who then turns elsewhere for supplies, as happened later with Black Looks who gave the suppliers only two weeks' notice.

3 Discuss the possible problems that Black Looks Ltd might have experienced as a result of making a quick decision to switch from the small-scale producer in Littlehampton to the larger supplier in Cardiff. (15 marks)

In moving to this supplier Black Looks gained a 20% saving in product costs, but might have lost out on quality. The products made were not as good and caused side effects on customers. The resulting bad publicity might lead to a decline in turnover and smaller profits per store.
The move was made too quickly without finding out enough about the new supplier. Therefore the new Purchasing Manager's appointment was probably overdue, given the rapid expansion of the business. Certainly his visit to the large supplier from Cardiff seemed to highlight the motivational problems among its workforce and poor employee relations that had led to mistakes in the mix of ingredients.
Supplier relationships were good with Littlehampton. This business was able to respond more effectively to short notice additional orders and seemed more flexible. However, a move from Littlehampton was necessary as this supplier was struggling to get production volume up, and prices down. Cardiff prices were 20% lower than Littlehampton and volumes were greater. Some of the savings in costs could be passed on to customers who in turn would demand more.

There was some use of data as evidence with the 20% saving. With 15 marks available evaluation is required, so it is good that the answer considered the benefits of switching suppliers as well as discussing the problems. The answer would gain from mentioning the type of information Black Looks should have found out before making the switch.
A good evaluation comes up with judgements or recommendations. For example, suggesting using Littlehampton to continue to provide some supplies and give it a chance to try to match Cardiff's prices in the medium term. Perhaps this is what Lily would have gone for even if it didn't save as much as the complete switch.

4 Analyse how the Purchasing Director's performance might be improved by the introduction of management by objectives (see Sections F and G). (8 marks)

Objectives are targets that can be measured. If the Purchasing Director is set 'management by objectives' that are clearly linked to Black Looks' business objectives then these will help the Purchasing Director prioritise and drive his activities. One of his targets should relate to sorting out supply problems that have arisen from the rapid expansion of 50% growth per year. Other targets could involve matching supplies to the growth of the business, ensuring deliveries are on time and reducing unit costs and maintaining quality. Such targets would provide the Purchasing Director with a clearer focus when investigating the Cardiff suppliers. The targets would need to be quantifiable such as reducing waste or faulty products by x% within 6 months. Without such targets and with limited managerial experience the Purchasing Director may choose to direct his effort at matters that are not high on Black Looks' main concerns.

This is a good answer as far as it goes, but performance is also related to how well managers are motivated.
You can argue that working towards targets may help motivate the

Purchasing Director to be successful. It will allow for recognition of his achievements and provide a sense of responsibility especially if he is given the chance to put his ideas into practice. These, according to Herzberg, would be strong motivators. Using relevant theory will help to raise marks. However, don't forget that the Purchasing Director will receive a bonus of 4% of the share of profits. Perhaps the bonuses might be linked to him achieving his targets (performance related pay), so long as these help to deliver more profits.

5 To what extent would Black Looks Ltd benefit from more effective human resource management? (15 marks)

Where has Black Looks been successful? The company has used the local college to get part-time recruits who are young and also fit in with the image of the business. It also recruited a Purchasing Director who has the skills and enthusiasm for the job. The company seems to have managed to employ the number of staff it needs during its rapid growth.

However, the recruitment is unplanned and last minute. For example, in the rush to open the first shop there was no opportunity to shortlist staff. There was also little to suggest an induction programme to settle them in and let them understand the ways and workings of the business. They may not have recruited the best and their labour turnover might be higher than desired.

Karen had to learn the hard way when she took over managing a shop. She arrived without having all the skills and lacked experience of running a shop. That could have been largely provided by training. She had a few hard knocks and, what is more, was blamed for not doing things correctly. On the job training alongside the manager of the Brixton store for the month before the change in job role might have helped.

The owners seem to have a different attitude to the way the business is being developed. External management training might have allowed them to develop a shared strategy.

Black Looks' human resource management may be viewed as a bit hit and miss. They are surely big enough to employ a specialist human resources specialist. The Human Resource Manager would add value to Black Looks because he or she would take responsibility for workforce planning, recruitment, training and motivation. A more motivated and effective staff in relevant job roles would more than compensate for the extra salary of the Human Resources Manager. Also, a lower labour turnover would reduce the costs of recruitment. There is no point in having good products if the staff is poor at customer relations.

This is a good answer in that it attempts to look at the effective and ineffective management of staff who are an important asset to the business. The answer shows an understanding of more than one aspect of human resource management which have been applied to Black Looks. Using evidence has enabled analysis and further the answer comes up with a recommendation. Perhaps some mention of a lack of any meaningful and planned training for all staff would provide an opportunity to comment on types of training.

External influences

Part A: The market and competition

1 What evidence is there that demand to see films has changed? (2 marks)

Cinema admissions measure the number of customers in a year and data indicates this was lowest in 1984 with 54 million admissions, compared with a high of over 142 million in 2000. Closure of cinemas in the 1980s and expansion of multiplexes since then also suggests the market has changed.

2 a How has demand changed? (2 marks)

Cinema attendances had dramatically halved between 1980 and 1984 suggesting the market was volatile, but since then the market has more than recovered and is now showing a steady growth.

b Suggest possible causes for this change. (6 marks)

The cinema became less fashionable in the early 1980s. TV and home videos were seen as substitute goods and offered a cheaper, more attractive, alternative. Matters changed when the cinema industry fought back by making better films, having more successful advertising and through raising the quality of the cinema experience with the introduction of multiplexes. This was matched by a growth in earnings leaving people with more money to spend on leisure activities.

3 Demonstrate the change in demand between 1980 and 2000 using a diagram. (8 marks)

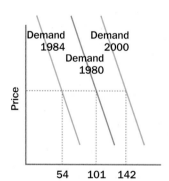

The demand curve had shifted inwards between 1980 and 1984 meaning that considerably less people attended cinemas for a given price. However, after 1984 the attendances grew so that by 2000 the demand curve had shifted outwards well beyond 1980 levels.

4 How might the cinema industry react to the trends in the short run and in the long run? (8 marks)

In the short run it is difficult to change the supply. Therefore during the early 1980s cinemas might have reacted by putting on fewer shows to lower costs or

cutting prices to entice back customers. Failure of this strategy meant that some cinemas closed. As shown in the data there were over 100 fewer screens.
Improved attendances in the short run may have been met with cinemas raising prices or by putting on extra performances. In the long run new multiplex cinemas were built in response to the continued growing demand. Some cinemas that failed to invest may well have still closed down.

5 Demonstrate the change in supply using a diagram. (6 marks)

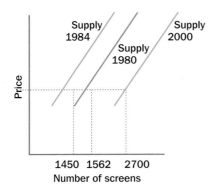

In the early 1980s many cinemas didn't have enough customers to cover costs and went out of business. Some became derelict and others took on different uses. The supply curve had shifted inwards. During the 1990s there was renewed investment in cinemas mainly in building multiplexes often on the edge of cities near good road links. The supply curve had shifted outwards.

6 To what extent is there a danger of over supply in the market? (6 marks)

There is always a risk when entrepreneurs invest in new businesses that there will be over supply or excess supply. This occurs when there is too much being supplied in the market. In cinemas this may result in them being unable to fill seats on release of a new blockbuster film. Demand might go down in the short term, for example in a period of good weather. Cinemas would have more empty seats than before. A temporary over supply may be overcome by lowering prices until the market clears. There will, however, come a point when the market becomes saturated or mature. This is a long-term position of over supply. In the 1980s it was caused by a drop in demand. Today it might be caused by investors getting it wrong and simply building too many new cinema developments for the market. Finally, a new competitor in the market with a different and exciting strategy may attract customers from existing cinemas causing them problems.

7 a How is easyCinema attempting to gain a competitive advantage? (4 marks)

Competitive advantage means having something more than your competitor. You might have a better product or lower costs. easyCinema feel its competitive advantage will be both. Firstly, all bookings are through the Internet and secondly, this will help it cut costs and it promises to pass these cuts onto the customer.

b What effect will easyCinema have on the competition should it be successful and open cinemas throughout the UK? (8 marks)

easyCinema's pricing policy is likely to create more demand for cinemagoers. This is because lower prices increase demand. A proportion will be new, but some of these will be attracted from existing cinemas and easyCinema is seen as a close substitute to them. The reaction of the other cinemas will depend on how many customers they lose. They may feel they are aiming for a different type of customer. Their product, although more expensive, is better and multiplexes are well-known brands with a good reputation for comfort and service. You can also see new films as soon as they are released, which fits into their heavy promotion. Many have close links with the film distributors. Some small independent cinemas may go out of business or seek a new competitive advantage such as screening specialist films.

Part B: Macroeconomic issues in relation to businesses

1 What is meant by the terms 'business cycle', 'recession' and 'boom'? (3 marks)

The business cycle shows the pattern of growth and decline in the economy. It creates the fluctuation in demand for many products. During a recession demand is growing more slowly or even declining and during a boom output increases to meet a rising demand. The business cycle takes several years to run.

2 What decisions did Terry make during a period of economic growth? How might such decisions if adopted by most businesses affect the inflation rate? (6 marks)

Terry wanted to take on more orders. He worked out that increasing overtime would not be a sufficient measure to be able to meet deadlines. Terry introduced another shift. To attract the right staff he had to increase rates of pay and passed on the increase in costs to his customers in the form of higher prices. If other businesses were making similar decisions the inflation rate would increase.

3 a Why might a skills shortage lead to a rise in wage costs? (2 marks)

b What effect will such rises have on businesses? (4 marks)

A skills shortage in, say, computer engineers would mean that the recruiting employers would have to pay higher wages to attract potential recruits and the other employers would need to match this to retain them. An increase in wages represents an increase in business costs. At a time of high economic growth it may be possible for businesses to pass this on in increased prices to customers. This will increase inflation. If the economy is sluggish such price increases would result in a significant fall in demand. In such circumstances the business would try to absorb the wage increases by cutting costs elsewhere or accepting a drop in profits.

4 a How will a rise in interest rates affect businesses? (4 marks)

b If raising interest rates affect businesses why might the MPC bother to increase them? (6 marks)

A rise in interest rates will increase the cost of borrowing. This makes investment projects more expensive. Some businesses will be put off making investments and for others who already have a loan they will see their overheads rise. Raising interest rates also makes it more expensive for customers to borrow money in order to buy. They will therefore buy less than before the interest rate rises so reducing demand for products and services. Raising interest rates will dampen down business activity and reduce business confidence. Making borrowing more expensive will also reduce the demand for houses. Overall interest rate rises reduce the level of economic growth. The MPC has responsibility to keep inflation levels low. It uses the interest rate as a tool to control inflation. The MPC might raise the interest rate to reduce inflationary pressures that might be building up as a result of continued house price rises and maybe skills shortages.

5 Evaluate Terry's strategy of looking for new markets in Europe. (8 marks)

Terry's business may be in danger of collapsing unless he finds new markets. Looking for customers in the Eurozone may give him a competitive advantage because the fall in the value of the pound has made UK imports cheaper to buy for customers in countries like France and Germany. There are some difficulties including the fact that importing businesses need to pay transaction costs when exchanging euros for pounds. Terry would also be wary that exchange rates could move in the opposite direction. The value of the pound may rise making his exports less competitive. He may prefer the UK to join the Eurozone.

6 How might an increase in the UK exchange rate affect UK businesses? (8 marks)

An increase in the UK exchange rate would mean you would get more foreign currency for your pounds. It would make imports cheaper, but exports would be more expensive for foreigners to buy. In the very short run businesses may find it difficult to change suppliers or be reluctant to do so if they believe the exchange market will soon move in the opposite direction. One way round this is to hedge your bets and reduce the effects of currency fluctuations by buying currency now for delivery at a future date. If the exchange rate stayed high then domestic suppliers may find their position less competitive against importers. The exporters may also find their demand squeezed.

7 What effect will changes in interest rates have on Terry's business and on the economy in general? (8 marks)

Terry would be concerned at interest rate rises, because converting vehicles requires him to pay for materials and labour long before he receives sales revenue. The effect would be more significant if he had a large overdraft. Higher interest rates make investment in new equipment more expensive. Higher interest rates also means less

borrowing and lower spending. He may have fewer orders as a result. In short Terry's costs would rise, the demand for his products fall and he would be more reluctant to invest in his business. The aggregate effect of such business decisions would be a slowdown in the economy. Interest payment is a cost to a business. Therefore an interest rate decrease has the effect of reducing his repayments and therefore his costs. Low interest rates make investment more attractive because the cost of borrowing has fallen. It also means people and organisations are more likely to borrow and spend more. The aggregate effect would be to lead to an increase in economic growth rates.

Part C: UK and EU law, social responsibilities, business ethics and technological change

Case study A

1 The E-Commerce Directive is one of many laws that support the consumer. Why might some businesses welcome laws like these while others see them as yet another burden? (8 marks)

Laws are necessary to protect stakeholders like shareholders, employees and consumers. Consumer law sets out a minimum of good practice. Given an option many businesses would not follow good practice either out of ignorance or simply because following it can add to the business costs. However, such laws will provide an even playing field. It allows the consumer to receive the products they think they are buying and makes it fairer for businesses like Goodnessdirect.co.uk who already look after their customers' interests. Businesses that do not provide good practice before a law change will be worried about increasing costs. Some laws are very excessive and the extra costs may be enough to force some out of business. Finally, laws need enforcing and this means local authorities setting up trading standards offices and financing these.

2 Why might small rural businesses that do not have access to broadband be concerned at it not being available? (4 marks)

The cost of having broadband is not too expensive for a business so it is a commonplace expense. The benefits of having broadband are particularly significant for businesses involved in e-commerce in terms of speed of exchanging documents and in receiving customer orders. It is no longer necessary for such businesses to be close to their customers and suppliers. For example, The Wentworth Wooden Jigsaw Company sends its products all over the world and also uses the Internet to receive files with drawings and artwork from suppliers. However, not being able to access broadband put it at a competitive disadvantage.

3 How has the growth of information technology led to new opportunities for businesses like Goodnessdirect.co.uk? (4 marks)

Information technology may well require an initial increase in investment and consequently some overheads, but it will then lead to greater efficiency and cost savings overall. For example, Goodnessdirect will use IT to help link customer orders to restocking. It might find that the initial investment pays back in less than a year as it needs less staff than if it had not used the system. Efficiency savings give these businesses a competitive advantage. This is increased when the technology enables it to target marketing and reach its customer audience more effectively. Niche products can now cost-effectively promote nationally. It allows small businesses like Goodnessdirect to survive alongside large businesses like Amazon. One of the beneficiaries of this change in technology will be the distribution firms who deliver the products to our door.

Case study B

1 Why did the government want to improve working parents' rights? (2 marks)

The law applies to all organisations and is designed to protect working parents' rights so that they can be with their children at a fundamental time without fear of being pressurised or bullied by their employers. Also, having such employment laws means that no one employer can gain a competitive advantage by exploiting their workforce.

2 Evaluate the effects of the new working parents' rights to a small business and a large company. (8 marks)

The new working parents' benefits will increase business costs, as businesses will be responsible for paying these benefits. At the same time they will suffer a lack of continuity in the work place. This may place a strain on employees who have to cover the workload. Some tasks may not be covered so well and the business will be less efficient. This could be significant in a small business where the absence of one or two employees can have a large impact. Larger businesses can cope with the changes, as it will be easier for them to arrange cover and cope with job share and other flexible working requests.

3 What is an employment tribunal? (2 marks)

An employment tribunal is set up to decide whether people have been treated fairly by their employers. The tribunal for Mr Mead decided to reject his claim, as a contract worker does not have the same rights as a full-time employee.

3 What is meant by a contract? What arguments are there for and against the swimwear workers' case against their former employer? (8 marks)

An employment contract is a legal agreement between the employer and the employee. It lays down the rights and responsibilities of each party to the contract.

The swimwear workers' union has gone to court because it believes the employer has broken his responsibility by failing to pay the workers what he owed and also by making them redundant when he then set up a similar business. It looks like he was ethically and morally at fault, but he may argue that his previous business failed and once his limited liabilities have been met he is free under the law to set up a new business. The tribunal will have to decide who is right.

Case study C

1 What is meant by a stakeholder? List three stakeholders for Shell and say what they might want from Shell. (6 marks)

A stakeholder is any individual or organisation that has a direct interest in a company's performance. For Shell this would include environmental groups such as Greenpeace, employees and customers. The environmental groups would wish that Shell minimise the environmental damage of extracting the oil, its distribution, refining and end use. Employees want to have motivated jobs with security with good health and safety standards. Customers want good quality products at a reasonable price.

2 a What motives does a company like Shell have for trying to be ethical in the way it behaves?

Big businesses have become increasingly aware of the need to satisfy a broad range of stakeholder interests especially when they are a well-known brand like Shell. Clearly they have to work within the framework of the law, but it may also make sense to be ethical. Politically the government is promoting sustainable growth, which means not putting at risk future resources. Hence Shell is researching new energy sources. Socially it has clear views on bribery. Shell can also use its research and development resources to produce cleaner fuels.
This ethical stance makes it easier to recruit employees and provides it with a stronger socially responsible brand. The CEO sees this as being in the interest of the business and presumably its stakeholders. On the environmental side Shell is aware of pressure groups targeting it as a polluter. It is looking at its actions on climate change, biodiversity and pollution.
Not all businesses will try to minimise the social costs of their actions. Smaller businesses on the margins of survival will be very reluctant to accept any unnecessary increase in costs. They would view this as making them uncompetitive. Big companies would be showing greater responsibility if they only bought from suppliers who themselves were socially accountable.

b Is there any potential conflict between having an ethical approach and satisfying shareholders? (8 marks)

Moving towards a more social and ethical approach will often add costs to a business. For example Shell promises to not tolerate corruption and bribery. To carry this out it will have to closely monitor its workforce. It will also risk losing business in certain countries where corruption is endemic. Being more innovative, such as in researching cleaner fuels, will increase research and development costs. However, the result might be the development of more environmental products that will give the business a competitive edge. Working with rather than against pressure groups means the company is less likely to receive bad publicity and is more likely to do the right thing first time.

Being upfront and transparent requires that the information is available to all stakeholders. Shell includes its actions in its annual report to shareholders and in published environmental audits. Pressure groups will keep a close eye on them and may be all too willing to publicise things that have gone wrong. For example, it looks like Shell was not too upfront when it allowed T-Mobile to use its petrol stations to erect disguised masts.

3 What would happen if the government increased the restrictions of erecting mobile phone masts? (4 marks)

The risk of ill health from living or working near masts would be reduced. The trade-off would be a poorer national coverage for users of mobile phones. The mobile phone companies may research new technology that would allow them to use fewer masts or even share them.

4 What does Unilever mean by 'the practices of suppliers must be in line with our own'? (6 marks)

Unilever needs to buy raw materials from a range of suppliers. The cost of purchasing these forms a significant part of Unilever's total costs. Unilever believes it would not be sufficient for it to be socially and ethical responsible for its own actions without its suppliers following the same practices. For example, Unilever wouldn't want to buy fish from boats that broke fish quotas or used nets that caught young fish.

Objectives and strategy

Case study A

1 What might Daniel's business objectives be? (2 marks)

Daniel will want to break even by six months and make a profit over the next six months. He must gain customer loyalty as well as gain new customers, so building up a customer base. Long-term objectives might be to expand by opening new outlets in other towns.

2 What budget is required to cover Daniel's start-up costs and what might the start-up costs include? (4 marks)

Daniel has estimated he will require a budget of £15,000 to pay for start-up costs such as refurbishing the grocery store, buying the specialist cleaning and ink filling equipment, buying a van or motorbike for deliveries and marketing so that potential customers are aware of the product.

3 What ownership would you recommend Daniel should consider? (6 marks)

Daniel needs an extra £10,000 to cover his start-up costs. It is unlikely that the bank would finance all this so he should consider going into partnership. He would have

to share responsibility and decision-making. The partner would need to invest £5000 and offer different skills to Daniel, perhaps a marketing expert. The downside of a partnership (or sole trader) is that the partners would face unlimited liability should things go wrong. He would probably only consider becoming a private limited company if he needed to open up new shops in other cities.

4 How can Daniel reduce the risk of failure? (8 marks)

Planning cannot guarantee Daniel success, but it reduces the chance of failure and it will allow Daniel to monitor his progress against his forecasts. For example, he would check to see if he kept inside his start-up budget. Also, as part of his finance budget he will need to produce a cash flow forecast. It will allow Daniel to see if he has enough funds to pay bills and it will help him secure a loan. Planning helps Daniel decide what to do and when. For example, a key part of his planning would be his marketing plan. Within this he would want to know the required sales per month to break even. At least his contribution is high because his variable cost would only be packaging, the ink and the £1 cost of buying the used cartridges. The price seems very competitive. Once he knows how many sales are needed to break even Daniel will plan to attract the required number of customers and more.

Research will have enabled him to determine what they want from his business. He will set up a budget to inform his potential customers about his business. Leaflets and radio adverts might be the most cost effective at first along with a website and entry in the Yellow Pages.

Case study B

1 a Provide two pieces of evidence that suggests Amazon is a market-oriented business. (2 marks)

  b Is the Royal Mail market or product oriented? Explain why. (2 marks)

A market-oriented business aims to make a product that matches what the customer wants. Amazon calls itself a customer company and is highly innovative in its efforts to provide 'an unparalleled online shopping experience'. The Royal Mail might be regarded as more product oriented as its focus was on its product, namely delivering mail. However, it must change this focus especially in the light of losses and increasing competition.

2 What is an aim? Give an example using Amazon. (2 marks)

An aim is the idea or vision of where the organisation needs to go if it is to be successful. Amazon wants to be the world's most customer-centric company. It's a very challenging aim. Aims are sometimes incorporated into mission statements.

3 What is an objective? What objectives did the Royal Mail set itself? (4 marks)

An objective is a target that can be measured. It is used to drive activities. The Royal Mail had an objective to turn its loss into a profit. Other objectives might be to reduce the number of strikes by its employees and to lower the pollution by a set level of its activities.

4 Suggest an objective that Amazon might set itself.
(2 marks)

Amazon might have an objective to grow by a certain amount each year. This should fit in with its aims of being the world's most customer-centric company. Happy customers will buy more and so the business will grow.

5 What is a strategy? What change in strategy did each of the organisations have? (6 marks)

A strategy is like a plan in that it shows how the objectives will be met. Amazon felt the need to change strategy even though its aims and objectives remained the same. This change was required to keep it competitive. It involved the company becoming distributors (holding stock and being responsible for delivery) as well as e-commerce sellers. A high investment was required for this long-term strategy. For the Royal Mail the objective of turning a loss into a profit required a strategy to improve efficiency and involved cutbacks in staffing and also closure of loss-making sub-post offices. It also wanted to improve employee relations and might have set objectives on absence and strike days.

6 Construct a simple SWOT analysis for each organisation. (8 marks)

Amazon		Royal Mail	
Strength	Super well-known website that is easy to use	Strength	Infrastructure in post boxes and sorting offices
Weakness	Complex IT system could go wrong	Weakness	Inefficient
Opportunity	Extended range of products sold	Opportunity	Develop the post bus in some urban areas
Threat	Too dependent on the Internet as an outlet	Threat	Much more competition soon

7 Contrast the culture differences between the two organisations. What recommendations would you make for the Royal Mail in order to improve its culture? (10 marks)

Amazon claims it has a positive culture and treats its employees with respect. The cross-functional teamwork means employees have a chance to meet and work with employees from other areas of the business. They are encouraged to be creative and exchange good ideas. The workers are likely to be more motivated. If they own shares they may work more efficiently to help Amazon improve its profits, since they will receive a share of this. The past strike record of the Royal Mail suggests that the culture has not been a positive one. It is difficult to change things around, especially when the organisation has to cut back the numbers of workers it has. The lower strike rate may reflect some success in the Royal Mail changing attitudes. Perhaps the Royal Mail needs to listen to its workers more and let them come up with some ideas to improve its competitiveness. This may help to bring about a more positive culture.

8 What is meant by social responsibility? To what extent is the Royal Mail meeting the social objectives of stakeholders such as its customers, the community and owners? (8 marks)

Social responsibility is the business's agenda to meet the needs of its stakeholders. Royal Mail customers want letters delivered on time at an affordable price. They will also want to use local post offices for transactions involving pensions, licences and the like. A more efficient mail service may achieve more reliable delivery, but to be cost effective some rural areas may lose out, as deliveries in these areas are expensive. Closure of post offices must mean longer journeys for many. However, the post bus would be seen as something positive for the community. Being a public sector organisation the owners are the government. It wants the levels of pollution to fall and would give the thumbs up to the Royal Mail's strategy of having fewer journeys and using less polluting fuels. Recycling its old bikes for charity is a socially responsible action, but even better would be to encourage greater use of bikes to deliver mail.
There seems to be a trade-off between some stakeholders especially at a time when the organisation needs to reduce its costs.

End of Module 3 assessment

Unit 3: Summer 2003

1 Outline two significant strengths in the way Lily and Seyi started up Black Looks Ltd (see Sections A and B). (6 marks)

They seemed to be well organised and had prepared and researched carefully for the start-up. This included working out their start-up costs and compiling a cash flow forecast. As a result of their detailed plan and forecast they were able to establish how much cash they needed to raise and seek ways of doing this.
They had recognised that they could provide a niche product because there was a clear gap in the market and they could fill that by providing accessories for black women. The name Black Looks and the atmosphere would appeal to black women.

Other strengths could have been used, such as the limited liability helping to reduce the effects of failure or the use of branding, or how the marketing strategy seems to fit together well.

2 Analyse whether C.C. plc's strategy for launching the range of cosmetics and toiletries should be regarded as fair or unfair competition (see Section G). (8 marks)

C.C. plc's strategy for entering the same market area seems very unfair. They are a national chain and can afford to heavily discount at prices 45% lower than Black Looks. It is an obvious example of predatory pricing as they are going for exactly the same market and in similar locations such as Birmingham, Lewisham, Tottenham and Brixton. If Black Looks matched these prices they would make a loss. Black Looks can possibly maintain higher prices than C.C. plc because of its branding, but faces serious difficulties.

It is a price war that Black Looks cannot win as C.C. plc can subsidise its new range of cosmetics because it has such big sales elsewhere from its product range and from other chemist shops. Its actions should therefore be against the law.

The answer does not go far enough as it considers only one view. The answer must look at the case both for and against. There is no mention that it may be fair competition on the grounds that it is selling in those shops because that is where the main black customer base is found. Being a national chain C.C. plc may be able to gain economies of scale and make great savings on bulk purchases. C.C. plc may suggest its lower prices reflect these economies plus a need to establish itself and gain the competitive advantage.

3 Discuss the possible effect on Black Looks Ltd of exchange rate changes proving to be in line with the minimum figures forecast by City economists. (15 marks)

In both cases the pound will buy less, but it is a greater drop when buying euros. Each pound will buy 3 cents less of the American currency in December 2004 compared with 12 months earlier, but 12 cents less of euros. The biggest drop in the value occurred in the first 6 months. If the value of the pound drops then each dollar and each euro will buy more pounds. There is about a 2% drop in the value of the pound against the dollar so that will increase the cost of importing cosmetics made in the USA (the brand Sleek). Since this brand is popular Black Looks may well pass on these increased costs to its customers. Each euro can buy more pounds, thus making it easier to sell Black Looks' own label products abroad. One option would be for Black Looks to increase the profit margin by keeping prices in euros the same. This would provide about an extra 13–14% increase in wholesale revenue.
An alternative would be to reduce wholesale prices so that the profit margin is maintained. This should lead to an increase in sales as the prices in the Eurozone are cut.

The answer has shown an understanding of exchange rates and applied these sensibly to the case study.
It demonstrates an ability to analyse, drawing upon theory about profit margins and using data. Some implicit inference is made to price elasticity of demand leading to the only real evaluation in this answer. The section about the euro has no evaluation. The answer needs to make a recommendation for either maintaining or decreasing euro prices based on the elasticity of demand for own label products, the competition abroad and the fact that exchange rates can both fall and rise. Also the value of the change in the dollar against the pound is much smaller than the change in the euro and will have less impact. The extent of the change in currencies might be lessened if the competitors are getting their supplies from the same countries.

4 Seyi's long-term hope is to turn the business into a public limited company. Explain how Black Looks Ltd might benefit from this. (6 marks)

Being a plc will allow Black Looks to raise more capital from the issue of shares. This capital could be used to help Black Looks continue its ambitious expansion programme, both in the UK and abroad. The capital might also be used to support diversification into different products that might allow it to survive the competition from larger competitors like the chemists, C.C. plc.

Alternatively it may help with cash flow. Black Looks will also be able to take advantage of greater economies of scale. All the economic forecasts indicate that the economy will continue to grow and Black Looks want to be able to take advantages of this.

Although the question asks for benefits it would be useful to briefly point out some drawbacks. Since the question is only worth 6 marks don't spend too long on this. It is enough to say that there are problems with going public. For example, there will be a loss in personal ownership of the business and it will be ripe for take over bids. Therefore Black Looks could consider becoming a franchiser.

5 Some experts believe that there is an inevitable conflict between the aims of shareholders and those of the other stakeholders. To what extent did this prove true in this case? (15 marks)

A stakeholder is any person or organisation that is interested in the way a company is run and performs. The shareholders who own the company represent just one type of stakeholder. Shareholders usually have aims to maximise their dividends and increase the value of their shares should they need to sell them. Sometimes shareholders have longer-term interests, such as how well the company will perform in the future. Seyi is one of four shareholders and owns 26% of the shares. He has been ruthless in trying the maximise profits. For example, at short notice, he changed suppliers so destroying supplier relationships with the Littlehampton business. When this did not work out he could not go back. He was also too firm with managers early on. His drive was to reduce business costs even if this was at the expense of many stakeholders' needs. Lily, however, believes that getting a range of stakeholders on board, such as developing supplier relationships, supporting and empowering staff (through management by objectives) will actually help boost the performance and therefore the shareholders will also benefit.
The company seemed to change its attitudes and demonstrated greater responsibility when it chose a supplier who could produce high quality goods and care for the environment (e.g. through its recycling programme). Letting customers know about this will help to add value to the brand and hopefully increase profits, thus making shareholders happy. It could be argued that conflict is therefore not always inevitable between stakeholders. Companies like the Body Shop have proved this.

The answer looks at the conflicts and relates this to the early practice of the company, but then goes on to to indicate that more recently the company, by meeting the needs of a range of stakeholders, can also meet shareholder needs. It even makes an application to a real business. However, the argument could be extended to discuss how the company might behave when it has got its back to the wall trying to survive with the threat from C.C. plc. Would it be ruthless again and close down or sell off the UK retail outlets to concentrate on activities abroad? This has parallels with companies like Barclays moving call centres abroad.

Index